All Mare and Muck-Cart

AS EXPERIENCED BY

Derek Bumfrey

Published by
Robert Boyd Publications
260 Colwell Drive, Witney
Oxfordshire OX8 7LW

First published 1998

Copyright © Derek Bumfrey

ISBN: 1 899536 26 4

by the same author

A Boys Eye View of Norfolk Village Life

Printed and bound by the The Alden Group, Oxford

Contents

	Preface	7
	Acknowledgements	8
Chapter 1	A New Beginning	9
Chapter 2	Beauty, the Only Girl for Me	18
Chapter 3	Rats Hall Calls Once More	28
Chapter 4	Swede Pullers	38
Chapter 5	Land Army Girls Come to Soigné	48
Chapter 6	I Follow the Girls to Abbey Farm	58
Chapter 7	Days Away at the Shoot	67
Chapter 8	Back with the Thresher	77
Chapter 9	Spring Cultivations	88
Chapter 10	Summer Jobs for Us Boys	98
Chapter 11	Harvest – Still My Heaven	108
Chapter 12	More Harvest on Farm and Garden	119
Chapter 13	Autumn Mud and Mangolds	129
Chapter 14	Taking to the Beet Field	139
Chapter 15	National Service	169
Chapter 16	Back in Civvy Street	179
Chapter 17	Old Seasons, New Methods	189
Chapter 18	Heroes in Yellow and Green	199
Chapter 19	More Muck-Cart and Merriment	209
Chapter 20	Almost the End, but not Quite	219

My Dad with the "heir to the Bumfrey millions".

Pat Easter with the Rats Hall Water Cart.

Soigné Farm

Preface

After having written "A Boy's Eye View of Norfolk Village Life" which recorded school and farming memories from 1933 to 1949 as seen and recalled by a boy, I felt it well worthwhile relating a few facts from my own experiences as a farm worker. This book will cover the years from 1949 to 1958 with a slight hiccough when National Service took me away from my natural countryside surroundings and, unfortunately or otherwise, sowed seeds of discontent into my fairly primitive and non-worldly, basic life-style.

I shall try to give careful details of many farming jobs in the period mentioned, as they are with us no more, and if I were to begin work again in farming tomorrow, I would be just as much a greenhorn as I was on that first October morning in 1949, when I exchanged my grammar school blazer for a thick, multi-purpose, working jacket and set off for the farm to which my grandfather, Alfred Bumfrey, first brought his large, working family in October 1927.

The farm in question had the very unusual name of Soigné, probably named after some French conflict, but why I've never known. It was, and still is, I presume, a large mixed farm with plenty of woods and similar game cover, intermixed with large fields, as it was part of the extensive Westacre Estate owned and farmed then by Major H. A. Birkbeck.

I suppose the countryside could be called "rolling" as the often-held picture of Norfolk being flat was certainly not held by us, and anyone having to cycle around as we did would soon realise this fact. The steep Tumbler Hill, which led out of Westacre village to Pretoria Cottages (my home) and Soigné Farm was the bane of my school life and never improved much in all my days as a cyclist, no matter how many gears I tried.

I hope that I won't be accused of looking back "with rose-tinted spectacles". Yes, we did have happy days, but also many wet, cold and miserable ones. The work was hard for scant financial reward, but on the plus side fellowship between the large number of men employed was great and job satisfaction was there to be savoured and enjoyed. Great changes have taken place on the workfront and, with the coming of time-and-motion studies, a certain "x" factor in the difficult-to-define "enjoyment of work well done" has been lost, much to the detriment of modern life. Worthwhile work in a happy environment is to me real life. How often I hear the wishes of men for the clock to turn back to the days when work went with a whistle and a smile.

Preface

My real hope with this book is that I can help my readers recall those other days when working life was geared to the speed of the heavy horse and not to the horse power of the modern high-speed machine. In doing this I also wish to leave a written record of someone just fortunate enough to work at the very end of that long history attached to the working horse. Or perhaps it wasn't the end; who knows what the future has in store? We must leave others to assess just where our experiences fit into the jigsaw of life, but without a record they will never be able to judge.

Finally I would like to point out that this book, as its predecessor, has been written entirely from memory 45 years on, and no serious research has been undertaken. So if any reader has a better memory than me I must stand corrected on any points of detail, but no poetic licence has been used by me to make it more readable. So prepare your mind to charge down a few gears and enter another age at a steady, pedestrian pace. Now you are ready to read on and enter our world where the house had no piped water, sewage disposal or electricity, and "Shank's pony" and pedal-power were our only personal modes of transport.

Acknowledgements

Firstly, Jean and Ian Little must receive grateful thanks for deciphering my longhand scrawl and transferring it to their computer. Since the publication of my first book, "A Boy's Eye View of Norfolk Village Life", several readers have offered photographs for possible inclusion in this volume. Leslie Richardson, Iris Gooderson, Colin Deasley, Ethel Meachin, Mrs. Easter, and Ethel Abel spring to mind.

Many encouraging letters asking for this sequel spurred me on to complete it.

Special thanks must also be given to Ian Victor-Smith of Country Ways, Darkwood Farm, Nettlebed, for allowing the author to be photographed with the two Suffolk Punch horses used on the front cover of this book. Colin Bough acted as our official photographer.

PART ONE
October 1949 – November 1951

Chapter 1
A New Beginning

Slowly, very slowly, I unlocked the bike-shed door and stepped into the earth-floored, gloomy interior. Carefully extracting my left pedal from the frame of Mother's "sit up and beg" machine, I drew my trusty steed into the semi-darkness of a mid-October morning. The muscles of my stomach seemed to be in knots, and this all too common anxiety had already sent me into the old bucket toilet twice since rising just after six o'clock.

Why, oh why, had I surrendered the security of the known conditions in the sixth form at Hamond's Grammar School, Swaffham, to start work on Soigné Farm? Why indeed, had been the question on everyone's lips from the new Headmaster to my family, friends and neighbours. Why had I given up the chance of a "good job" just to work as a farm labourer? It had seemed such a good idea to me when the stresses and strains of passing the Cambridge School Certificate suddenly hit me and any additional learning required to join the R. A. F. became unbearable and I had dropped out of school after only about six weeks in the sixth form.

Now faced with the imagined terrors of the unknown at Soigné my head pounded and I felt the "first-day" migraine already taking hold and causing my limbs to seize up. Taking a deep breath I rode down the path on one pedal (we never pushed a bike if it was somehow possible to ride) and skirting the house, slid to a halt at the front gate. We always secured the gate in order to keep Waggs, our cross-bred spaniel, off the road. This extra security meant an aggravating need to dismount from our bikes in order to open and shut the gate. This may sound very strange to my readers, but our attachment to the saddle of our bikes was such that my father once wondered why we didn't ride them upstairs to bed.

Turning my head up the hill towards the farm I stood on the pedals to get extra purchase and rode on my way. The big, heavy, working boots, made of tough leather with hobnail soles and heels, seemed cumbersome on the pedals and I wondered how my rather thin legs would carry them around all day. But, as it was Saturday morning, the official starting day in Norfolk farming, I only had to last out until twelve o'clock, so that would be a bonus. Leaving the last of the ten houses at Pretoria on my right, I continued to the brow of the hill, down the slight slope to White Gate corner, following the road right down into the farmyard. The coarse surface of the road gave way to a thin film of mud as I skirted the farm buildings and glided into the open cart-shed where the men normally gathered to take orders for the day from Charlie Wilson, the farm foreman. But on this momentous (for me that is) morning the shed had a rather deserted air and only Uncle Will Bumfrey stood there to greet me. It appeared that almost all the staff had arranged to go on a trip to London and Charlie had decided to absent himself as well. It would seem that someone up above had taken pity and given me my favourite Uncle as both foreman and workmate for the morning.

"Morning, Derek", said Will, "looks like the farm is all ours today. Leave your bike in the corner, bring your coat and bag and we'll go and yoke up." Making our way down to the only stable left for working horses, I felt a great relief spread over me as a morning with Will was going to be O. K. My Uncle Will Bumfrey was one of the kindest men both to us boys and to the animals under his care.

Entering the "bottom stable" as we called it, the sweet smell of hay, coupled with an ever-present tang of horses' urine greeted me almost as a friend. I loved the stables and the horses even when they made life as awkward as possible for me, knowing I was only a novice at the start. Handing me a rope halter Will said, "Catch Gipsy and bring her in and we'll get on". As only one horse was needed that day, he had left them loose in the strawed yard. Opening the half door I slithered down the cobbled ramp and picked out the docile Gipsy, having been acquainted with her during my harvest work a few weeks before. But the mare, sensing she was the only one to be put to work that morning, had ideas of her own and made every effort to keep her head well away from the halter. After raising the temperature inside my thick ex-R. A. F. trousers and even thicker labourer's jacket by several degrees, I managed to corner my quarry and we came up the cobbles again with a fair amount of scraping from my hobnails and her iron shoes. Straight to her stall at the end and a quick tie around her neck completed the first task in my new world.

Each horse's harness hung on a peg behind the stall; collars and saddles were kept for each individual animal, as rubbing from a strange piece of harness could be very painful. After the disasters in harnessing horses, recorded in my first book, "A Boy's Eye View of Norfolk Village Life", a great improvement now prevailed, so the next step in the job held no hidden terrors. Balancing her collar upside down by the sails (the wooden pieces to which the chains for pulling a cart were attached) I quickly manoeuvred it over her head, and unbuckling the head stall, reversed the collar and pushed it back to her shoulders. Then, taking up the bridle already on my arm, I slipped the bit into her mouth, her ears through the top straps, and buckled it on to her head. Now

A New Beginning

for the saddle and breechings, after I had retied my charge to the hayrack by means of the leading line on the head halter. Up on her back went the heavy, padded, wooden saddle, to be tied with a strap round her belly, and over the back end went the breeching harness with chains to hold a cart back or to reverse the load as necessary. A flick of her tail over the harness and Gipsy was ready for the road.

Whilst I was keeping busy, Will was rooting around behind the partition which housed the wheat chaff used to mix with rolled oats for horse feed, finally emerging with a scythe and two pitchforks. The former looked to spell some difficulties for me at least, but the two-tined forks were well known and oft-used implements.

"What's on then?" I enquired of my Uncle.

"We are off up the top of the Hulver to cut some green hay for my stock in the top yard."

Not bad, I thought, at least a nice long ride there and back.

With Will carrying the tools and leading the way, I led Gipsy round to the cart-shed where the dark-green, pneumatic-tyred tumbrils were housed. Turning my horse round, pushing her bridle backwards, I slowly forced her between the shafts, taking great care to keep four very large iron-shod feet off the woodwork. Many an embarrassing situation has been caused by a horse's weight on an ageing cart-shaft. When in position we took up station on either side, lifting the shafts up level with her chains. I threw the back chain over the saddle, settling it into the wooden groove on top. Will connected the appropriate link on the other side to hold it in place. A chain, called the bellygatt, was already in position underneath and this would prevent the two-wheeled cart tipping backwards when loaded. After connecting the front chains or tees from collar to shaft and the breeching chain likewise at the rear, Will just checked to make sure the linkage was equal on both sides so the pulling would be level. Catching hold of the tipped front of the tumbril, we gave it a sharp pull, and as it dropped into position on the back of the shafts a metal bar or trap-stick was then shot home and secured with a pin. So far, so good; all this work had been done before when on harvest duties — nothing new to overcome and certainly nothing to send my knotted stomach muscles into a frenzy, or my bowels into overdrive.

Will tied the long, rope driving reins to the metal ring at each side of the bit in Gipsy's mouth, after threading them through supporting rings on each side of the collar sails. All tools, sacks and dinner bags were safely stowed in the cart, and we mounted ready to leave the cart-shed, remembering just in time on my part, to duck my head under the timber eaves.

Straightening up, we headed out of the yard and past the two houses of Charlie Wilson the foreman, and Dick Welham the cow-man-cum-pig-keeper and barn man. The rubber tyres hissed gently on the gritty road surface with

A New Beginning

Gipsy digging her feet in to gain momentum up the slight incline. The yard itself was almost silent that morning, and only the occasional bawling of a cow separated from her calf disturbed the peace, painting a very different sound-picture from the normal hive of industry at the beginning of a working day.

Charlie Wilson looked out from his back door as we passed, his very white, bald head, uncovered for once, shining in the increasing sunlight. "Morning, Will. Got your apprentice with you then." "Morning, Charlie, nice morning", was all my Uncle could manage as we skimmed past at a good, brisk walking pace, for Gipsy was no idler. My terrible shyness prevented me from uttering a word, my only reaction to the exchange being a rushing of blood to my face and a slight sweat breaking out under my shirt. My wretched nerves never let me rest for long.

But never mind, this was the life, cutting across the corner of the unploughed Bottom Hulver, past wheat stacks already showing signs of a heavy infestation of rats, whose gnawed pathways on the sides, and earth spoils under the bottom, promised much sport at threshing time. Although there was a permanent cart-track running up beside the wood, we kept to the stubble as parts of the track were so rutted one would be jolted silly after a few hundred yards. Water stood in many of the deep ruts, and would remain there for most of the winter months.

How strange that the first morning of my real working life should bring me to exactly the same field as did my first harvest morning at the age of nine.

No conversation passed between us as we both enjoyed the peaceful surroundings. A few pheasants pecked around on the stubble. Cocks and hens fed together with very little to fear on this closely game-keepered Estate. Not until the first gun shots were heard in November would they skulk in the wood. Then the wily old cock birds would run away to isolated pit-holes and keep a very low profile until the sporting fraternity put away their guns at the end of January. Then, to the day, you would see the cock birds strutting around in all their developing finery, calling hens to join their harem for the mating season.

Top Hulver consisted of a three-cornered piece of land, ten or so acres in area, with the point running away from Soigné Wood to meet up with the green road leading to East Walton. The crop left on was a second hay crop, rye grass and red clover.

"Whoa there, Gipsy", commanded Will as he pulled his horse's head into the side of the wood. Climbing down, he tied her to a sapling and prepared to get to work.

"I'll cut some grass, Derek, and then you can pile it up ready for loading."

After deftly sharpening the scythe blade by rubbing alternate sides with a carborundum stone Will removed his jacket and set to work. How easy it looked as each swing laid a swathe of fresh, green fodder in a neat line. As the

A New Beginning

cut area grew the sweat began to show on Will's forehead, and an occasional stop to mop his brow showed it was not as easy as it looked.

"Let's have our breakfast now, shall we?" the slightly breathless voice of my companion suggested.

Laying the scythe and my fork back on the cart, we retrieved our sacks and bags. Spreading his sack at the foot of a tree, Will plonked down with his haversack between his feet. Ever ready to take the weight of my big boots off my legs I made the same arrangements and opened up my bag. Two cheese sandwiches, a piece of cake and a flask of cocoa, Mum had packed to keep me going until dinner time. Breakfast on Soigné Farm was usually taken between 8.30 a.m. and 8.50 a.m. This morning we were a little later as we had only ourselves to please, and, after all, Will was the foreman for the morning. There is nothing to compare with the taste of cheese sandwiches and home-made fruit cake eaten in the open air and the wonderful peace of those far-flung Norfolk fields. Even on the coldest days, eating outside after working hard holds a very special feeling for me. Very little was said, for the Bumfrey family are poor conversationalists, and two together certainly did not help the situation. And yet the companionship of two born and bred countrymen was not strained in any way. The slight rattle of Gipsy's bit as she chewed and pulled at pieces of sapling made all the sounds necessary to turn what could have been a strained silence into a comfortable one. I wasn't to know that never again in my working life would I find a peace to compare with such mealtimes as these, tucked away in a field or wood corner. Nor would it last for much longer for agriculture was destined to change so rapidly over the next ten years that we two might well have been part of the agricultural Middle Ages and not farm workers in 1949.

After eating, Will produced his packet of Players and lit a cigarette. Everyone smoked then, it seemed, except for me, which tended to make me once again a bit of an oddball. But smoking was not for me. After listening to my father coughing his heart up on half an inch of hand-rolled "fag" every morning, smoking held no joys as far as I was concerned. But my Uncle seemed to enjoy his smoke and sat, with eyes half closed, at peace with life and with the world. He had been to India as a Hussar between the wars, and experienced life in other countries, but decided to return to farm work. This was the life he had chosen and as long as horses were part of the scene he was contented.

"Well, we'd better get on I suppose." Will rose and placed his bag down on the sack. "Leave your stuff here and we'll pick it up when we're loaded. I'll cut some more and you can start picking it up."

Once more the fodder fell before the scythe as my Uncle pulled the blade seemingly effortlessly through the standing crop. Leading Gipsy forward I forked the grass into the buck or body of the cart. As the load grew, Will stopped and leaned on his scythe. "That's nearly enough I think", he told me in his very low-toned voice. One had to listen closely to catch everything a Bumfrey said or else spend all day saying "What?" "You try this scythe and see how you make out."

Hoping not to cut my leg off, I clutched the handles, as instructed, and swung out into action. The blade just entered the crop before shuddering to a halt. Once more I tried, with more force but scarcely more success. "Not as easy as it looks, is it?" said my smiling Uncle. "Heel in and toe out", or was it "toe in and heel out"? I can't remember now as scything has never since been one of my pastimes. My efforts met with limited success after much sweat, and I was glad when a halt was called and our loading finished.

By this time the sun had broken out, giving us a calm, late-autumn morning. We gathered up our bags and Will showed me how to hang the haversack straps over the horse's sails where the flask could ride without fear of being broken. I then hopped up on the back of the shafts, made an indent in the load over the front-board, and placing my sack there prepared to drive back to the farm. "You drive, Derek, and I'll walk behind. Take it round to the milk house gate and then we can go into the top yard under the arch." Off we went with Gipsy striding out in the direction of home, with head nodding away and me feeling like "Lord Muck" sitting up above. Don't rush, Gipsy, I thought, I can stick this all morning. Even now the memory brings back the smell of freshly-cut grass and the fine sight of animal muscles rippling under the horse's fine skin. As I rode I enjoyed the panoramic view set out before me, the deep Soigné Wood on the left showing off rich autumn colours and shedding a few leaves which slowly drifted to earth. Before me, rising up from the light-brown, unploughed stubble foreground, were the majestic elm trees, gold against the blue sky. These magnificent trees stretched from Sixteen Acre Belt corner on the left, down to the East Walton green road near Twenty-four Acres, a length of almost half a mile. Who was to know then that a tiny, unknown beetle would come along in future years and kill them all in a season? Now that scene lives only in the memory of those, fortunate enough to have worked the Hulver on a sunny autumn day, and possessed the eye to appreciate their simple beauty. Their desecration cannot be blamed on the greed of modern man, except perhaps those timber merchants who inadvertently imported the Dutch Elm beetle, which caused trouble and death for those lordly trees.

On then we went, along the road, through the farmyard, round the barn corner and sharp right past the milk house and under the arch which supported the second floor of a barn extension. "Whoa." Gipsy stopped instantly and I scrambled down. Rolling up the long driving reins I looped them round the sails out of the way and prepared to lead the horse into the yard as soon as Will unfastened the black double doors. Inside, the young stock were kicking up a terrible noise, knowing by instinct their food was on the way.

A New Beginning

Open went the gate and in we went, with the bullocks pushing each other around in an attempt to pull a mouthful of feed from the cart. As we sped well into the centre of the strawed yard they all followed, allowing Will to re-fasten the doors without fear of any stock escaping. Gipsy's ears were laid back as the cart was bumped about and she herself had to endure a few pushes by over-enthusiastic, bovine scavengers shoved off-course by larger yard inmates. After a few forkfuls had been thrown off into the big, free-standing, wooden, feeding troughs some semblance of order returned and Gipsy was left in peace to pull her fast-emptying cart from trough to trough. Back we went through the doors, leaving the cattle chewing away and slavering over long pieces of grass which hung from their mouths.

Pausing outside Will looked at his pocket-watch. "Just half-past-ten — time we were off to Fifty Acres to load up some beet tops for tomorrow. I'll just put this scythe away and bring four-tined forks. Pull round into the yard, I won't be a minute." Leading Gipsy by her halter I carefully negotiated the gateposts and turned up the yard. Tractors stood silently in the cart-shed bays, waiting for action on Monday morning. The drivers were all in London, so the internal combustion engines were silent. The horse ruled today and was far more useful in the confined spaces of bullock yards than a cumbersome tractor and trailer. Anyway, neither Uncle Will nor myself had the least idea of how to drive, and even less inclination to try. We were horse lovers and had no wish to move into more modern times.

Jumping up into the cart once more we set off in the same direction as before, except we turned right along the road at the Hulver gateway. A couple of hundred yards on brought us to the Fifty Acres and into the field we went, rocking through pot-holes in the gateway. The crop of sugar-beet had been harvested by hand, leaving severed crowns and leaves lying on the ground. Someone the previous day had turned some tops into thick rows and this enabled us to load our cart quite quickly. By quarter-past-eleven the job was complete, and after a quick drink we plodded back to the farm where Will carefully reversed the loaded tumbril up to some bales of straw which formed a prop to prevent the cart from tipping backwards when Gipsy was unyoked from the shafts. Using the small wooden legs slung under the shafts, Will propped them up. The chains securing horse to shafts were then uncoupled and Gipsy eased forward, leaving the shafts up level, thus enabling Will to reverse the procedure by himself, on Sunday morning. As cattle had to be fed seven days a week the tender always tried to cut Sunday working time by preparing as much food as possible on Saturday mornings. Gipsy, who was well-versed in these procedures, began to walk off towards her stable, leaving us to follow her this time, carrying our bags, coats and precious sacks, along with the four-tined forks.

"You unyoke the horse and I'll rack the others up with hay", directed Will, and as my old watch showed only fifteen minutes to leaving-off time, I set to with some urgency, replacing her harness on the peg, then opening the door into the yard, I watched the mare clatter down the slope once more. All the other horses had to gather round and make sure Gipsy was one of their own before tackling the sweet-smelling hay being forked into the wall-racks under cover. Another working week was over for them. For me a working life had just begun, a life that would take me far beyond my present environment to see changes beyond my, or anyone else's, wildest dreams.

Carefully shutting and bolting the door, Will and I donned our bags, walked to the cart-shed and prepared to cycle home. As Will also lived at Pretoria, he at No. 9 and myself at No. 6, we set off together. "Are you coming down to the stack bottom in the Squire's field this afternoon? I'm going to dig the last of my potatoes, so you could finish Freddick's" (my father, Fred's). "All right", I replied, "see you there about two o'clock."

We parted at his gate and I free-wheeled a little way down the hill and in at No. 6.

"How did you get on?" queried my mother.

"All right. I was with Uncle Will so I had a good morning. Only saw Charlie Wilson as we passed his gate. I'm going to finish Dad's "taters" on the Squire's field this afternoon. Will is going down."

After a good dinner I collected my wheelbarrow, fork and sacks, and set off down the road to the end of our row, turning along Westacre road for fifty yards, and then left into the field. A stack bottom was a corner where a cornstack and later the threshed straw had remained until after the rest of the field had been sown. This land was then given over to any worker who required an allotment in addition to his large cottage garden. Will and Dad usually shared one, planting potatoes after Will had ploughed it with his one-furrow horse-plough. Handily a plot remained in the Squire's field this year, so we hadn't far to push our crop home. A more distant plot would have meant borrowing a horse and cart for the purpose. Horse-power and implements were always available if required. Nobody was ever refused, as long as permission was sought from the foreman.

Not many people then thought of recreation on Saturday afternoons, especially the Bumfrey family. Occasionally Will went to King's Lynn; Dad, who worked on Saturday afternoons, might visit Carrow Road for Norwich City's only evening match of the season. Floodlights were still away in the future, so games could only be played when daylight permitted. Our recreation usually consisted of gardening, more gardening, wood sawing or hedge trimming, and we never thought of anything else. So I was quite content to labour away, sweating in the October sunshine, because it was all free — as yet I had no money of my own to spend anyway, and even after pay-day on Friday I wouldn't have much either.

A New Begininning

So we dug our "taters" out of the raised rows which had been moulded up by hand earlier in the summer. All care had to be taken to avoid any green tubers, you understand, as the crop had to last us the year round. Potatoes were never bought in — our belts were just tightened according to the state of the stocks. The larger tubers were carefully bagged and then the very small ones put into a separate sack for chicken feed. Nothing was wasted in our economy, which was well-versed in living within very limited means, and surviving on wartime rations, many of which were still operational even near the end of 1949.

Just as we two labourers were completing our task, brother Michael, and his mate, John Thaxton, ambled out of the wood — Michael, tall and fair-haired, John shorter and dark, made quite a contrast. "Trust you two to turn up now the job is finished", quipped our Uncle. "Never mind; perhaps you can bring your truck and carry the chicken potatoes home. You'll manage them alright." Ever ready to be of help as long as the job involved wheels in some shape or form, the boys nipped off home and returned with a couple of trucks consisting of wooden boxes on old pram wheels. So wheelbarrows and trucks set off for home carrying the last of our crop to be harvested. I felt tired but proud of the fact that now I was a working man who could earn money and also pull my weight with the many chores that made our family life a fulfilled and happy one.

Saturday afternoon wouldn't be complete without the football results. Dad returned from work as cow-man at High House as soon after 4 o'clock as possible in order to catch the end of the football commentary. The large radio set run by two dry batteries and an accumulator would be tuned in to bring the latest action from a First Division game. Then later the treble-chance pools were checked with the usual negative result, leaving him to work for another week at least. But would he have been happy in any other environment? I doubt it, and in my mind then, neither would I. My world was complete with nothing to tax my tired and exam-sick brain.

My father never changed, but the days would come when dissatisfaction would sour my relationship with the land and my surroundings, but not until I had enjoyed many seasons of work and fellowship in the far-flung fields of Soigné Farm.

Chapter 2
Beauty, the Only Girl for Me

Having whetted your appetite by taking you through my first, and very typical, working day on the farm, I think perhaps I ought to fill in a little back-ground information, before donning work clothes once more and setting out on Monday morning — not that our usual Sunday clothes were any different to weekday ones, except if we were going out. Otherwise Sunday meant work of some kind around the garden, so there was no need to dress up. There were one or two exceptions to this rule and I expect we will come across them later on.

Our home village of Westacre was at the centre of Westacre Estate, which also took in the neighbouring villages of East Walton and Gayton Thorpe. Westacre itself stood by the meandering River Nar, approximately twelve miles from King's Lynn, and six miles from Swaffham, the town to which I had cycled when attending the Grammar School. We lived about a mile-and-a-half beyond the village at Pretoria, which consisted of a row of six cottages and two pairs of semi-detached houses slightly further up the hill. By continuing up the incline towards Massingham one would see the turn-off to High House Farm on the right. By turning left up past our houses, another half mile on would bring into sight the buildings of Soigné Farm; these consisted of a central block containing the barn, stables, bullock-and horse-yards, with cart-sheds and pigsties on the north and west sides of the farmyard itself. Rising up above the buildings was the unmistakable silhouette of a metal windmill, which pumped water up into large metal tanks. It was on this water that the people and animals relied for their sole supply. My, how those metal sails rattled and whistled if the tail wasn't pulled in when a gale blew. Dick Welham had to keep an eye on it to make sure no damage was caused by leaving it turned into a very high wind.

A row of squat cottages ran on from the bullock-boxes in the north-eastern corner. Albert Richardson's family lived in the first one and Charlie Andrews, the shepherd, at the far end. The centre cottages had various short-stay tenants after Archie Easter moved away to Gayton just after the war. On the north-west wing a semi-detached block housed Charlie Wilson and Dick Welham. A large farmhouse, let out privately, stood, complete with stables and walled garden, in the south-west corner looking out over the Horse Pasture (now arable) to the south. The last tenant farmer to occupy this house was Alfred Lewis in the early 'thirties. Since his move to Ashill the farm had reverted to

Beauty, the Only Girl for Me

the Estate, being farmed by Major Birkbeck and run in conjunction with High House by Willie Thaxton as bailiff, and Charlie Wilson as foreman.

So you see, we "lived, ate and slept" Westacre Estate. Our house was tied to the job, which in turn depended upon us all living by the rules of the Estate — not difficult for those born and bred in that environment, but not so easy for those of us who went away later on and came back with new values. Anyone with what were considered disruptive ideas was soon moved on, but more of this later.

All too soon the weekend had passed by and my shoulder was being shaken at 6 a. m. by my mother, who rose at 5. 30, winter and summer, without the aid of an alarm clock. The fire in the grate was already going well and a tin kettle singing away promised a nice cup of tea. A quick swill in cold, soft water from the rainwater tank outside the back door swept sleep from my eyes. At half-past six Mum would call Dad from his slumbers. After several shouts, each one louder than the previous one, he would arrive downstairs rubbing his hair around a near bald pate and coughing his heart out as the smoke from the first puffs at a sparrow's-leg, hand-rolled cigarette met his lungs. As every day began in this manner, can you wonder we younger members of the Bumfrey clan never took up smoking? In between his spasms of hacking I managed to decipher the fact that Charlie Wilson had not sent any pig-meal to High House as requested, and could I ask him to send some up. During this daily ritual Mum served breakfast and packed my dinner-bag with food to cover the 8. 30 a.m. breakfast and 12 o'clock dinner, along with a flask of cocoa and a large bottle of milky tea. These supplies had to be sufficient to feed and water a growing lad for the day, for there were no convenient corner-shops to pop into should hunger strike by mid-afternoon. For this was the land where a bus passed once a week and the nearest shop was a couple of miles away in the village.

6. 45 a. m., and it was time to pull on my heavy, leather boots which this morning, being Monday, were clean and freshly-blacked. The thick leather laces stood plenty of pulling and were long enough to knot and turn a couple of times round the top before I tucked the ends well into the turns. The hard leather of the boot uppers would bruise my legs above the ankles well before the day was out, and already I could feel where they had rubbed on Saturday morning. Seeing me wince slightly, Dad advised, between coughs, that they would be comfortable once they were "broken-in". Personally, I felt it was my legs that were being "broken-in" and not the boots.

At ten minutes to seven it was jacket on and bag straps over my shoulders. My heavy Army coat was folded on the bike handlebars and off we went to Soigné. Dad would go in the opposite direction to High House where, as cowman, he was technically his own boss and so didn't have to adhere to strict timekeeping. The road to work wasn't so quiet that morning as men from

Castleacre and Westacre were streaming in, as well as us from Pretoria. Bob Clarke and Uncle John, both tractor-drivers, set off from Nos. 10 and 9 respectively, and from No. 1 Georgie Wright, the head gardener's son, would sail into the farmyard as near to 7 a. m. as it was humanly possible to be. George never gave the master an extra minute of his time, so unlike his father who was an Estate man twenty-four hours a day. Up the hill and through the autumn mist we cycled in dark clothing, and without illumination on our machines. There was no traffic to worry about at that time in the morning. It was our road and we knew it as we sped along, two or three abreast, and swept into the cart-sheds like sparrows going up to roost in the rafters.

Now came the trouble. How on earth was I going to pluck up courage to ask the foreman about Dad's pig-meal with all those other men present? How did I address him? I had always been taught to call him "Mr. Wilson", not "Charlie" as the men did. My back was in a "muck sweat" and my stomach was churning. Even that morning the seething cart-shed didn't contain the full complement of men as all the piece-work sugar-beeting gang would have gone straight to their field.

On the dot of seven the sound of Charlie's size twelve boots could be heard crunching down the slope. "Morning, everybody", came his opening speech. "Morning Charlie", mumbled the assembled staff.

After a moment's pause the orders were given out.

"Gerald and Derek Winner, yoke for beet-cart. Laddie, you and your father take a load of straw to High House. Pick it up from Pretoria Breck; Bert Chase needs it round the yards." And so it continued until I was the only one left.

My mouth was dry and it wouldn't start working. As Charlie stood scratching his head with trilby tipped up I managed to put Dad's request to him.

"Mr. Wilson, Dad urgently needs pig-meal this morning."

"Right, my fellow, get some from the barn and take it. See Will about a horse."

Then, as if suddenly touched by a cattle probe, Charlie accelerated across the yard towards the tractor-shed to issue more orders there.

As tractor engines burst into life the farmyard quickly became a hive of industry. Each driver tried to get mobile as quickly as possible to be first in the queue for paraffin near the barn door. One driver filled a bucket with fuel and passed it up to another, who poured it into his machine. This rattle and roar continued for half an hour at least, every morning, as the relatively modern, rubber-tyred tractors prepared for work. Prior to this period all tractors had metal spud wheels and, staying in the fields, were supplied with fuel in forty-gallon drums.

While all this internal-combustion engine mayhem took place I made my way to the more peaceful bottom stable where Will was allocating horses to us "boys". Gerald and Derek needed three animals for beet-cart, so Violet,

Beauty, the Only Girl for Me 21

Traveller and Prince went with them. Gipsy of course was Will's horse and stayed round the cattle yards with him. Beauty was kept back for me as she was a very quiet and reliable Suffolk Punch mare, of a rich chesnut colour, with clean legs and a white forehead. Derek and Gerald were quickly harnessing their charges in order to reach the beet-field as soon as possible. The men there were at piece-work so they needed to get started as soon as they could. Of this fact I was very glad, for, although Gerald was a close mate of mine of many years' standing, Derek Winner and I had a bit of a history, and I wasn't looking forward to meeting him, although, to be fair, any bad feeling was on my side and all my fault.

Now Derek Winner was postman Sculpher's grandson and lived down in the village. By our quiet standards he was a bit of a "tearaway", being involved in any mischievous prank taking place down there. Once he unfortunately broke his leg falling out of an apple tree. When told of it, the Major's son, Captain Harry Birkbeck, remarked with a wry smile, "I'll bet it wasn't his own apple tree".

Derek had been a paying pupil at the King's Lynn Grammar School, but spent most of his time playing truant. Eventually he became a farm worker, much the same as myself, but for a differing reason. One day when we were both still at school we met up at harvest time on a field belonging to the Warren Farm. I had just caught a rabbit and blood was still running from its nose as Derek approached. Before he could say anything, for some unknown reason, I hit him across the head with my rabbit and ran off at high speed, hotly pursued by a naturally irate, fellow rabbiter. Why I did it I've no idea, but having escaped at the time I gave Westacre a wide berth if Derek Winner was likely to be around. With this unfortunate incident uppermost in my mind I was rather wary of my newly-acquired workmate. But, to Derek's credit, he never took revenge on me, but rather was always helpful on the numerous occasions when my ham-fisted efforts at work landed me with problems.

Both Derek and Gerald were great pranksters, taking every opportunity to play practical jokes on any unsuspecting fellow worker. There was no malice aforethought in their actions, but occasionally the jokes misfired. On one occasion a relatively new employee, namely Walter Back, from Massingham, spent his dinner-break picking blackberries into his food tin. During the afternoon, whilst Walter worked out in the field, the boys emptied the tin into one of their own and replaced Walter's now empty container back into his haversack. At the end of the afternoon the unsuspecting Walter shouldered his bag and cycled home to Massingham. Imagine his surprise and rage when he presented an empty, juice-stained tin to his spouse, already preparing to make blackberry and apple tart. It would appear that Walter's sense of humour wasn't tickled and his temper was short and long-lasting, for as soon as Gerald arrived at the field next morning Walter punched him in the face knocking the practical joker to the floor. Although this drastic reaction wasn't the norm, everyone agreed that justice had caught up with the culprit. I doubt if either of our pranksters meddled with Walter after that.

On another occasion a mock battle broke out on Twenty-five Acres with our two heroes leading an attack, using part of the potato crop for missiles. One stray tuber hit Larkie Bennoitt on the leg. Larkie was a very tall, morose man from Castleacre who always sat alone at mealtimes. It was reported that Larkie looked up, scowled, and marched off the field, mounted his bike and went home never to return. This incident occurred before I joined the Soigné workforce, so I never had the pleasure, if that is the correct word, of spending a period of work-time in the company of the silent Larkie. I remember his cycle had a double crossbar support, as it was a very high machine. The man himself sported a wide-brimmed hat, and his legs were almost always protected by wrap-around, canvas leggings or "states" as we knew them. I doubt whether our two heroes were reprimanded on this occasion by either the foreman or their workmates. Thinking back I wonder if the potato was launched by hand or with the aid of their catapults which were always carried in their pockets. If the latter was the case, perhaps Larkie considered a leg bruise was enough to go on with, and left before a second shot took his hat off, or worse.

Joe Bly was another innocent victim of Gerald's occasionally misguided sense of humour. Joe drove a spud-wheeled tractor, which needed fuel delivered to the field. One summer's day Joe was working near Field Barn and Gerald went with horse and tumbril to deliver the said fuel. Arriving at a time when Joe was at the far end of the field, Gerald thought what a good idea it would be if he hid Joe's bike. Lifting the machine up into the cart, he stood up and hung the bike on a branch. Leaving the scene of the crime before his victim returned, Gerald set off for the farm. As well as being a tractor-driver, Joe Bly was a leading bowler with the village cricket team, and as it happened they had an evening fixture that day. As we waited on the coach to go to Rougham for a match, Gerald was bursting with some very funny situation, known only to himself. The senior team members were fretting at the lateness of their star bowler. I kept asking Gerald what was so funny. Eventually a sweating Joe appeared on the scene. "Come on, Joe! Where have you been?" queried the captain. "Blooming well ask Gerald Andrews", gasped Joe. "I suppose he thinks it's blooming funny." One look at Gerald confirmed his guilt as he laughed and wheezed with merriment. Eventually Joe regained his breath and composure enough to tell us what had happened. At four o'clock Joe had stopped the engine of his tractor and covered up for the night, then, shouldering his bag, had looked for his bike under the hedge where he had parked it that morning. As no bike was there he remembered who had delivered the tractor fuel, and searched along the other side of the hedge, but to

Beauty, the Only Girl for Me   23

no avail. After much searching and sweating, but definitely no swearing for Joe was a devout Chapel man, he looked up to see the missing machine perched in a tree. Being unable to reach it from the ground, he had to crank the tractor to re-start, drive it under the branch, stand on the mudguard and retrieve his trusty steed. This of course all took time, and by the time our victim had cycled home, washed and changed, he was late for the coach. I have an idea that when Joe bowled that evening Gerald had all the running to do in the outfield as the veteran cricketer extracted some revenge on his very junior team-mate. I don't think I played on that occasion, but sat under the surrounding trees providing a meal for the very sharp Rougham flies which were especially trained to feed off visiting supporters. I only played when numbers were short, as my nerves weren't geared to positive actions required on the cricket field. My very first innings resulted in my running out a fellow batsman. Who was it, you may well ask. Derek Winner, of course. He must have wanted to hit me over the head with a dead rabbit, but he took the blame for a bad call instead. The local officialdom sighed with relief when Derek joined the Royal Navy, but we missed him, and life on Soigné Farm was the poorer for his leaving.

But I transgress and leap on too quickly. On this first Monday morning I was speaking of, Derek and Gerald were soon away with their three horses and I was left to yoke Beauty at leisure across the yard in the far stable.

"Everything all right?" called Will as he came across the strawed yard.

Beauty was ready for off, and my uncle gave me some long reins, which would enable me to sit up on the tumbril for a more comfortable ride.

"Where are you off to this morning?" he enquired.

I told him about the pig-meal and asked where I should get it from, as Charlie, in his unique style, had failed to give either directions or information.

"It's in the barn, but you will have to wait until the tractors have finished re-fuelling. I'll give you a hand to load as Dick Welham will be milking and Barney Hooks is sugar-beeting."

So, after putting my horse in the tumbril, I tentatively hung around waiting for the crowd to clear. When the last tractor had roared out of the yard I backed Beauty up to the meal-dust-covered door and entered the dark barn interior. Inside at the bottom of a flight of wooden steps were several open-topped meal-sacks. As if by magic, and in answer to my prayer, my uncle appeared through the gloom at the back.

"Did he say how many you were to take?" he questioned.

"No, he only said to take some", I replied.

"Well, if Freddick has run out, then you had better load a dozen. Jump up and I will lift them up to you."

Dragging the dusty sacks to the cart-front I was soon covered with itchy barley-meal, my rough Air Force-blue trouser legs taking up enough to feed a litter of pigs. Will's blue "dust jacket" also changed colour and the air became thick as we beat the offending dust out of our clothes. "Right, off you go before those hungry pigs shriek their heads off", were my Uncle's parting words as he disappeared through the back to continue feeding his bawling cattle.

Clipping the tail-board back in position, I picked up the dangling leading line, and half-hitched it safely on one of the collar sails. Shaking out the long reins I mounted the front-board, arranged my sack, and set off out of the yard in fine style. As I didn't need the hard road all the way I was able to take the cross-country route to High House – up to the Hulver corner, past the end of Sixteen Acre Belt, and as far as the Big Strawberries gateway. A green road-cum-cart- track led along the top of the aforementioned field, which ran down from the track to the left. On the right was a thorn hedge separating Little Strawberries from its big namesake. The cart tipped and bucked through the ruts made by tractors, and on one occasion an extra deep chasm tipped a couple of my open-topped sacks over, sending a cloud of meal across the back of the cart. Damn, I thought, now I've got a fine mess to clear up. A thin trickle of dust found its way through a cracked floorboard so that by the time I reached my destination my dozen bags had reduced to ten and two halves. Never mind, the birds could enjoy an unexpected feast. An occasional long-trailing bramble tried to pull my cap off my head, but, all things considered, I was enjoying a very pleasant if bumpy ride through the autumn mist, which promised a sunny day later on.

At the end of the first field the track deviated slightly to the right, and entered Honeypot Lane proper, which ran between high hedges inter-spersed with large hedgerow trees. The lane surface certainly didn't improve, but there was more width to help in avoiding the worst of the ruts. Between Lightning Breck on the right and Long Elbreck on the left I jolted along, to the third section of the track which took me on between Forty Acres and Honeypot field. The mist shrouded any activity in the fields, and only the sound of a labouring tractor engine broke into my reverie, although on one occasion a wood pigeon, clapping his wings as he flew out of a tree, made Beauty shoot her ears forward and me to jump on my hard sack-cushion. The slight rattle of my cart and gentle jingling and creak of harness was very soothing, feeling like heaven compared with the worry of school lessons only a few days before.

As we prepared to emerge from the lane end and cross the Westacre to Massingham road I pulled Beauty to a halt in order to listen for approaching traffic, taking special care as visibility was poor. It was all clear, so a touch of the reins and a click of the tongue sent Beauty forward across the road and into Farm Drive. The sun, just breaking through the mist, gave me a wonderful picture across the Park to the right. Huge trees loomed out of the mist and fat cattle blew steam from their nostrils as they moved slowly in and out of view. Several tried to run along the fence with a vain hope of food arriving, but soon gave up as we disappeared into the farmyards. Having spent many schoolboy afternoons up there with my father I knew the pigs were kept opposite the cow-house in the centre buildings.

As we passed the pond away to the right, the ever-noisy geese gave warning of our approach. Sitting up high on the cart my legs were safe from the attention of that fierce old gander whose predecessor made my life fraught with danger when I was small and lived over the High House pasture.

"Whoa Beauty. This is it", I informed my faithful companion, pulling her in by the meal-shed door which had a large padlock through an even larger hasp and staple.

"Why do you always lock that door, Dad?" I had once asked my father.

"Because that meal tends to get legs and walk away", he replied, leaving me even more baffled than when I'd first asked. Now, of course, I am slightly more worldly-wise, and realise that domestic fowls can live on barley-meal just as well as pigs. I also realise just how hard life on very limited money could be, and there were times when one had to live off one's wits in order to keep the wolf from the door.

Jumping down from my perch I tied the horse to a post and set off in search of the key-holder, namely my dad. The weaner pigs nearby made a terrible noise as they realised that at last breakfast was near at hand. Even the docile Beauty got agitated by the racket, and would have liked to be off, but my precautionary, well-tied, leading line prevented any silly antics. Lesson number one had been learned — never leave your horse without tying it first.

I didn't have to look far for the key-holder because the noisy pigs had alerted him to the arrival of his meal. We soon unloaded the sacks and swept the cart out in readiness for the next job.

"Take those empty bags back to Dick or he will be hollering his head off", were my strict instructions.

"Have you had your breakfast yet?"

"No."

"Then leave the mare here and sit in the cow-house and have it. I am going to the dairy after I've fed the pigs so you will have to be on your own."

Sitting in the dusty section on the end of the cow-row I felt quite at home. Pouring a cup of hot cocoa from my flask I had a few welcome sips before delving into my dinner tin. Cold beef sandwiches were soon disappearing as I realised the chilly morning had given me a good appetite. A nice, thick shortcake of pastry and currants soon followed the first course. Gazing around, my eyes found the familiar cards stuck on the wooden partition, depicting footballers of the 1930s. The Thaxton boys had been keen football followers, and as their father, Willie Thaxton the present bailiff, had preceded my dad as cow-man, they had also spent much time in these sheds. The thick legs, padded like tree trunks, of Frank Soo, Alex James and Eddie Hapgood stood four-square as their owners, with arms folded, showed off their team-shirts in all their glory. None of the present day changes of strip every week — Arsenal wore red, Everton blue, and of course the Norwich Canaries yellow and green. Unfortunately teams of the lower leagues were not represented, so none of the heroes playing for our local team were displayed. A medicine chest, smelling of the traditional remedies such as green oils and Stockholm tar, adorned another wall, and beside it an old roller towel and a tiny piece of hard, yellow washing soap. The latter two items, combined with cold water from a drinking trough, represented the only token show to the cow-man's hygiene in 1949. A couple of thick glass pantiles let a little light through past the cobwebs adorning the unlined rafters. The only other light admitted, came via wide cracks around an ill-fitting door, which kept the shed well ventilated, especially when a lazy, north-east wind rattled its hinges — but not on that morning as peace reigned after the pigs were fed, and only the rustle of greaseproof paper lining my tin broke the silence. That very slight disturbance caused a thin-faced cat to peep round the open doorway leading into the milking shed, but even she crept away leaving me to my own thoughts and devices.

When my old watch showed me to have had my allotted twenty minutes break, I loaded bag and sack into the tumbril, and after untying Beauty, turned her towards home, retracing our steps along the scenic route which now displayed all its late autumn colours in the strengthening sunshine. Then I could see the Standard Fordson tractor turning grey corn stubble into dark brown earth by means of a trailer plough. White gulls and black-feathered rooks swooped and squabbled over worms and pests revealed for a moment by the ploughshare. As the tractor turned on the headland, the sun's rays caught on the shiny mould-board rising up out of the earth, and the labouring engine gasped its respite as its load was eased, until it turned into another land, and the two furrows sank into the ground at the pull of a rope attached to the back of the driver's seat. Slowly the return journey began across the wide expanse of Forty Acres, and I left the lone ploughman to his task as we plodded on towards Soigné.

Turning out of the Big Strawberries gateway on to the road my thoughts began to race on to what form my next job would take. A well-known churning started up below my belt as I worried away to myself. Would I find Charlie Wilson when I got back? Where would he send me next? Would I know what to do or where to go in order to do whatever it was I was going to be ordered to do? It was a wonder that huge ulcers didn't grow in my stomach. Certainly, if worry and stress caused them, then here was a case for King's Lynn hospital in the very near future. Fortunately I disproved any such theory, for despite all my worrying no medical problems developed, and I am still here forty-five years on, all in one piece. Perhaps the constant worry kept me as slim as one of "Pharaoh's lean kind", and the need for dieting never bothered me.

Now the question is, can your nervous-systems withstand the waiting to find out just what traumatic job I would have to face next? If you can stand the suspense, the following chapter will reveal all.

Chapter 3
Rats Hall Calls Once More

Beauty began to increase her pace as we passed the end of Sixteen Acre Belt, sensing her journey would end in the farmyard. Even allowing that working-horses had a very good sense of time, which caused them to become very agitated as 4 o'clock approached, she had the hope that stabling time might come early on that occasion. Swinging into the seemingly deserted yard I pulled up by the cart-shed, dismounted, and tied my mare to a ring staple conveniently situated on a wooden stanchion. Gathering up the empty meal-sacks, I then made for the barn door, which stood open. Entering the gloom, my eyes could hardly focus after the bright autumn sunshine of the yard outside. A voice to my left made me jump violently, and except for my heavy size 9 'Zugg' boots, my feet would have left the ground.

"Ah, Derek, Charlie said you were to help me bag some meal until he comes back." It was Dick Welham who appeared as an apparition through the gloom and dust-laden atmosphere. Now I wasn't to know then, but Dick almost always gave this kind of message to unsuspecting workers returning to the yard. Being a vulnerable victim, I quickly fell for his ploy and held the returned empty sacks for him to fill with meal, using a large shovel. You see, the system of grinding was rather primitive, although fully automatic, apart from this very dusty part. A large diesel engine provided power for all barn machinery by means of various belts. This monstrous, shiny green engine needed two men to turn its flywheel when starting. Once started it continued to run for most of the day until the need for power was over. Sacks of barley were hauled to the top of the barn by sack-hoist, flying up through trapdoors in each floor. The barley was then tipped loose into a hopper, which slowly released a dribble of grain into the mill below. On the ground floor the meal dusted down into a heap under the machinery. From there we had to fill the bags which were propped, open-topped, against the wooden steps leading to the first floor. Soon my clothes, hair, eyes and lungs were full of fine meal-dust as Dick shovelled away with gay abandon, getting his work done in double-quick time. The sound of size 12 boots crunching on the yard surface alerted Dick to the foreman's approach. "That will be enough for the moment", he said, and dropping the shovel, disappeared towards the cow-house.

"Derek", roared Charlie Wilson in his best fire and brimstone chapel-sermonising voice. "Where are you?" Knocking the dust off my clothes I flew out into the sunshine. "That's enough time spent in there my fellow", the voice

Rats Hall Calls Once More

went on. "Drop your tumbril and take Beauty to Rats Hall, collect the water-cart, fill it under the tank, and set it back again." Without further instruction he turned on his heel and strode off towards his house. Wondering what I had done wrong, I set about his bidding. What I didn't then realise was that Charlie had an unfortunate habit of upbraiding youngsters when it was a full man who had upset his temper. As his then barn man made a habit of enlisting help without first asking the foreman, he was the man to tell off, not we innocents. Anyway, Charlie's bark was much worse than his bite, and really he was too easy-going for his own good, and sadly, in the long run, for the men under him.

Backing my vehicle under the shed I retrieved my bag, coat and sack. Hanging the bag on the collar sails as instructed by Will, I placed my coat and sack on Beauty's back, making a comfortable cushion. Then, releasing her from the shafts and lowering them to the ground, I gently drew her alongside a convenient cart-wheel and climbed up to sit side-saddle on her broad back.

Off we went out of the yard and back the way we had come half an hour before. As the hopes of an early release from work had receded, my faithful mare wasn't in such a hurry now. But it was fast enough for me as I sat, facing so that my right hand was on the rein, hooked when resting on a leather knob between the collar sails. I believe a horse should be ridden to meet oncoming traffic on the highway, but as there wasn't anything of a vehicular nature likely to disturb our peaceful ride, I sat looking left over the Fifty Acres, and plodded along on the left-hand side of the narrow road, past the Big Strawberries' gateway this time, and down the slight incline to Waterpit corner. I could see the sugar-beet gangs at work on part of Little Elbreck, two gangs topping beet with hooks, the white roots seeming to be constantly in the air above the cart or trailer as if a fairground juggler was at work. Further across, two lone figures were pulling lifted beet from the ground by their tops, knocking them together to remove surplus earth, and then laying them out in a neat row for the toppers — a busy, yet peaceful scene to the onlooker, but, as I was to find out a couple of years later, a back-breaking and tiring job.

Approaching Waterpit corner I could see Gerald, or Dilberry as everyone nicknamed him at school, unloading beet in the corner of Big Strawberries. The beet remained there in an open hale until the red lorries of Sommerfeld and Thomas arrived to convey loads as allocated, to King's Lynn Sugar-beet Factory for processing. Gerald gave me a friendly grin as I turned off the hard road on to the cart-track leading to Rats Hall. The track was rough and uneven, running between hedges of old, twisted fir trees with dense skirts of dead brushwood at the base, and large gaps where old age had allowed wind to blow down trees in past winters. Half way along, the trees finished and the track ran alongside Donkey Hill Wood on the left, with a grassy bank on the right, allowing a clear view of Rats Hall barn and cottages nestling in the hollow. It was to here that my Grandfather Bumfrey had brought his wife and family in 1927. That was in the days of Alfred Lewis who farmed Soigné, as a tenant before moving on to Ashill in the early 'thirties. The Bumfreys no longer lived there, but had moved to the more civilised Pretoria Cottages, at the instigation of Aunt Ivy who kept house for her father and two brothers. I know the menfolk would have liked to continue living in the back of beyond, but were threatened with the loss of a good cook and housekeeper if they didn't get into a roadside house at least.

Down the grassy slope, horse and rider made for the huge barn in which the water-cart stood as the sole drinking-water supply for three cottages and two bungalows. Originally a pump over a well did the job. I remember very clearly going to get water in two large buckets on Sunday evenings with Grandad who was very tall and broad-shouldered, and I used to crane my neck to see his weather-beaten, moustached face under a flat cap in winter and a large, battered trilby in summer. Rats Hall was the scene of many a happy family tea when we walked the three or so miles from High House on Sunday afternoons.

Sliding from Beauty's back outside the barn, I held her with one hand and opened one of the huge black doors with the other. Leading my horse into the barn I found the water-cart propped up on legs just inside. It was a round, galvanised tank, set across a wooden frame, with hinged lid on top and tap below to allow buckets to be filled when required. I've no idea as to the capacity of the tank, but it was usual to take a new supply weekly. Quite often Charlie forgot to send a load down, and had to be reminded by either Nobbie Easter or Harry Ashby who lived there. Charlie would strike his forehead with the ball of his hand and utter those famous words of his, "My fellah, it slipped my mind. I'll see to it right away". This could mean within the next two days if it slipped his mind again.

Anyway, he had remembered on this occasion, and I was here to prove it. Carefully uncrossing the support legs and placing them slightly out from the shafts, I backed Beauty into position and fastened her chains in place. Having satisfied myself that everything was equal and level for comfortable pulling, I looked around to see what else was stored there. One end of the barn itself contained a quantity of loose straw. At the back another door led out into a bullock yard, now full of stinging nettles and high weeds. Under the covered surrounds where fat bullocks had originally fed from troughs or "bings" suspended along the wall by chains, stood a motley collection of outdated horse implements: a faded blue root-seed drill, which could sow four rows spaced about fifteen inches apart; an old corn-drill looking tiny compared with its much wider successor now pulled by a tractor; an old binder with a broken sail looked very forlorn beside a collection of small harrows and a rusty grass-cutter. What a prize they would be today for one of the many agricultural museums. They seemed to have a sad fascination for me, and, of course, I now realise I was standing in a horse-age implement graveyard, looking at machines which had once been the pride and joy of some team-man as his horses proudly pulled them across the wide acres now tilled so much more easily by the tractor.

Breaking out of my reverie, I realised that time was progressing, and after consulting my pocket-watch, found the hands pointing to quarter to twelve, almost time to consider making dinner plans. Deciding the barn was too dark and cold for dining in, I led my trusty friend out into the sunshine. The water-cart came with a good rattle because I forgot to remove the two bricks in front of the wheels, holding them steady. As Beauty was of a very docile nature, the sudden noise only resulted in a couple of quick forward steps. A more spirited animal could well have shot off at speed, taking me and the barn doorpost with it. Sudden, unidentified noises and horses do not go together, I was learning.

After closing the door I once more mounted my charge and set off up the hill towards Soigné. The first plan was to stop for my break at the top of the slope where I could tie my mare and sit in the sun for half an hour to eat my dinner, for which I was more than ready. Choosing a young oak as a backrest, I spread out my sack and thick Army coat for a cushion. It seemed an age since I had last "fed my face" in the cow-shed at High House. More cold beef sandwiches, and then an apple turnover quickly disappeared, washed down by the last of my lukewarm cocoa, and then some cold, milky tea. An apple from the bottom of my haversack finished the meal, and after feeding the core to Beauty, who lifted it from the flat of my hand with her velvet-soft lips, I settled down for a peaceful rest.

Rats Hall — what an awful name for such an idyllic spot. I don't think for one moment I sat there waxing all poetic over it, but in my mind's eye I can still see it all before me. Many people today would give anything to leave the madness of modern, so-called civilisation, and plonk down at a place as peaceful as Rats Hall. But, having experienced living miles from anywhere, with no transport, piped water or proper sanitation, and being paid very little money for a continuous treadmill of hard, monotonous and often soul-destroying work in the 1930s, perhaps the then incumbents could be excused for wanting to move out. My Granny Bumfrey sat down and wept when she arrived at such an outlandish place in 1927. But this lovely, golden autumn day painted a very different picture. The flint-walled cottages sat very squat alongside the dirt roadway, with grassy areas in front. Paths with long clothes-lines dissected these uncut islands of cock's-foot and other coarse grasses. No movement caught the eye, and only airing clothes on Mrs. Ashby's line gave any clue to human occupation. The two bungalows on the other side of the barn were hardly visible, being tucked under the ever-encroaching arms of trees in Half-Moon Spinney. Rising up behind the tiny settlement were the unploughed stubbles of Heron Hill and Sixteen Acres, which led up to a narrow belt of trees on the skyline, and a green track wound away over the horizon to the small village of Gayton Thorpe. I often wondered if a heronry once crowned the hill, hence the name; if this was the case, it was well before my time. An occasional wood-pigeon flew from one cover to another, bringing back memories of Sam and Susie, two tame pigeons that once lived in a wooden box on the front of Grandad's middle cottage. One day, Sam flew off across this same vista, and one shot from a keeper's gun ended his short life in a puff of blood and feathers. Susie waited in vain for the return of her mate, but in a time when keepers shot anything that moved which wasn't a pheasant, these things were normal, run-of-the-mill on large estates. That, of course, was before World War II. As I sat looking over the landscape in 1949, keepering was becoming much more humane, and our pet cats were less likely to suddenly disappear under Clem Softley or Ernie Deasley than in the days of Charlie Welham. Perhaps Ernie, at least, had seen enough senseless killing during his war service to take a more "live and let live" view of life.

Taking my watch out, I saw that my dinner-break was almost over as the statutory thirty minutes had expired, and only the unwritten, but universally recognised, extra ten minutes were ticking away. The warm sun and comfortable seat made rising a difficult exercise, but needs must when the devil drives, so my bag was packed and hung on Beauty's collar once more, and with me seated on her back, off we went down the bumpy track between stunted fir trees, with the empty water-cart rattling behind. Turning out at the end, I could see the sugar-beet gang already hard at work, all in shirt sleeves now as the sun had taken on a real summery heat. Merrily we bowled along with the iron-tyred wheels making a not unpleasant, crushing noise on the rough-surfaced road.

On reaching the farmyard I pulled under the dangling pipe from the water tanks, and after dropping the leading line to stop Beauty wandering off, inserted the pipe into the top of my conveyance. Climbing the metal steps I carefully turned the valve and released water, which rushed down the pipe. In a very short time, water cascaded from the top of my cart indicating a full load. The valve was then hastily reversed so as not to waste any more precious liquid.
On windless days, water conservation was needful as the windmill pump was out of action until the air started to move again.

Just as we prepared to return once more to Rats Hall, Charlie came out of his gate, having finished his midday meal. "Derek, stable your horse when you get back, and finish the afternoon rowing-in tops on Fifty Acres. Borrow a fork from Will if you haven't got one." I should point out here that the men had to supply all their own hand-tools, so I would be expected to get a pitchfork and four-tined "muck-fork" as soon as my finances allowed. As Uncle Will had a good supply of hand tools, Charlie took it for granted that boys without tools

Rats Hall Calls Once More

could borrow from Will. Most of the youngsters didn't abuse the team-man's kindness, and soon visited Plowright, Pratt & Harbage, Ironmongers, in Swaffham to purchase the tools of their trade.

The return journey to Rats Hall proved uneventful. Nothing seemed to have moved in the tiny settlement. The sun still shone warmly, the airing linen hung motionless, and no sign of life disturbed the peace. I noticed once again the strange fan-like scratch marks on the concrete rendering alongside the stable door, which once housed Grandfather Welham's horse. The gentleman in question had been head gamekeeper before the war, living in one of the bungalows and travelling the Estate in his horse and trap. On the other side of the barn a lean-to shed now housed Harry Ashby's little car, in place of the pony trap. Man, horse and trap, were all long-since gone, but I remember them well when I visited my grandparents as a small boy. But the fan-shaped scratches that had so puzzled me on that wall remained. Well, it appears that a tall elder bush had once grown from a seed dropped at the foot of the wall; this bush had swayed backwards and forwards in the wind, making marks on the concrete. One day it was decided that the fast-growing bush was steadily blocking the stable door, so it was removed, leaving a bare wall with strange and unexplained marks to puzzle a small boy whenever he visited his grandad. I wonder if they are still there on this sunny October day in 1995. I don't suppose anyone cares, except me, that is. It's surprising how small things remain so plainly in the memory, whilst world-shattering events pass into oblivion quite quickly.

It seems the tranquillity of Rats Hall is causing my mind to wander, so I had better return to my work.

After setting the water-cart back into position with bricks either side of its wheels, and the shafts propped, I closed the barn doors and turned for home. Just one slight problem reared its head as I tried in vain to remount my steed. Having no stirrup or mounting block, my feeble attempts to leap up physically from the ground failed to achieve anything except to pull the breeching harness off to one side. Hoping no one was watching my amusing antics I sought inspiration and found it in the form of a raised bank from which I managed to haul myself up by the saddle and flop down on Beauty's broad back.

The sugar-beet gang had almost finished the crop on Little Elbreck. Only the part rows, or 'scutes' as we called them, remained. These were the short rows caused by one side of the field being longer than its opposite number. Soon the sugar-beeters would move to the next field on another part of the farm, leaving the severed beet tops to be eaten by folded sheep, which were already sectioned off at the far end of the field. I could see Charlie Andrews, the shepherd, knocking in net stakes in readiness for the next day's fold. Charlie was married and lived in the far end cottage at Soigné, as previously mentioned. His son, Gerald, had been my friend at school and now worked on the farm, whilst younger daughter, Jean, was still attending school. After crowing a hole for the stake Charlie placed it in position, and then with a few deft clouts on the top with the flat edge of the bar, firmed it in the ground. The shirt-sleeved, broad-backed figure made seemingly light work of lifting and dropping the heavy metal crowbar. As the bar hit the top of the post a distinct gap occurred before the sound reached me over half a mile away. A black and white collie dog lay close to its master, and the shepherd's horse and cart stood quietly tethered to the occupied fold. After setting up his square of stakes Charlie would roll out the sheep netting, and then clip it on to the hooks, one at the top and one at the bottom of each stake. The flock of black-faced sheep would then move to fresh feed the next morning. After the move, down would come the net, to be re-rolled, stakes would be pulled up, and all loaded on the cart for transport round the far side of the occupied fold. This process would then start all over again in constructing next day's pen. Many shepherds did not have the luxury, if that is the correct word, of a horse and cart. Nets and stakes would have to be manhandled over the uneven ground. Even with some horse-power thrown in, shepherding with folded sheep entailed a lot of hard labour in adverse conditions. I have seen Grandad Alfred Bumfrey come in from the sheep with his leather boots sodden and hands cracked wide open after using a cold, iron crowbar in windy, frosty conditions. Leather gloves were unheard of for him and Wellington boots hadn't become common either prior to the war. But as Charlie worked away, conditions were ideal, and winter was but a bad dream and seemed a world away.

After stabling my horse and borrowing a four-tined fork from Will, I hopped on my bike and set off the short distance to Fifty Acres. Propping my bike inside the gate I stripped off my jacket and set to, flinging beet tops into thick rows, leaving room for a tumbril to run up the centre between them. Only an hour and a half remained of the day, and already the sun began to dip slightly behind Soigné, Wood, leaving half my work in shadow at the Ash Tree Shift end. Working quite hard I soon made a show and was pleasantly surprised to see my watch pointing to four o'clock and leaving-off time. Riding easily down the slight incline to the farm I called in at the stable to return the fork and pick up my heavy coat left there earlier. Sitting on the corn bin top I watched Will preparing feed for the returning work horses. Using a large straw sieve he mixed wheat chaff and rolled oats, tipping some into the manger where each returning horse would stand. Gipsy soon snuffled her way through her rations and tried in vain to reach along to pinch Violet's, but her head-stall prevented the portly lady from eating more than her share. After turning out in the yard they would be free to eat their fill of sweet hay from the wall racks, but too many oats would make a horse hot-blooded and skittish, too dangerous for work. Moving me off the corn bin, Will set about preparing another sieve for the far stable where Beauty whinnied occasionally to alert Will to her presence, just in case he had forgotten her feed.

Just as he returned across the yard and I prepared to set off for home, a loud clatter of hooves and jingle of harness sounded out in the yard. It was a fact that Derek Winner and Gerald Andrews had to bring their horses back in the evening after four o'clock, when the piece-work gang packed up. On fine days the gang, working on the basis of the more crop harvested the more money earned, always continued up to four o'clock. Derek and Gerald, who were paid on day work, were expected to bring the horses back to the farm in their own time, with no additional pay in the form of overtime. This expected free labour, especially after a pretty hard day's work, began to irritate them. Sometimes the distance of homecoming might be in excess of three-quarters of a mile, meaning that at least thirty minutes of their own time was taken up. Management, in the shape of Charlie Wilson, could see no injustice here, and had made it very clear that any additional financial reward was totally out of the question. Hadn't men in charge of horses always returned to the farm in their own time when serving piece-work gangs? It was traditional, as were many other operations that favoured the farmer and not the worker. So it was then that this irritating sore continued to fester.

Anyway, back to this particular evening, and the sounds very reminiscent of a sheriff's posse riding into town. Poking our heads out of the door we beheld our two semi-militant heroes racing into the yard astride their respective mounts. One horse had breeching harness trailing, and they all blew steam from flaring nostrils. It was eventually construed that, to speed up the journey home, a race had developed, and with the spirit of youth taking over from common sense, they had galloped the last furlong in order to be the first past the post. But now it appeared a steward's enquiry was very much on the cards, as Charlie strode across the yard with a face like thunder. "My fellows", he barked, "what do you think you are doing galloping tired horses?" Before the now slightly shamefaced amateur jockeys could reply, he stormed on, "If the Major had met you it would have been the sack on the spot. You are worse than a couple of boys. Get those animals into the stable and cool them off". Turning on his heel the foreman strode away, without allowing the two miscreants a chance to speak in their own defence. It has always struck me as ironic that Charlie should accuse them of being "worse than a couple of boys" when they were just that — two boys on boys' money, doing men's work. Now, rather crestfallen they led their mounts into the stable, fully expecting another broadside from Will, as any rough treatment of animals met with short shrift on his part. But, realising very little harm had been done, he apparently put it down to high spirits, and said very little, apart from a very quiet, "Don't let this happen again. It's not the horses' fault you don't get paid. Have it out with Charlie". Whether it was ever resolved I don't remember, but I reckon "tradition" won the day, and no extra cash left the farm coffers. Anyway, within a couple of years the beet-carters were speeding home on tractors each evening, so not much time was lost by them.

And so the working day was done once more. It seemed a long one to me, more like a week in fact. Gerald walked off towards the cottages, his head very much to one side as he passed Charlie in the yard. Ever since his early school days, Gerald had this habit of dipping his head to one side if in trouble. The deeper the trouble, the more pronounced the head angle. We two Dereks set off round the corner and away on our bikes, just like two lifelong comrades, with the rabbit-slapping episode seemingly buried and forgotten. As I slid to a halt at No. 6, Pretoria, I felt part of a new team, and had rather enjoyed my day, despite my groundless worries along the way. Waggs stuck her nose through the bars of the gate to welcome me home and my thoughts turned to a cooked tea, which would soon be on the table. Ah well, let's get this bike in the shed and these heavy boots off my feet.

In the darker, winter afternoons we had our tea soon after returning from work. This was the main meal of the day for all of us, for there were no school dinners yet, so Michael had sandwiches, as of course I did. Dad, who came home at dinner time, had only a light meal then, so we were all looking forward to sharing in some substantial but simple fare. As the afternoons lengthened in early Spring, our system changed slightly for a time, to enable us to go digging on the garden while daylight lasted. Then Mum made us a cup of Ovaltine first to keep our energy levels up, and when bad light called an end to our outside work, we sat down to enjoy our tea in peace. My father always begrudged any precious daylight being wasted by him sitting indoors. Grandad Eke used to comment on his annual visits to us that if darkness never fell Fred would never stop working. He could always find a job to do outside whatever the time of year, as long as it was light enough to see. On occasions even a bright, dry, moonlight evening would tempt him outside again to saw logs under the leafless branches of the Dr. Harvey apple tree which supported his lengths of firewood. He never came home from work without a fallen branch on his shoulder. His eagle-eye would spot a likely length lying in the wood between Pretoria and High House, and this would be perched on his shoulder as he cycled home down the slope either at dinner time or at night. His firewood collecting genes must have been passed on to me, for even today I can't pass a fallen bough without transporting it to my own wood pile. It would seem that old habits die hard, even in a different environment.

The one exception to our ongoing work routine was enacted at 6.45 p.m. Monday to Friday, when all action ceased as if by magic. Spades and forks were abandoned, and play stopped for younger family members, and the inhabitants of Pretoria disappeared indoors like rabbits into a warren if a warning stamp of the foot was given. The reason – Dick Barton, Special Agent came on the wireless. Dick, Snowy and Jock drew us like magnets. Old and young alike, we were held mesmerised by the daring exploits of this trio. Rumour had it that anyone passing No. 4, Pretoria would hear Diddie Frost yelling, "Come on Snowy, get him Jock", at the top of his voice. This was hotly denied by our diminutive neighbour, but tension and excitement did run high for those fifteen minutes. When the B.B.C. hierarchy decided, in their wisdom, that Dick & Co were much too violent for the public's delicate ears, and replaced the programme with "The Archers", there was a public outcry, but to no avail, and life in our community was never quite the same as we heard our own lives being re-enacted in Ambridge.

Chapter 4
Swede Pullers

The next morning dawned with a sky of pink and mauve showing in the east over Pretoria woods. "Red sky in the morning, shepherd's warning", sprang immediately to mind as I pedalled my way towards the farm. I must say the air seemed to be of a more damp nature than of late, but the clear sky up above gave a false promise of fine weather.

Once more the size twelve boots crunched towards the cart-shed, and my stomach began to do a crazy dance beneath my khaki shirt.

"Derek, I want you to help Will with his stock this morning, and then you and he can fetch a couple of loads of swedes this afternoon."

This sounded a very promising day, so off I went to the stable without delay. As it was Tuesday it transpired that Charlie planned to visit King's Lynn cattle market and needed to give me a full day's orders.

"You're my helpmate for the day then, Derek?" Will greeted me, in his usual quiet and friendly manner. "We'll get on while it's still dry — I don't think it will last."

I spent a very pleasant morning leading Gipsy in and out of the yard with sugar-beet tops first of all, and then with barley straw for bedding. Since the coming of the combine harvester, most straw was baled, as opposed to the loose straw stacked after threshing. The only disadvantage in these oblong bales was the fact that the straw divided into sections which needed shaking out by fork. These sections had been made by the action of a ram compacting straw into the bale, which was then held together by two lengths of thick twine. This twine had to be collected up and removed to prevent stock chewing it, thus causing a blockage in their digestive systems. If straw was slightly damp when the baling process took place, it came out in slabs, resembling compressed cardboard, and would never shake out however much one shook or kicked it around. There is no finer sight than well-fed stock contentedly chewing the cud on a bed of fresh, golden barley straw. Some of the straw served as additional fodder, especially if there had been some grass content in the barley crop. As the fresh straw soaked up the moisture and became well-trodden, rich farmyard manure was being made. This "muck" was the basis of the farm crops to be grown in forthcoming years, and may have been instrumental in the well-known saying, "where there's muck, there's money".

Swede Pullers

These particular young stock were mainly pure-bred Red Poll cattle, an old and well-established East Anglian breed which was especially pleasing to the eye. A deep red colour, and hornless heads were their trademark, and they were generally kept as very useful, dual-purpose animals. Unfortunately the standard of stock kept on the farm at this time had fallen, due to various financial reasons, but the Major was still very proud of the Red Poll breed.

As Will Bumfrey was a first-class stockman, as well as horseman, he had these classier animals under his care. Being by nature a quiet man, Will had the basic essentials for a good stockman. He always talked gently to the animals as he moved around the yard. His low-toned voice indicated to his charges just where he was, and, being aware of his position, it was less likely that a bullock would bump into him or tread on his feet. Sudden movement or loud noises were out, for not only did disturbance disrupt the fattening process, it could also spell danger if heavy and often horned animals decided to stampede in a restricted yard. Frail man stood little chance against half a ton of very fresh beef on the hoof, and ribs were easily crushed when sandwiched between bullock and wall.

All the Bumfrey family were born and bred stockmen. Grandfather Alfred Bumfrey had, in his time, been a shepherd at Soigné, and also fed bullocks for several seasons in the yards at Elbreck Barn, a group of buildings right in the centre of the farm land. John had held the post of head team-man during the war, but had now relinquished this job to become a tractor-driver, and incidentally the only family member to be mechanically minded, until my brother, Michael, came along later. Will we have already mentioned, and my father, Fred, was cow-man at High House and overlooked all the grazing stock and suckler cows out in the extensive pastures around the other farm. Dad had also fattened bullocks at Elbreck Barn along with Will just after the latter had left the Army to return to farm work. It would seem also that younger brother Fred had taught Will a few lessons in stockmanship in those early days. The system used then to fatten stock in yards was to feed them copious amounts of mangolds or swedes placed in mangers around the walls. To tempt the appetites of these overfed animals, the roots were sliced in a hand-operated grinder, and mixed with chaff, then left to ferment very slightly for a few hours in a pile. This was very hard work and also very time-consuming, especially at weekends, for the process was continuous over a seven day week. On one particular weekend Will wanted to go out somewhere, and to speed the process up he persuaded brother Fred, much against his better judgement, that by feeding whole roots they could get away early. So skeps of mangolds were carried round the yard, and the bings filled in double-quick time. All was well until the next morning when a yard of bawling cattle greeted the two brothers as they biked down the rough track to their place of work. You've probably guessed it; yes, the uneaten mangolds still filled the troughs whilst the bullocks roared out their disapproval as they waited for a supply of sliced roots for Sunday's tea and Monday's breakfast. By the time they had cleared the troughs, carried the heavy mangolds back into the mixing house, ground and prepared fresh food, with their ears being assailed by a continuous cacophony of bawling cattle telling the whole Estate of their discontent, tempers were slightly frayed. Will never quite lived down the disaster of his bright idea as Dad used to bring it up on occasions if he was in danger of losing an argument involving the care of cattle with his elder brother.

Going back to the cattle kept on the farm in 1949, these store Red Polls were the exception rather than the rule. Quite a number of store animals were being bought in to augment the steers raised from suckler cows. Often the quality of animal wasn't that good, and I can well remember some gangling North or South Devon bullocks which resembled hat stands, with large horns at the front, and protruding hip bones at the rear, and very little meat in between. Willie Thaxton used to try to reassure all and sundry that they would fatten, but Dad wasn't so easily convinced. "They will soon fill out, Fred", Willie would tell him. "Not in my lifetime or yours", would come the reply, and often the poor-doers would return to King's Lynn market in the same state as they had come home after having consumed a couple of years' feed in between. Not that Willie Thaxton didn't know his stock, because he did, but financial restrictions had started to cloud his judgement, which was very unfortunate for the farm and the bailiff's standing amongst the men.

It seems as if we have drifted into general farm policies and away from our day's work in and around the Soigné, yards, which I was enjoying. At about twenty minutes to nine we stopped to have our breakfast, which was taken in the quiet of the stable. A companionable silence had settled over the whole premises; tractors had roared off to all parts of the farm to carry out various field duties; cattle and pigs were all fed and watered, which meant they rested at peace for a while. The dimly-lit stable itself gave out a peaceful feeling as we enjoyed our simple fare. Will still preferred his pure white linen bag with a drawstring at the top for his sandwiches; I had progressed to a more modern dinner tin, lined with rustling greaseproof paper.

As I stretched out my long Air Force-blue clad legs my uncle suddenly noticed the stains of bullocks' muck on the bottom of my trousers. Even though I had taken the precaution to tie the bottoms with binder string, the mess had still found its way upward.

"What you need is a pair of states to keep your trousers clean", announced my uncle.

Without more ado he began rummaging in his horse medicine cupboard. Out came a roll of canvas which, when unrolled, became two lengths about 15" x 12".

Swede Pullers

"Put these round your legs and tie them in the middle. No sense in mucking up your clothes unnecessarily." So that's how I acquired my first set of states, and felt much more of a workman now dressed for the part. Canvas was a much sought after commodity in farm workers' circles. Whenever a binder canvas became unserviceable it quickly ended up around several pairs of legs in the workforce. Our serviceable leg guards would never have passed muster under a sergeant-major's eagle eye, but they did a good job for us.

Feeling twice the man I had before breakfast, I had even more reason to feel proud later in the morning. "Take Gipsy and a cart down to Waterpit and bring some hay back for the horses while I mix up concentrate feed in the barn." I could hardly believe my ears because it was common knowledge that no one besides Will ever had charge of his beloved mare. "You will find the hay knife on the stack. Just take your fork and bring a handy load back." Not quite knowing what a hay knife did or how much constituted a "handy load", I set off for Waterpit corner. I had noticed a partly-cut haystack on my way to Rats Hall the previous day, so I did know where my destination was. Sitting up on the cart I drove out of the yard feeling like two men. The much broader back of Gipsy rippled before me, and her soft ears were cocked intelligently forward. She wasn't a true-bred Suffolk Punch, but of mixed ancestry, having just a slight feathering on her legs, light brown coat and darker mane and tail; highly intelligent, perfectly tempered and ever eager to serve, she was a beautiful workmate. It was no wonder Will kept her as his partner.

The sky had clouded over and a sharp wind began to move in from a north-easterly direction. As I had been sweating in the sheltered bullock yard I stopped the cart and put on my thick ex-Army coat. All was quiet on Waterpit corner this morning as the sugar-beeting gang had finished opposite and moved on towards High House. A short ladder was propped against the cut third of the stack. Can I explain here that one didn't take down a complete 12yds. by 6yds. haystack all at once because water would penetrate the dry hay and spoil its precious food content. Instead, one-third was taken at a time, using a broad-bladed knife with a wooden handle, offset at the top end, to cut down. The main cutting edge of the knife was situated on the bottom, and by driving this implement down into the stack the hay was cut cleanly and could be divided without tearing. A sharpening carborundum stone lay by the knife, and with this I endeavoured to make a razor-like edge on the tool. After a few abortive attempts at making a cut, the sweat began to rise under my coat. Discarding my outer blanket and then my thick jacket I puffed and swore as the only half-sharpened knife made very little impression on the stubborn haystack. Eventually I made some sort of a cut and was able to lift away slabs of sweet-smelling clover hay. The size of my "handy" load was governed more by the lack of depth on my cut than anything else. Setting off back to the farm, at least my load didn't shake off or settle down below the side-boards of the tumbril to look too small. Anyway, Will made no comment, so I presumed my efforts were classed as adequate. At least my newly-acquired leggings had prevented hayseeds filtering down into my boots, and saved me an age that night picking sharp seeds out of my thick, woollen socks.

Dinner was taken in the blacksmith's shop where a fire could be lit in cold weather. As we walked up the yard from our stable a few spots of rain flicked our faces. The "red sky in the morning" sign had begun to take effect, and nasty weather seemed to be in the offing. I noticed that Will carried a large bundle of discarded baler twine. I wondered at this, but could come up with no feasible solution. Soon all was revealed as the bundle was placed under the smoke canopy of the cold forge. After emptying a quantity of waste sump oil over the string he lit the mixture and, despite a few initial splutters, a nice blaze developed, making shadows dance around the very gloomy smithy. As the temperature had by now dropped considerably it was very pleasant to eat, and warm oneself at the same time. Wind and rain began to rattle on the cobweb-covered window as if hell-bent on blowing away the last vestiges of summer, which had been with us during the previous few balmy afternoons.

At a quarter-to-one Will sighed and indicated we must make a move. As Charlie was safely at King's Lynn market we weren't being pushed, but it seemed that needs must when the devil drives. Charlie's plan for us involved pulling a large stack bottom crop of swedes on Big Ashbreck. These had to be cleared that particular afternoon to enable the tractor ploughmen to finish turning over the field. As explained in an earlier chapter, land with stacks on was often planted with a later crop, and this had been the case here.

"There's nothing for it, Derek. We must get the job done today, rain or no rain. You yoke Beauty and we'll get off." Sitting up on my tumbril with a chaff sack over my head and shoulders, and my legs pulled into the front-board, I huddled against the heavy rain. This was indeed a different world to the one I had been in twenty-four hours previously on the way to Rats Hall. After passing out of the shelter provided by the end of Sixteen Acre Belt I could feel cold and damp penetrating my thick coat. The dead potato tops lying on their ridges made a very depressing picture on Little Strawberries. Here was another crop waiting to be harvested, well past the optimum time. With so many labour-intensive tasks to perform seemingly at the same time, it was inevitable that some jobs slipped behind schedule. Riding on down the slope towards Waterpit corner my glorious view of yesterday across Little Elbreck and beyond was veiled in a grey curtain of almost horizontal rain. The sheep-folds were shrouded, and there was no sign of Charlie Andrews or his faithful dog. Up the hill towards Long Plantation we went where Will bore right to set off along the hedge separating Big Ashbreck and Little Elbreck.

Swede Pullers

Stretching away to the left I could see the ploughed land which would run down to an unseen Massingham Heath. The sound of a labouring tractor engine heralded the approach of Uncle John Bumfrey, hunched on the seat of a Standard Fordson hauling a trailing plough. John had a chaff sack forming a hood over his head and shoulders, but there was no protection in the form of a cab on these very basic machines. The stubby Standard Fordson had been a wonderful servant to British agriculture during and just after the war years, but was now being superseded by the higher and more powerful Fordson Major along with hydraulic implements which gave a new dimension to mechanised cultivation. Meanwhile the elements poured down on the unprotected operator as the faithful servant hauled a two-furrow plough slowly along the trench formed on the last trip. Heads were nodded in recognition, and the machine receded behind us as we made our way to the swede patch situated half way along the length of this large field. As we passed the folded sheep I could see Charlie Andrews under copious amounts of coats, struggling to get rolls of netting on to the cart. A new fold had to be set up whether it was wet or fine. A very miserable looking face peeped out from under the cart where the dog tried to find a dry spot of shelter.

Will eventually pulled up under a couple of overhanging holly trees and dismounted. As the wind blew from the north-east the trees gave little shelter, so it was decided to press on with the task in hand, and get it over with as soon as possible. Under instruction I tied Beauty to the hedge in order to help Will fill his cart first. Now my Uncle was always in the front line when it came to modern weather protection garments. He visited the Army & Navy surplus store at King's Lynn to buy any useful items likely to make life easier at work. Today he covered himself in a long, camouflaged, sleeved cape. The material resembled a stiff version of our plastic mac and had been designed to keep a soldier safe from contact with various gases, which might have been used by the Nazis during warfare. This cape was reasonably lightweight, and shed water perfectly, although quite a bit of it ran down the legs. My thick ex-Army coat kept out rain for quite a time by soaking up water, but of course it became heavier by the minute, and eventually needed a Herculean frame to carry it. Also, as one moved inside it, the water worked through to join with sweat from inside to give its occupant a wet back.

We had to pull the round, purple-crowned swedes up by their long necks and sling them into the tumbril. Soon my frozen hands were mud-spattered as were my legs, coat and face. The heavier my coat became the more the bottom scraped the mud every time I bent to uproot a swede. Heave, sling, clump, heave, sling, clump — slowly the tumbril filled until it was Gipsy's turn to be tied and my cart took her place. Periodically the two tractors at plough laboured past getting closer with each furrow completed. I believe John's ploughing mate was Artie Keeley, but I was too wet, cold and miserable to take much notice. The water, which ran down my neck, joined that soaking through my coat. The chaff sack, which started as my hood, became such a soggy encumbrance that it had been discarded long since. So, I thought, this is work on the farm in winter; what have I let myself in for? My spirits sagged even lower than my trailing coat flaps.

Eventually the last wretched swede had been chucked into the cart. Stiff, sore and thoroughly miserable I straightened my back and surveyed the sodden countryside.

"Nice day for ducks, Will", a cheery voice came from the other side of the fence. "You bringing me those swedes for my sheep?" It was Charlie Andrews peering out from under his sack hood. Drops of rain stood on the front of his black, curly hair where his cap had been tipped back by the sack's weight.

"Like hell I am, Lop", retorted Will whose temper never stood much human leg-pulling. "They are for my bullocks." A characteristic gurgling laugh bubbled out of Charlie who, winking at me, said, "I never thought you would come out of your dry stable on a day like this. They tell me you have a snip in that yard with those few bullocks". Charlie could never resist pulling Will's leg if he got the chance, and had splashed across to the hedge especially to get Will's rag out. It is educational to note here that both stockmen referred to their animal charges as "my sheep" and "my bullocks". Major Birkbeck never came into the equation at all. He just bought and sold the animals, but in between they "belonged" to whichever stockman had their welfare in his hands. There was a very strong bond between man and beast at that time.

Having nothing of a warming nature left in our bags, Will suggested the best way to keep up our body temperatures was to walk and lead our horses back to the farm. So off we squelched to the road with Gipsy leading the way and Beauty keeping her nose as close as possible to the tail-board of the first tumbril. There was no let up to the driving rain, but at least it was at our backs now. After propping our carts and releasing our mares, all four of us made for the shelter of the stable, leaving the wet and fast-darkening afternoon behind. Derek and Gerald had returned and stabled their horses earlier in the afternoon as sugar-beeting had been abandoned soon after the onset of heavy rain. The piece-work gang would return home, dry, but without pay until they took up their hooks again. Judging by the noise issuing from the barn as we passed, the two chaps accused of being "worse than a couple of boys" were acting out their alleged age group and were indulging in some kind of loud horseplay, probably at Dick Welham's expense. No doubt a look-out had been placed at an elevated window in order to give warning of the foreman's approach as he returned from King's Lynn. "Boys will be boys", but some of our boyhoods lasted well into our twenties, as will be disclosed as this narrative unfolds.

Swede Pullers

At sharp on four o'clock my bike sped off towards Pretoria. Having suffered endlessly from ferocious colds all my life I knew staying in wet clothes was fatal, so I made for home with all possible speed. When my sodden and forlorn figure entered the back door my over-protective mother went off into one of her tirades against everyone in general: myself first of all for being stupid enough to work out in the rain; Charlie Wilson (I think she labelled him "Old Thump Skull") for sending me out; finally poor old Will came under the hammer for taking me out with him — no matter how many times I tried to explain that it was dry when Charlie issued the order and there was a need to clear the swedes today. My Dad met a blast of hot temper when he tried to pour oil on troubled water, and I soon gathered both he and his innocent and soaking wet brother, Will, had very little brain content between them! I wonder if Will's ears glowed along with Charlie Wilson's. But the storm soon abated and clean, dry shirts came forth and plans were laid on how to dry my clothes for work on the morrow.

As luck would have it a clear wall of the back kitchen backed on to the chimney-breast which was well heated by the range in our living room. By stretching my weighty coat on strings, it hung close to the wall, which acted as a radiator, and soon steam rose and a rather foul smell of drying wool permeated the lower part of the house. The coat in the scullery, and trousers in the living room set the smell up, and it was helped along by a jacket over a chair-back and a cap on the hob. But soon the appetising aroma from beef pudding took over and set our taste buds dripping. Charlie Fitt had called in the morning leaving some shin of beef and kidney. The shin had been cut up small with Mum's very sharp knife on that well-worn, wooden chopping board. Real butchers' beef suet had gone into the pastry which lined the basin, and this was filled with the beef and kidney and some thick gravy, and then cooked for four or five hours. The old black-leaded cooking range may have been primitive, but it produced some mouth-watering meals even under wartime and post-war food restrictions. I expect most of our meat coupons would have been taken up in purchasing that evening's fare. Sitting around the deal table, covered first of all with an American oilcloth sheet slightly worn at the corners, and then a spotless, carefully ironed table cloth we experienced a taste of heaven, and the foul weather and hard work were left behind. The large Aladdin lamp standing in the table centre gave both light and heat. This more modern type of paraffin-oil lamp had a round wick and worked on the same principle as a gas light, using a cone-shaped mantle to give off a very white glow. If a slight draught affected one side of the lamp a patch of black soot would appear, causing a partial eclipse of the light, but would soon burn off when the draught was removed. Any slight knock on the side of the glass, or chimney as it was called, would result in the disintegration of the fragile mantle. A new one then had to be fitted, this being pink in colour as it was coated with an inflammable material to keep it rigid during transport. The pink colour burned away immediately it came into contact with heat from the wick, and one was left once more with the white, very fragile mantle. But despite this rather expensive replacement drawback, the light and heat given out were a big improvement on the ordinary single or double burner oil lamps of past decades.

The wind continued to roar through the fir trees, which made up the narrow belt at the rear of our cottages. Rain rattled on the scullery window, which faced north. "I told you we would suffer for that weather breeder on Monday." My Dad had a fixation about a lovely, warm, out-of-season day heralding a spell of rough weather. I must admit that this "Job's comforter" type of forecast often proved to be very accurate, but we liked to enjoy our fine weather bonus in blissful ignorance of what might follow, and anyway, forewarned or not, we couldn't do much about it, could we?

During the long, dark winter evenings we sometimes listened to radio programmes, besides Dick Barton Special Agent. But one thing we always did, and that was to enjoy a game of Ludo — one game only per evening, no matter how short or long the duration. A league table was kept by Michael, who always played red, whilst Mum was blue, Dad yellow and myself green. Just as the green shirt of Wilson's House won the wooden spoon for me at the Grammar School, my lack of Ludo-cunning left me rooted at the bottom of our family league. The wretched yellow barriers set up at strategic points by the head of the house confounded us continually, and he was unanimously voted the villain of the piece. Sometimes we played dominoes, and at one time whist became quite popular. The well-filled grate burned a mixture of coal and sawn logs, and cast a good heat out into the top half of the room, but because it was at the end of a rather long living room, the unfortunate at the far end of the table — me — often had cold legs in extreme weather. A thin, wooden spill, lit between the bars, kept my father's half-inch of hand-rolled cigarette going for a couple of puffs at a time. He spent hours carefully splitting down these spills from sawn pine logs, with his knife. I always thought that he burned more wood than tobacco, but as he insisted that smoking was his only bit of enjoyment in life, we desisted from interfering most of the time, that is until his life-threatening coughing fits broke our resolve, and we all expressed our doubts as to his sanity in persisting with such a silly habit.

Slowly the fire burned down, and the nine o'clock news came and went. The still heavy, half-dried coat was turned for the last time. Mum usually took her pre-bed nap sitting upright on a dining chair, snoring with increasing velocity as she slowly settled to a very acute angle, only to right her equilibrium with a snort and shuffle. Stone water bottles were filled from singing tin kettles on top of the range. Remember, rubber, hot water bottles disappeared as soon as the pre-war purchases perished, and these flat-bottomed, stone bottles, with a knob on one end, and a screw-cork in the top, replaced them by necessity. When the Japanese overran South-East Asia all the rubber plantations perished in more ways than one. Warm feet in bed came very low on the Government's priority list in dark days of war.

As Waggs made her way up the garden to her box of straw in the shed, the mellow lights at the windows of Pretoria were fast being extinguished, as most people, like me, were only too glad to pull the bedclothes up round their ears, and forget about the sharp reminder of approaching winter, which they had experienced that day.

Chapter 5
Land Army Girls Come to Soigné

By work-time next morning the weather had resumed a more hospitable face, giving promise of a dry day, although, of course, everywhere was soaking wet. Charlie seemed to be almost apologetic about the previous day's downpour as he joined us in the cart-shed. "What an afternoon yesterday, my fellows", was his opening gambit. "The wipers on my windscreen would hardly clear the water on the way back from Lynn." After a bit more small talk he began to give out orders until at last he reached me.

"Did you and Will manage to clear the swedes?"

After receiving a reply to the effect that we had, he proceeded, "Put a good half of your load down by Will's yard, and then take the rest to the old sows behind the pigsties. Throw them well out on the grass at the top. Then make sure Beauty is in the blacksmith's shop by half past-eight. Walter High should be here to do some shoeing today". Walter High was the ageing blacksmith with a forge at East Walton, which was also part of the Estate.

On acquaintance with Charlie's plan, Will decided he had a better idea in order to save time and labour. "You take the load on to the pig pasture first, and then come back to me and I can use the rest in the yard today. That will save putting them down, only to pick them up tomorrow. I'll leave my load propped and borrow your cart while Beauty is being shod. Gipsy has to go next, so it should all work out."

It all sounded very complicated, but putting my trust in his judgement, I yoked up and carefully backed my mare into the precariously balanced, cream-coloured shafts. Leading Beauty through the ever-present mud around the farmyard, I suddenly remembered my states. No man worth his salt started work on muddy days without first binding his trouser bottoms. How could I have forgotten after only one day? The omission was soon rectified, and away we strode up past the milk-house door, and past the open yard to the gate leading into the sows' pasture behind the two rows of black-painted pigsties. These sties held the farrowing sows tended by Dick Welham. The heaps of soiled straw outside each door steamed away in the damp morning air. The "in-pig" sows, accompanied by the much larger boar, came shrieking and grunting to the gate at the sound of my approaching cart. Opening the gate, which needed dragging through the thick, churned-up mud, was one problem, as was keeping the old sows from coming out. Of course, the ladies in question weren't interested in escaping at all. Their one great interest of the moment

Land Army Girls Come to Soigné

was the contents of my cart, and after running under the wheels, then through Beauty's legs, they followed us into the field. Leaving my poor mare, with grunting pigs making free with her legs as a short cut from side to side of the cart, I ran back to close the gate, once more having to lift it clear of the ruts. Drawing away from the permanently muddy delta around the gate, we reached firmer ground. Here a few blades of grass had survived the constant rooting which all pigs love to do, so I threw some food around the cart, causing much chasing and squealing as one greedy pig tried to race her neighbour to the delicacy. Much crunching and slobbering continued in our wake as I threw off about one-third of my load in as wide an arc as possible. All the pigs were far too busy to bother us on our way out, so we could negotiate the muddy gateway at a much less frenetic pace this time.

After helping Will distribute the roots in the store cattle yard I parked my tumbril and led Beauty into the narrow stall or "travis" on the side of the blacksmith's shop. Tying her leading rein to a ring-fastening on the end wall, I settled down to wait for the reputedly elusive Walter High. At twenty-to-nine I ate my breakfast, sitting in the dark, fireless forge. At ten-past-nine Charlie crunched his way down from his house.

"Isn't Walter here yet?" The conspicuously empty and silent smithy meant his question needed no answer from me as I shuffled uncomfortably from one foot to the other, feeling that somehow it was my fault the blacksmith hadn't arrived on time. "You'll have to wait a bit then." Having uttered this next piece of pretty obvious mental deduction, he swung away towards the barn loudly humming a favourite hymn tune to disguise his irritation at having his day's plans messed about by a man who couldn't get up in the morning.

At nine-thirty a horse and trap pulled into the yard, and a very surly man of advancing age got down. A grunt acknowledged Charlie's good morning, as the latter emerged from the barn.

"I want four new shoes on this mare, and then a couple on Gipsy", the foreman rapped out in a tone that brooked no disagreement, but sounded rather as if some was expected.

"Can't do all that today, Charlie. There isn't even a fire started yet."

I visibly shuddered as Charlie drew in a large breath and prepared to blow the ageing blacksmith back to East Walton.

'He" (that meant Willie Thaxton) "told me this morning that you knew about the six shoes to be fitted, Walter. He'll expect it to be done." Then, having put the onus of the order on to the boss from High House, Charlie strode away, leaving Walter to weigh up whether Willie knew about the horses or not. Muttering oaths about foremen in general, and chapel preachers in particular, he set about raising a fire. With me on the bellows, a bright blaze soon lit up the smithy, and Walter, now clad in leather apron, set about his task, but without, I am sad to record, any of the cheerful personality associated with the traditional smith in all the best stories of rural life. Very soon life returned to the forge as the sound of hammer on metal rang out, and the smell of burning hoof drifted out of the open stall door. Beauty did nothing to upset the already fragile temper of the tradesman, although I did hold her head just in case. Her feet came up in turn in answer to the tug on the tuft of hair on the back of her leg. I breathed a sigh of relief when the last nail was driven home and clenched over on top of the hoof. A few strokes of the rasp and her feet looked a picture.

Just as I was wondering if it was safe to have my dinner beside the fire, or whether I should suggest collecting the other horse, Will came up the yard leading Gipsy. Tying her outside, he carried his bag into the warm forge.

"Hello, Walter, going to have some dinner now?"

Without replying directly the smith grunted at me, "Fetch my bag from the cart". When he opened his bag, it was evident that a very caring wife had provided his fare, along with a thermos flask of tea. After a bit the atmosphere thawed as he and Will discussed life in general on the Estate. I just sat as usual and listened to the "experts" on running the large concern, not really caring or understanding anything about it. To me the Estate was there when I arrived, and presumably would still be functioning long after I had passed by. Like Great Britain, it was indestructible, untouched by outside influence, and in a nutshell, "just there". It went without saying that the Estate would provide work for anyone, young or old, who required it. Farming operations were carried out using all the labour available, but with the lowest financial outlay possible. This system of estate management had worked to the satisfaction of owners for hundreds of years, and to a degree, on an estate such as Westacre, to the satisfaction of employees. Yes, the system had its flaws, but overall it provided a rather primitive kind of social security. The key to it working, of course, was extremely low wages compared with other industries. In 1949 it still worked, but was beginning to show signs of breakdown in the form of small spots of irritation amongst the younger elements in the labour force — a good example being shown in one of the previous chapters when Gerald and Derek Winner felt they were being treated unfairly over the non-payment for extra time worked. I don't believe anyone on either side realised at the time the need for positive ideas of change before radical economic stresses would threaten to destroy that which provided work and a living for practically the whole of the Westacre population, most of whom were reasonably satisfied with their lot. Nor did I then realise that I would become progressively the most radical-minded man employed there within a decade. All that was to come, after much listening and much thinking and soul-searching.

To return to our dinner time discourse in the blacksmith's shop, as Walter High mellowed following his hot tea and sandwiches, Will broached the subject of two shoes on Gipsy, and the blacksmith agreed to complete that before

Land Army Girls Come to Soigné

returning to whatever urgent business awaited him at East Walton. He also excelled himself by offering to put a new handle into a muck fork that Will mentioned rather furtively in passing, promising to return it next time he had to come to Soigné. Packing up my meal tin, I waited for Charlie to finish his dinner and give me orders for the afternoon. Meeting me in the yard, he seemed rather pleased to see the broad beam of Gipsy protruding from the travis door, heralding the fact that the unpredictably-tempered blacksmith intended to carry out the full shoeing programme without additional bidding.

"Derek, take your mare to High House and bring back the green cart they've borrowed. We shall need that tomorrow for 'tatering". Then look in the bullock boxes just before Laddie's house and load all the baskets that are usable ready for the morning."

So, off along the familiar track to High House we went. There was no difficulty in finding the cart and a nice, steady ride back found me outside the now unused bullock boxes stretching from the pigsties to Laddie Richardson's garden. As I said, these fattening bullock boxes were now unused for that purpose at any rate. They were specifically designed to fatten one animal per box, and were, I suppose, the very beginning of factory-farming ideas. Each small box had a sunken floor into which the bullock, usually the very stocky, black Aberdeen Angus, was put at the beginning of autumn. The individual stalls were placed on either side of a built-up walkway, from which the tender placed sliced roots and rich oilseed cake into bings which were hanging on adjustable chains inside each box. As the straw-bedded floor of the stall rose under its occupant, the level of the feeding trough could be adjusted to suit each individual animal. The mangolds were sliced in a central shed, and then mixed with wheat or barley chaff. This shed had wide, double doors through which loads of roots were tipped in readiness for grinding in the hand-turned root-slicer. I imagine the best animals from this type of fattening system found their way into the pre-war King's Lynn Fatstock Shows, then on to the Christmas meat market. Probably the outbreak of war killed off the demand for extra prime beef animals for I know these particular boxes were empty in the early 1940s when our local salvage collections were stored there, awaiting collection for the war effort.

This afternoon all was quiet in this blue-slate roofed, one-storey building. Dust was everywhere, and the adjustable chains were rusty and hanging with age-old cobwebs. Several pieces of yellowing newspaper showed where a corner had been used as a makeshift toilet by a worker finding himself a long way from his bucket lavatory at home. A few rusty tins lay in the first one, reminding me that our last salvage collections of 1945 had never been needed for the war effort. Ragged tails of house sparrows' nests hung untidily from rafter ends, and piles of white droppings indicated the position of a neat, round, mud cup nest of the swallow. Having so many "sweet smelling" pigsties around the farm attracted clouds of tiny insects which, in their turn, provided plenty of food for our swooping, diving, summer visitors, whilst convenient beams in the open sheds made perfect nesting places. The only drawback to the system was the fact that any implements parked directly underneath these sites were soon coated with a liberal amount of excreta released over the nest edge. But I am sure everyone would agree it was only a small price to pay for the sight of these wonderfully versatile flyers, displaying their skills over the farmyard as they scooped up beakfuls of insects to feed hungry youngsters.

Finding baskets flung "willy-nilly" in one box, I began to sort them over. To say they represented a very mixed collection would be an understatement. Certainly they roughly divided into two categories — wire and woven, but their condition of repair defied description. The wickerwork baskets were caked with mud, often with handles bent or broken. In size they resembled a large shopping basket, whilst the wire variety could have been rejects from the modern supermarket. By degrees I sorted, straightened and loaded the best of them. By banging the muddy bottoms on a wall I managed to dislodge most of the adhering dry clay soil. On one or two occasions the rotten framework left the handle so I realised care was needed with the banging process. Towards the end of my task Charlie came along to take stock of the situation. His rolling gait brought him to the tail of my cart where he stood, staring for a few moments, and then, raising his trilby slightly, he proceeded to scratch his head.

Muttering more to himself than to me he said, "There won't be enough there. It's too late to send anyone to the Abbey now". Then, with a sudden flash of genius and clear thinking, the problem was resolved. "I'll send a tractor and trailer in the morning". It wasn't until afterwards that I discovered what the baskets — or lack of — were destined for. They were potato baskets and they were needed on Little Strawberries the next day when a gang of land-girls was coming to pick up the crop.

This was all revealed the next morning when I was sent to that field with a tumbril and baskets. Georgie Wright and Leslie were despatched to the Abbey Farm to borrow their supply of baskets, with strict orders to return post-haste. Bringing a second cart to the field was Albert Richardson, or "Old Laddie" as everyone knew him. He was instructed to act as "haler", which meant that after the potatoes had been picked up and loaded into the carts he would form a clamp along the hedge side, where the tubers would be stored until later in the year. With great trepidation I set off behind Laddie to the twenty-eight-acre field situated behind Sixteen Acre Belt, which itself ran across the top of the small pastures at the rear of the farm. Work was to begin at the top end of the field where Honeypot Lane proper began. The potato rows ran across the shortest length of the field, beginning alongside part of Lightning Breck hedge, roughly north to south. The sun was just beginning to show with the

Land Army Girls Come to Soigné

promise of a nice day. Since the hale was to run down alongside Big Strawberries hedge, Albert looked to have a pleasant working position for the day. Joe Bly had his orange Case tractor parked just inside the gate with a potato harvester behind. Everything seemed to be confusion to me as we grouped in the top of the lane, awaiting the arrival of the picking gang. Joe, who was always agitated, began to get more agitated as eight o'clock came and went. Charlie Wilson arrived on his bike and paced around, making poor Joe even more uneasy with the unheard of occupation of "standing around". Charlie stamped, then kicked out at the potato baulks, muttering from time to time, "He" (indicating Willie Thaxton) "said they were coming today for certain". Laddie meanwhile had seated himself on an upturned wire basket, and looked comfortable enough to stay there all day. "Have your breakfasts, together", barked Charlie, "I'll go back and find out what's going on." With that he mounted his bike and sped off down the stubble of Big Strawberries and away to Soigné. Eventually it transpired the missing ladies had failed to finish the crop on their previous farm as estimated, and had to return for a couple of hours before setting off to Soigné. They arrived in an ex-Army lorry, with a canvas-covered back and wooden seats along each side. Needless to say the prettiest girl on parade sat in the front beside the male driver, with her mate squeezed in by the passenger door. Joe had already spun out one row of potatoes down the field and one back, but there was quite a lot of preparatory work to be done before picking began. Firstly, a canvas toilet needed to be erected behind the hedge from where we were working. This necessary item was something new on our horizon as the all-male workforce only needed to turn into the hedge to relieve themselves. With females present a certain amount of care had to be taken to preserve modesty on both sides, although I soon gathered our new recruits weren't all that modest, and soon shocked the rather reserved Joe Bly and Charlie Wilson with some of their language and rather forward observations. The two gentlemen in question were local Methodist preachers, and as such obviously had to appear shocked, even if they weren't. Anyway, back to work — as the girls stood around chatting and smoking, Leslie and Georgie Wright arrived with additional baskets. It appeared that Charlie's order for much haste had fallen on deaf ears, as far as George was concerned at any rate. George never hurried for anyone, except at five minutes to four so as to be ready for home at four o'clock. Neither did the two basket men hurry unduly in the transfer of their load into my cart, but rather stood feasting their professional eyes on the female talent adorning the fields, where normally nothing more exciting than Blackie's trilby hat or Barney's flat cap lit up the scenery. Of the two would-be local Romeos, George carried a reputation of being a Casanova on the courting scene. One tale circulating around that time recorded that George, whilst doing a spot of hot-blooded courting in the cart-shed at Soigné late one night, apparently dropped a vital piece of his safety precautions, and was frantically engaged in finding it with the aid of struck matches. Now, just by chance, Leslie Richardson was passing the shed to record these facts. Whether he offered to lend his electric torch to the two lovers or not, was never mentioned, but the somewhat exaggerated tale spread like wildfire throughout the Soigné fraternity. Leslie of course, in his best town crier's style, could tell us all in one go if he really put his mind to it. I can tell you, no stone was left unturned when an opportunity came to pull a mate's leg, and Leslie was always a leader in this department. Anyway, it appears that George's reputation grew in stature as a result of the story. But any romantic notions regarding the land-girls was quickly cut short as Charlie Wilson's arrival sent the two unattached young men away for a load of straw to cover the potato hale. I've no doubt the thoughts of a return visit sped them on their way.

Meanwhile, the girls' gang-man had collected a number of nut sticks from his lorry, and after pacing the length of the rows, proceeded to divide the distance into equal parts and marked each one with a stick. The divisions numbered equally to the number of girls in his gang. The system was for each girl to position herself beside a stick. After the digger had passed, exposing the potatoes, she picked along her stretch, filling baskets as she went and setting them to one side in a row. When the next stick was reached and the last potato picked she waited for the following round of the digger. But before this occurred the cart-men had to pick up and empty the baskets so that a line of discarded baskets was available for filling next time around. This was to be my job, assisted by the gang-man, Jim, who incidentally was rushing round to earn two pay packets, one from the Government and one from Soigné Farm. But there was no doubt he was a good worker hailing from the fenland part of Norfolk where piece-work was the norm, and fast workers earned the most money.

After slinging all my empty baskets at regular intervals along the entire length to be worked, I waited until they were filled for the first time. Jim then instructed me to stand in the cart and set Beauty walking along the side of the undug work, with the left-hand wheel in the potato ridge bottom. Jim meanwhile walked level with the back of my cart, his left hand holding the protruding metal side support. When the first basket was adjacent he lifted it with his right hand, and slung it up to me using the metal stay as a support to assist his easy, swinging action. I, in turn, caught the heavy basket, then tipped its contents down into my cart before discarding the empty container over the side, well clear of the tractor's path when the next row was dug. As we approached the end I took up my long reins, hooked over the front-board, and guided the horse into a return row on the far side of the land Joe had set out. The cart was then passed over to Laddie at the hale for him to unload, whilst we set off again using the second mare and cart. The whole system was designed to proceed at a steady, working speed. If the weight of crop varied across the field, then as the pickers moved around they would suffer where the crop was heaviest, and gain on lighter areas. Each end section was only half the distance of the centre ones. This meant that our end picker went half way down to the headland, and then round into the second half on the way back. I must say I marvelled at the simplicity of it all as everyone moved along like clockwork. But of course there had to be a snag somewhere. Amongst all this hard, manual work, there was one man who was fully mechanised, and that was Joe. Normally agricultural workers had a built-in work speed regulator which matched each integral job of work with its partner. But Joe seemed to be very out-of-cog with everyone else wherever he went. He was a very nice man indeed, but an eternal worrier. It was certain he had never read the passage in his Bible which says, "Can worry add even one cubit to your height?", for Joe worried from dawn to dusk. Well, on this job, it was obvious he could drive his tractor across and back much faster and in less time than the heavy crop could be picked. Common sense should have told him to wait on the end until the clearing cart was well on its way, but not Joe, and he kept revving the engine quite close up behind our tail-board, much to Jim's obvious and mounting annoyance. The faster we went to get out of the way, the nearer the machine came. Jim stopped occasionally to silently make a point, but it didn't sink in. The girls were also becoming agitated as they were being driven on to work non-stop, and anyone who has ever bent double picking spuds will know just how back-breaking it can be. Jim and his gang stuck it until mid-afternoon, and then the ganger stopped and walked up to Joe's machine. Jim pointed out the error of Joe's ways, and Joe in return blustered on about keeping the job going. A group of nearby girls gathered and a couple of hefty lasses stepped in with a very serious looking threat. If work didn't proceed at a reasonable speed, the cause of the aggravation would be removed from his machine and then, have his trousers taken away for an unspecified period. I've no doubt they were serious and quite capable of carrying out their threat. Sitting on the side of my cart I found all this very interesting and highly entertaining. I quickly made a mental note not to upset these female Amazons in any way, and to work at whatever speed they thought suitable. The threat of de-bagging had, for a time at least, a marked effect on the speed of our digger and Jim became his normal, cheerful and matey self once more as tension eased.

Laddie was kept busy building the potato hale or clamp. Potatoes are mostly round by nature, and tend to roll downwards no matter how often and how high they are thrown upwards. Even with the help of heavy straw bales along each side, it wasn't easy to keep the tubers in a neat, pyramid-shaped pile. Using a special potato fork with close steel tines and metal knobs on the end to prevent damage, Old Laddie built his clamp. After the potatoes settled a bit he could move the bales forward to form a barrier once more. Even then some escaped by rolling from the apex and bouncing over the top. George Wright and Leslie Richardson returned with a large load of bundled wheat straw. This type of bale was loosely compacted and tied with binder twine across the width near both ends. By laying each bundle lengthways up the sloping side of the hale, a thatching effect was obtained, and a frost-proof layer covered the tender tubers, eventually being itself enveloped in a layer of soil.

Leslie stood surveying his father's handiwork with a professional eye, which turned out to be highly critical. "Not very level along the top", said son to father. "You'll slope to ground level by tomorrow night." With this statement of fact he seized the fork and proceeded to hurl more spuds on the top to achieve a level line. To be fair to Mr. Richardson senior, his shortage of breath due to a lung disorder and the poor tipping qualities of the long-bodied, pneumatic-tyred tumbril hadn't helped him cope with the job too well. By mid-afternoon his efforts were becoming more laboured, and his apex line sank as a consequence. But son Leslie liked to see things done perfectly, and produced a short burst of energy as potatoes flew through the late afternoon air. George thought it highly amusing as the family jousting became rather heated. Eventually Leslie, who was recovering slowly from his terrible experiences as a prisoner of war in the Far East, also ran out of puff and peace returned to the scene. These little exchanges helped to pass the day away, and very soon, a halt was called by the ganger. Into the lorry piled the girls; Laddie and I unyoked the horses and followed the tractor and trailer back to the farm. Joe was left in the field to cover his spud-wheeled tractor for the night quite thankful I am sure to be able to cycle home to the Warren still decently attired in his overall trousers. The mind boggles at the thought of Mrs. Bly greeting her white-legged husband had his bags disappeared in the back of that ex-Army lorry. I felt very happy with my day and thoroughly enjoyed working with a gang from outside the Estate.

On reaching the stable I met up with Gerald and Derek, and was provided with a few more laughs as the two wags told me about their experiences the previous year when they worked with the Land Army. Gerald thought it was hilarious to use the girls' canvas toilet for target practice whilst it was being occupied. A shower of well-aimed potatoes thudded into its soft sides making the young lady inside scream out in mock terror. But, unbeknown to the ambusher, a counter-attack was planned, and after a short scuffle, half a dozen lusty land-girls succeeded in subduing Master Andrews and did actually remove his lower garments for a short time thus cooling the ardour of the missile aimer. Derek also told me how he had slowed down Joe Bly to deter him from pressing too close to the cart-tail. It appeared that as Joe closed in behind Derek my namesake suddenly hauled his horse to a halt and pulled him backwards. As a result, the metal-covered toe at the back of his tumbril went clean through the tractor radiator as Joe failed to stop in time. Water and steam flew into the air, and Joe almost died in his seat. Derek, who cared for no one, carried on regardless and left the crippled tractor in his wake. Actually he had only planned to frighten Joe, but as the operation worked so spectacularly, he allowed the girls' adulation to cast him in a much more clever mould.

Chapter 6
I Follow the Girls to Abbey Farm

The potato harvest continued without serious interruption for about eight days. One morning a band of heavy showers sent us scampering for shelter – the girls to their lorry, and us under one of the large oaks along the hedgerow, and as the leaves were fast disappearing, we fared the worse, but the rain soon passed and apart from making everything wet and the soil sticky, not much harm came from them. On most days we were blessed with some pale sunshine which made the job much easier. The land tended to be heavier under the trees at the far end, but horses and tractor had no real difficulty as regards traction. The wickerwork baskets became encrusted with clay soil in these wetter conditions, and were consequently heavier for the girls dragging them along between their legs as they picked the crop two-handed for increased speed. Even for those poor souls who were used to it, the job was a back-breaking one, so I'm sure that the invention of more sophisticated harvesting machines eventually brought only tears of relief to the manual workers. But, by the time progress was made in this direction, potatoes were no longer grown as a crop on Soigné Farm.

At some time during the day we managed to find an extra large tuber and this baking potato found its way into our dinner tins after the food contained therein had been consumed. I believe the crop was Majestics, a white potato equally suited to boiling or baking in the jacket.

As the operation approached the road hedge and the end hove in sight I felt quite sad. Firstly, I had enjoyed working with the lively gang, and secondly, I knew where I should be all day and every day until the job finished and this was a great bonus to my nerves. As the last rows were levelled and their hidden, white harvest shaken out on top of the ground, Charlie arrived on the scene.

"Load all the baskets into your cart, Derek. They want you to go with the gang down to the Abbey and help with their potatoes. You'll find the field opposite Tumbler Hill sheds."

Setting off first thing in the morning I made my way up to White Gate corner, then struck off along the green road between Lower and Middle Thirty Acres. This track led to Westacre village, but was so rough that no one, unless on foot or horseback, used it as a short cut but rather took the longer, more comfortable route via Pretoria. I left Soigné land behind after passing between the two Thirty Acres, and continued along the top of a large field that ran

I Follow the Girls to Abbey Farm

down to Shortrow Plantation which bordered the Pretoria to Westacre road. As I approached Tumbler Hill sheds, which were protected from the north by a small wood known as Old Covert, the potato rows appeared on my left. Up the track from Westacre came another cart driven by Claude Miller. With him was Lou Reynolds, brother-in-law of Joe Bly being married to Joe's sister, Edie. Claude Miller was team-man at the Abbey Farm and always wore a bow tie both for work and going out. To see anyone around Westacre wearing a bow tie would be surprising, but to wear a tie of any sort to work was unique. I must say I approached this man with a certain deference, but found him very easy to work with once I got to know him. Claude was a fairly large man with a healthy, rubicund complexion. Lou, on the other hand, was much slighter in build and looked very unwell. I wasn't to know, at that precise moment, that he was the victim of a terminal cancer in quite an advanced stage, and must have been suffering intense pain. Looking back, Lou's example emphasises my point that a person born into the working classes was expected to continue with labour of some kind right up to the time that either old-age or terminal illness took them to their permanent rest. This ingrained, traditional thinking didn't just come from employers because, generally, it was considered a weakness to show concern for a labouring body, unless that body was in the shape of a horse, and not always then. The modern concept of the new National Health Service, which paid a man wages if he was ill, and continued to do so until he became strong enough to work again, hadn't really sunk in through this strange, historical idea carried by a majority of agricultural workers. If a man, or woman for that matter, didn't work for whatever reason, they were silently deemed to be lazy by their own workmates. Not so with the rest of the country's workforce as the wonderful, idealistic, revolutionary N.H.S. idea was abused so badly that it has been eventually brought to its knees, to the detriment of us all.

The much lighter, sandier soil of Abbey land helped the harvesting continue, despite a slow deterioration in weather conditions. A nice brushwood fire at dinner times kept the girls' spirits up, and we all enjoyed the week or so working together. There was ample time to collect wood from the fir belt running alongside the field, and this made a lovely crackling fire. This time we took turn about with Claude and Lou collecting up the full baskets, thus having only half as much work as at Soigné. Tom Abel drove the tractor at a good, steady speed throughout, helping the job to run smoothly. Tom was a cousin of the Thaxtons on their mother's side, married and living in the village. The Abels were the first family to live in the school after it was converted into a house in the early 'fifties. Tom also served the cricket team behind the stumps for many a season.

We were joined at dinner times by Harry Boughen, the long-serving tractor-driver, ploughing next door with his large, orange-painted Allis Chalmers tractor. Harry was a rather stout man, taciturn by nature, and quite renowned for his care of money. We wouldn't have classed him as mean, but there was a noticeable air of thrift about him. Sitting by the fire on an upturned paraffin bucket, Harry began to recount a disastrous tale of personal anguish and pain. It appeared that Harry habitually placed his pay-packet containing a week's wages behind the mantle clock every Friday evening. His dutiful wife then took the contents out to pay her weekly bills. But, on this occasion, she had only removed the coins from the packet, leaving the £1 notes inside. For some unknown reason, early the next week Harry had taken the packet, supposedly empty to his mind, and thrown it onto the open fire. Mrs. Boughen, almost unable to believe her own eyes, managed to cry out the fact that it still contained notes. Harry, galvanised into frantic action by the thought of money going up in smoke, grabbed at the blazing packet with bare hands, but, alas, it was too late, and only charred, numberless ashes remained for both husband and wife to shed anguished tears over. Poor Harry's face became longer as the tale unfolded, and I'll swear there were tears in his eyes as the thought of his money burning, welled self-pity up inside him. His enthralled audience tried very hard not to burst into uncontrolled laughter, which even now threatens to break out from me. Claude said, in a very solemn voice, "Well, I never thought I'd see the day when you burned money, Harry". "Bugger, nor did I", was the reply. "I'll make damn sure it never happens again." This was said with much feeling and total conviction, as the sufferer, both mentally and physically, examined his scarred hands. Whether it was God or the Devil who placed the thought into Harry's mind to burn the packet, I don't know, but whichever it was had a very twisted sense of humour. Jim and I displayed a like humorous trait when we almost burst our sides laughing after Harry had laboriously mounted his machine and returned to plough. I could never see Harry after that without conjuring up a picture of the victim slapping away at the blazing pay packet. It may have been a case of "titter ye not at the afflicted", but we couldn't help it, could we?

All too soon, for me at any rate, the job drew to a close. The Abbey foreman, Jack "Pont" Softley, thanked me for my help, and gave me a few shillings extra for travelling back to Soigné after hours, which was the precedent Charlie Wilson was so reluctant to set. Mr. Softley was a tall man of rather stern countenance. He always rode his very high bicycle, never resorting to horse or motor vehicle. "Pont" was the nickname reserved for him only when he was out of earshot. I had been at school with three of his four children, namely Jean, Dan and Eileen. Myrtle, the eldest daughter, had left before I started school. Eileen, being the same age as me, often had her long pigtails dipped in the inkwells by yours truly when sitting behind her. She and I were the first two pupils to win secondary school places after the grant scheme began. Jack Softley was a traditional foreman, dedicated to understanding and caring for

I Follow the Girls to Abbey Farm

the land under his command. He left in the early 'fifties when his superiors became men learning farming from the top. It appeared that Jack would rather move than change his lifelong and proven methods of husbandry, so he took up a similar post in North Norfolk, at Stanhoe I believe. His unmarried son Dan, a very experienced tractor-driver, went along with him.

These moves signalled a gradual changeover of management at the heart of the Estate. During the War the whole Estate was farmed by Major Birkbeck who had taken back the land from tenant farmers who found it impossible to farm profitably in the depressive 1930s. Then, after World War Two, renting agricultural land became a very viable proposition and once more the Estate divided up, from the farming angle at any rate. Warren Farm, Great Barn Farm, Gayton Thorpe, and Abbey Farm, East Walton became independent items under tenants, as did three smaller holdings, two at Walton and one at Gayton Thorpe. Abbey Farm, Westacre and Soigné Farm remained under the Birkbeck control. Captain Harry Birkbeck took over the former with Mr. Leslie Cameron as agent and Jack Softley then Albert Reynolds as foreman. Major H.A. Birkbeck retained the combined Soigné and High House Farms, with Willie Thaxton and Charlie Wilson as bailiff and foreman respectively.

So you see we workers at the very heart of the Estate were cushioned from any ideas of change, be they good or bad. Let it be said now that most rumours of change drifting up from Westacre were firmly bracketed in the second column. Any new theories tried with arable cultivations there were swept aside with the blanket coverage of "Soigné land is much too heavy for that to work up here". Most Soigné minds were very set against any change in 1949. Although everyone employed on "our" farm was allowed to and did criticise Willie and Charlie for almost everything, no one wanted to be shaken out of their own little rut. The one or two slightly progressive minds that did peep over the rut edge were soon pushed back down again into the self-inflicted time warp. Looking back, I suppose the majority of the workforce were either in or fast-approaching the autumn of their working lives, so were naturally against any change which might lead to learning new techniques. Having worked a lifetime using an almost unchanged method of farming, their experience would have counted for nothing if progress moved the goalposts. A slight adjustment of a petrol engine here or there to alleviate an extra tough manual job was alright, but much bearable hard work must be retained to ensure continued employment. The operations which lent themselves most readily to mechanisation were those jobs which were taken on piecework, the only chance we labourers had of earning extra money. Hoeing, harvesting and sugar-beeting were hard manual tasks, but quite honestly the extra money earned there was badly needed to lift very low wages above the poverty line. Modern, labour-saving machines on which employers might spend money were no more popular in the late 'forties than were threshing drums about a century before. Even with limited changes such as combines becoming more common and tractors speeding most other operations, there were certain times of the year when Charlie had to "hide" some of his older workmen to ensure employment for all. This "head in the sand" outlook to limited progress suited many, but the younger men became frustrated as they saw their efforts to press for a reasonable working wage, on which to keep a wife and family, stifled at every turn. The overall wages bill had to be kept to a certain budget level, whilst no one must be denied work. Obviously as pension levels rose under a Labour Government, there was less need for men over sixty-five to continue working until the undertaker called. The farm purse wasn't bottomless, and those putting the most work in felt their efforts should be rewarded on Friday and reflected in their pay-packet. In hindsight, new management blood would have brought fresh ideas, but none came and by far the largest majority of employees at Soigné didn't want to know. As for myself at that juncture, my thinking was of no consequence, even if I had done any. If Charlie said go, I went, and if he said come, I came, as docile a worker as you could wish for. Those same men who were still in command ten years later and had to deal with my bloody-minded obstinacy and "never give an inch" determination would say that National Service had a lot to answer for.

Those later events of 1959 may have soured my relations with the Estate for a time, but my fondness for the environment and the people I grew up with is still there, and has forced me to make the effort needed to record most of these memories and put them into print for others, I hope, to enjoy.

Having tried to set a background picture to the general workings of the Estate and Soigné Farm in particular, I must take up my story from a personal point of view. Whilst I was on my short excursion to Abbey Farm, Westacre, a new recruit had joined the Soigné ranks, a new family having moved into No. 3 Pretoria Cottages in the form of an Estate bricklayer by the name of Lane. This family included an elder daughter, Chrystal, whose good looks and outgoing personality caused waves amongst the numerous bachelors of our community, and a son aged about 16 who needed agricultural employment. Jimmy was quite a character who made up for his lack of inches by means of a wonderful sense of humour and friendly disposition. Charlie Wilson found he had another boy on his hands whether he needed one or not, which was the way things worked then, as previously mentioned.

Being of like age, Jimmy and I worked together quite often, and his outgoing nature helped to bring me out of my shell. One of our first jobs together was the most soul-destroying imaginable. You remember my description of the potato clamp on Little Strawberries? We left it with the tubers inside covered by a layer of straw bundles. After I left that field to go to the Abbey a tractor plough had been despatched with instructions to plough about six or so furrows around the entire hale length, turning the soil inwards so that the first furrow pushed over on to the base of the straw. This freshly-ploughed soil then had to be thrown over the straw by hand to an average depth of about eight inches. The two layers together formed an effective frost barrier to protect the vulnerable potatoes.

A dark November morning found Jimmy and I cycling towards the farm with no firm idea as to the type of job we would be set that day. No daylight penetrated the thick cloud layers, which remained invisible to us and would continue to do so for the next hour. It was what I would call a dead day, with nothing to commend it at all.

Charlie crunched into the shed where no artificial light, apart from a few glowing cigarette ends, helped him find his men. Standing together and hoping we would be teamed up, the long and the short of it (Jimmy and myself) awaited our fate for the day.

"Derek, you know the potato hales on the Strawberries. You and Jimmy can go up there and start moulding up. Take a muck fork apiece, and also a shovel. Put about eight inches all over. If you make a start then I'll come and see you later."

We collected our forks and the best shovel available, which incidentally was rusty and well worn. Pushing our bikes, with tools resting across the handlebars, we made our way towards the field in question without showing much enthusiasm towards the task. This limited eagerness to get started waned even more when increased visibility showed us the daunting lengths of three hales.

"I'm buggered", said James, "I hope he doesn't think we'll finish today".

"Not much hope of that", I replied, "It will take us the rest of the month."

Propping our trusty bikes by the hedge we took off our topcoats and set about the job in hand. Using the four-tined forks to start, we dug and flung earth up on to the hale sides. Then, with a little help from the rusty shovel, the loosened soil sailed up to the top, although most of the clay particles adhered to the rusty surface and came back down again, much to our frustration. If we had been issued with correct tools for the job we would have made better progress. A flat-tined fork would have held our forkfuls of soil together whilst lifting, as opposed to the round tines we used; a shiny shovel would have shed its load at the top of our throw depositing soil over the apex every time. But we struggled on until eight-thirty with Jimmy making various comical comments such as, "this bloody old shovel must have been the one Noah had on the ark", and, "I wish he had cleaned it after he landed".

Sticking our forks in the ground we looked around for a spot to eat breakfast. The hedge, which was now devoid of leaves, didn't give much shelter, although, as there was very little air movement, this wasn't a problem. A seat at the base of a hedgerow oak looked the best bet, so we plonked down on our trusty sacks and draped thick, army coats around our shoulders.

By the time our snack had been eaten, cold began to creep through to my back, which had been wet with perspiration when I stopped.

"Let's get on", I suggested, "my back's getting cold".

So back to our treadmill task we went, taking turns with the shovel and trying to get some rhythm into the job. It soon became clear that the bottom half of the hale side had about ten inches of soil and the top half barely four inches. When I raised the subject, Jimmy made light of it, so on we went without further ado.

By ten o'clock my back ached and the tender skin on my fingers and palms began to show red patches which soon developed into deep blisters. The hands on my watch (Jimmy didn't possess one) moved at a snail's pace as did our progress along the length of the hale. At this rate painting the Forth Bridge would have been child's play. After every second forkful of soil our eyes would glance towards Soigné in the hope that Charlie's burly figure would appear to give us fresh orders, but all to no avail, although he did arrive at 11.30 to check on our progress and to suggest more depth of soil was required at the top, which meant retracing our steps to follow his instructions. Watching Charlie cycle away towards the farm, rolling from one side of the road to the other, we were akin to a couple of castaways watching a likely rescue ship slipping over the horizon. With no reprieve likely the day stretched away in front of us like a wet fortnight.

Dinner at twelve followed the same uncomfortable pattern as breakfast. No firewood nearby meant a cold half-an-hour with sweaty underclothes cooling quickly and no hot food to counterbalance this effect. Thickening cloud and a rising wind did nothing to lift our gloom during the long afternoon. A tractor and trailer passing on the road allowed us the excuse to straighten our backs and watch its progress from the first sighting by Sixteen Acre Belt to its disappearance below the road hedge of Big Strawberries. As its engine died in the distance our only distraction of the afternoon disappeared. I remember at the time having been quite interested in reading of Stalin's purges in Communist Russia, and our present situation measured up quite well with the prisoners in Siberia, to my mind at any rate.

By the time rain began to fall just after half-past-three our spirits were almost broken. After spending the last few minutes of the day crouched behind a tree trunk, sheltering, we made our weary way back to the farm, both wishing we had never been led to take up this farming life, where rain and mud ruled, binding our feet with clay just as securely as any slave in leg fetters.

Shortly after I had shed my wet, muddy boots and hung my coat to dry, the smell of a hot tea had lifted my spirits. A steaming plate of rabbit stew and mashed potato is guaranteed to put life back into the most despondent soul. There was no doubt my mother knew how to care for a family out facing the elements from before dawn until dark. No quick-fix meals out of a tin for us.

I Follow the Girls to Abbey Farm

Her day was spent planning, preparing and cooking a good hot, wholesome meal for when every member could sit down together and replenish the energy used up in hard, manual work carried out in all weathers. In peace and in war the humble, wild rabbit helped her out on many occasions, either stewed, baked, or in a pie. All were caught with the aid of a stick always carried by my stockman father who very rarely returned without at least one rabbit tucked away in the large inside pocket of his jacket, having walked the pastures checking stock. This special countryman's accessory was known locally as a "hare pocket", but a "rabbit pocket" would have been a more accurate description.

The week dragged on with no respite from our tedious job, mainly because the risk of severe frost increased daily as November progressed. One or two helpers came for short periods as and when they could be spared from other jobs, but Jimmy and I remained the backbone of the taskforce, an honour we would gladly have foregone. When Old Laddie joined us things did look up a bit, not necessarily in the work department as the lack of oxygen able to enter Albert Richardson's lungs did nothing to improve the thickness of soil on the top third of the sides, but mealtimes improved quite considerably. Laddie soon arranged for some bales to be dropped from a passing load of straw. One of these well-compacted bales was used each mealtime to provide a fire. By cutting one string and slightly opening the straw in a fan-like manner on the windward side, a slow burning fire gave some warmth to our faces at least. Maybe our backs still cooled off, but life became more cheerful as a result. Making a seat from the reserve bales under the shelter of a bramble thicket made full use of the limited comfort available, teaching we boys a little bit of countryman's common sense into the bargain. Working with some of the older men became humdrum at times as they seemed to tell the same tales over and over again, but there was always something to learn in the field of self-preservation when working in a very harsh environment. Learning the hard way usually makes that learning stick, and it certainly has with me.

As the week wore on we were rewarded with the sight of endless potato hales gradually turning from grey to brown as earth covered straw. Dull November days, which left the far field edges shrouded in mist, seemed hardly to get light before fading into twilight by early afternoon. Blisters were rubbed raw and backs ached as muscles struggled to acquaint themselves with new physical demands. I had certainly divested myself of any semblance of brain strain. This mind-numbing job had brought me down to earth in more ways than one.

Dig, throw, dig, throw, move forward one step, and then dig and throw, dig and throw. Salt mines of Siberia, here I come! Even Jimmy's sense of humour began to fail him.

I Follow the Girls to Abbey Farm

A faint flicker of wickedness surfaced on the occasion when Laddie's bale seat caught fire. We were all seated in a semicircle enjoying the warmth from our straw fire and Laddie dozed slightly next to Jimmy. Very stealthily a cigarette lighter flicked on, and was applied to the rear of our companion's seat. As the first smoke drifted past Laddie and flames began to creep towards his back, he leapt up and began to beat at the fire, all the time using phrases such as, "stupid young bugger", and expressing the opinion that someone needed his arse kicked. We two youngsters thought the whole episode hilarious as our older workmate dragged bag, sack, and coat away, and beat out the small conflagration. Of course the whole episode was thoughtless as the sudden exertion set off Albert's cough which he could well have done without. "There's no rest for the wicked and very little for the righteous either", was Laddie's summing up after he regained his seat and breath. Jimmy vehemently protested his innocence, declaring a spark must have blown round the back to catch the bale, but his victim was unconvinced by the "silly young sod's" denial.

As our work on Little Strawberries approached completion a malicious rumour reached our ears to the effect that a mangold hale on Long Elbreck would be the next needing our attention. The mangold, like the potato, is not frost-resistant and so moulding up would be a necessity. This news sent our spirits way down past our heavy boots. Were we to be condemned to this accursed job for ever? But rescue was at hand, or part rescue at any rate, and from an unthought of source, as will be revealed in the next chapter.

Chapter 7
Days Away at the Shoot

I imagine if we could have been a fly on Charlie Wilson's wall at about 6.45 a.m. one November morning we would have listened in to this type of conversation when the 'phone bell rang as it did every weekday at around the same time.

"Hello", from Charlie.

"Morning Charlie, not much of a day again by the looks of it", would have been Willie Thaxton's opening gambit.

"No sign of frost though, thank goodness. Don't want that until all the hales are moulded up."

"Ah! Now that is what I wanted to mention to you. Fred Welham" (head keeper) "wants at least two brushers on Wednesday and alternate days up to Christmas. Could you spare those two boys, Derek and young Lane?"

"William, if you want to risk losing potatoes and mangolds, then let them go, my fellah."

"Well Charles, it's like this, the Major pays the wages and he expects...."

So the conversation would continue until Bailiff and Foreman agreed, or agreed to disagree on whom to send the next day and what farm work should be left.

At about quarter-to-eleven on a grey Tuesday morning we dug and threw, dug and threw soil over straw. Water filled the ruts where Joe Bly had turned his potato harvester, dead potato haulms lay strewn around, along with a few well-washed potatoes missed by the pickers and now awaiting attention by some hungry rooks when all human presence had left the scene. The rattle of cart and creak of harness heralded Charlie's approach as we prudently kept our backs bent to the task, not that his approach hadn't been noted long since. Keen young ears and even sharper eyesight had picked him up as soon as the conveyance appeared from the end of Sixteen Acre Belt. A hissed warning of "Hie up, he's about", had set us to work with heads down but with hooded eyes to watch his progress either straight on or into the gateway towards us. He sat for a moment watching our work, and probably thinking what frauds we were, as Charlie himself had been one of us until his promotion to foreman many years before. Eventually the silence was broken.

"Derek, Jimmy, they want you to go brushing tomorrow at Gayton Thorpe. Fred Welham needs to start at nine sharp."

With that, away he went, splashing through the ruts towards Honeypot Lane. As soon as his broad back disappeared into the lane we stopped work and were so pleased at our reprieve for a day at least that a highland fling would have been danced, except the heavy clay soil adhering to our already weighty boots prevented this kind of rash display. A ray of imaginary sunshine burst through into our mundane existence and gave us something to live for. Starting at 9 o'clock meant an extra hour in bed before biking the four or so miles from Pretoria to Gayton Thorpe. But most important of all was the release from mind-numbing monotony caused by the work before us. You, as my reader, may wonder why so many pages have been written about such an insignificant and uninspiring farming task. The answer is in order to accentuate the repetitive nature of many labouring jobs which eventually turned young men into non-thinking robots, or forced them to up sticks and leave the land in sheer frustration. As surely as dripping water will wear away a stone, non-use of brain cells will cause them to die leaving a clone with no wish to think for itself. Variety is the spice of life and there were many times I wished for a little inspiration to be added to our work allocation. A mundane or tiring job well done seemed to be rewarded by more of the same, which quickly killed enthusiasm and encouraged brooding and discontent.

At just after eight the next morning Jimmy and I set off for Gayton Thorpe with coats on our handlebars, and a good stout stick apiece tied along the crossbar of our bikes. Cycling through Soigné yards we made tracks for Long "Planton" (Plantation on the map), leaving the mud of Little Strawberries on our right with hardly a glance, but secretly hoping the shadowy figures at the hale would finish the job before tomorrow. Down the slope and up an incline towards the heath road, left at the junction opposite The Allsorts, we sailed down Norwich Hill, and past the Milestone gateway leading to Rats Hall. Bearing left at Patch corner we followed the narrow road into Gayton Thorpe village catching up with Ernie Deasley and his dog in time for him to tell us where the shoot intended to meet. The little, round-towered Saxon church reminded me that it was in its small churchyard that my Granny Bumfrey and Uncle Stanley lay at rest, having been carried from Rats Hall which lay just over the hill on Soigné land.

The farmyard seethed with men and boys dressed in all manner of waterproof garments. Each had a stick and looked as if they all knew just what was expected of them. Parking our machines in a convenient cart-shed we put on overcoats and joined our fellows, keeping very close to neighbour Ernie who was dressed in his best keeper's jacket and plus-fours, although he wore rubber boots and not the totally inadequate brown shoes sported by the gentlemen carrying guns. These men had to observe the ritual dress expected of a guest invited to the shoot — thick tweed jacket and plus-four trousers in traditional country colours, thick knee-length socks and heavy brown shoes. A deer stalker hat with ear flaps or a flat cap was the usual head gear. Mittens could be worn in cold weather. Sometimes, one was accompanied by one's wife, suitably attired for rough terrain, and usually a loader came along to carry a second gun and re-load when game flew over thick and fast. The whisky flask, so essential when standing around in the cold, would be secreted in one of the many pockets about one's person.

Here my reader may notice a slight sneering tone to my description of the landed gentry. This comes of course because I saw them at the time through very working-class eyes, which were more used to reading the views of contributors to the Daily Herald than to The Times. Perhaps the slight mickey-taking is uncalled for, because I really enjoyed the shoots, and always had done as a boy watching pheasants thumping out of the sky, collecting spent cartridge cases and now with the chance of beating game birds out of the woods. It was very much part of our country season and way of life. "The guns", as we called the gentlemen firing the twelve-bores, were going to have an enjoyable day and so was I struggling through bramble thickets and eye-swiping sapling branches. To me a quick death to a wild game bird which could be eaten was sport, but fox hunting on the other hand was barbaric and despicable, a straight view of a countryman which I still hold today.

Keeping close to Ernie we trooped out of the farmyard in the wake of Clem Reynolds, the local keeper, on whose beat most of the day's sport would take place. Clem had keepered this land for many years, and knew where every drive started and finished. As we passed the church once more the memory of Uncle Stanley came back to me as a fair-haired teenager who started work as keeper's boy under Grandfather Welham at Rats Hall. But for the rheumatic fever which claimed his young life after less than a year in the job, he could well have been here today as a full-blown keeper and leading us out into the fields.

For those who know nothing about organised shoots, let me explain the system. Prior to the day of the shoot, local keepers would mark out eight positions for guns in a semicircle around the end of the wood where a drive was due to take place. Each station had a nut stick bearing a number placed in a cleft at the top. Each marksman took up his position under the guidance of the head keeper, in this case Fred Welham, having drawn a number at the beginning of proceedings. Obviously more birds were inclined to fly over numbers three to six, which were centrally placed, but those wily enough to realise danger in the air would try to wheel away towards the sides. These seasoned campaigners flew at high speed, and consequently were harder to hit, calling for expert marksmanship from the sportsmen below. So, at each station stood one gentleman and one loader who was usually a keeper from the guest's own estate — although occasionally a wife or sister of county standing, well versed in sporting etiquette, loaded the second gun. Older men sat on a shooting stick, resting their legs between drives which were designed to limit the distance walked by guns but conversely caused considerable waiting time to allow beaters to reach the far end of a wood. The other important and very necessary occupants of a station were gun dogs, specially trained to ignore exploding shot, and who sat obediently waiting for their master's order to "fetch". Picking up shot and wounded birds took place only at the end of a drive, as any moving around during the drive itself was frowned upon and could be a highly dangerous pastime. Everyone at this end of a shoot knew the safety rules by heart and had been schooled in countryside ground rules from birth. These men had known money for generations, and despite their "silver spoon" upbringing were real gentlemen in every sense of the word. They always treated working men with respect and received respect themselves as a consequence. Major Birkbeck himself always kept to a strict conduct code, never giving direct orders to a worker but passing his wishes through the chain of command. One was always addressed by surname only, and I for one never took it as any kind of insult from the man who paid our wages. Strangely there was one exception to the Major's rule. He called his bailiff "Thaxton", his foreman "Wilson", but his High House stockman, my father, was addressed as 'Fred'. No one knew why, and I'm sure no one asked. Major Birkbeck was a real gentleman, and within the confines of his feudal-based upbringing, a very good employer. I can honestly say there were very few people who spoke against him personally.

Whilst all this preparation took place at one end, we brushers (beaters in other parts of the country) were playing "follow my leader" as Clem Reynolds led us in a wide circle well clear of the first wood to be driven. The weather was dry overhead, but recent heavy rain had made the slightly clay soil tacky enough to quickly add weight to our wellington boots. On reaching the far side of this particular small wood the order came to spread out in a line at not too many yards apart. Jimmy and I made sure we joined the section where Ernie Deasley supervised. Each keeper was spread out to keep us newcomers in check as the slow walk forward began. Clem blew loudly on his whistle as a signal for action to start, and also to warn the guns of impending birds overhead.

"Keep in line, rattle your sticks and stop if a flurry of birds go up at once", was the order given by our section leader. On Ernie's signal his dog moved forward, quartering the bramble-covered floor of the wood, rooting in the denser patches that we two-legged brushers had to circumnavigate owing to their thickness. Trailing brambles, rooted at both ends, caught in my boots and quickly taught me to lift the leg high before taking each step. Jimmy managed to measure his length, which wasn't much, almost at once after catching a foot in these natural trip wires. Scrambling up James rammed his brown cap back over his black hair, swearing the while, and trying to laugh with the rest of us.

"Bugger me, Jimmy, you been at the whisky flask already?" was the quip that came easily from Ernie who was always ready for a laugh. Needless to say, in Jimmy's language those brambles turned all sorts of red colours, especially when he tried to extract the hooks embedded in hands put out to save his fall. With Jimmy Lane and Ernie Deasley around, the day just couldn't be dull and promised to be filled with companionable good humour.

As we penetrated further into this wood, and its overhead canopy became thicker, brambles gave way to nut bushes growing out of a clearer floor, thus making walking much easier. The bramble carpet had stripped all adhering clay from our boots, which helped lighten our feet. As we reached this clearer section in the centre we naturally lengthened our stride, and were soon ahead of those less fortunate comrades on either wing still struggling through brambles whose growth had been promoted by increased light at the wood edges. Earlier orders to keep in a straight line were forgotten until a shout of, "Keep the line straight you boys there", brought us to the realisation that our minds weren't wholly on the job. Truth was that we were more intent on catching a skulking rabbit for the pot than serving up sport for our master's guests. We were lucky to be brushing in a line of easier-going under-keepers; Bob Chapman, and Ernie hadn't long left the Forces and Clem Reynolds was a very cheerful, elderly man. I'm sure that in earlier days, when the Welham family keepered most of the Westacre Estate, their regime would have hankered for a return of mantraps to keep their fellow farm and Estate workers in fear. Even Clem Softley put fear into we boys at times, and he was one step more humane than his predecessor.

So we continued to rattle and hiss our way through the undergrowth. After every burst of feathered energy that sent a pheasant hurtling into the air, a volley of shot could be heard. At the bottom of our wood a bundle of whirring feathers would plummet to earth as a direct hit of lead shot ended the life of another noble bird. All that would be left of the flight was a few coloured or brown feathers floating in mid-air depending whether the victim was a cock or hen bird. As each one thumped down on to the ploughed land, a dog flinched, but not one moved as good training taught their doggy instincts to be restrained until the command "fetch" released them from an invisible chain. Only on very rare occasions would a young dog forget the hours of training undertaken by a keeper, and involuntarily start off in pursuit of a fallen bird. A parade ground command of "Sit, sir, sit" would check the miscreant in its tracks, and one very chastened dog would creep back to its original seat.

Slowly the line of brushers reached the last quarter of the first drive. Now all birds that ran forward down the wood had to take flight. Care had to be taken to ensure a steady stream of sport was supplied, so the march forward was very slow, the foraging dogs were called to heel, and sticks stilled from rattling. If a sudden rush of birds should rise, the voice of Fred Welham observing from the side, called "Stop". It was his job to make sure the guests had ample opportunity to enjoy shots at all birds and for not too many to be flushed up at once over discharged guns. As the last brusher broke out of the trees, dogs were released to pick up all fallen birds which, in turn, were placed around the stick marking each stand. As birds sent over numbered well, the Major might have had a quiet word with the local keeper. "A good show, Reynolds, well done". Of course, at the end of a good day's sport, generous tips would go into the pocket of head keeper Welham's brown jacket, and a percentage passed down to under keeper Reynolds, and his colleagues, but in the meantime the Major's few words of congratulation would go a long way towards Clem's feeling of a year's work well done.

As the scene cleared with guns and brushers setting off for the second drive, a real blast from the past came in from the side. A brown, horse-drawn vehicle, closely resembling an old stagecoach, pulled up at the first stand. The ageing chestnut mare was deaf, and had no cause to take fright from the discharging of twelve-bore guns. Jimmy Reynolds (no relation to Clem) looking every inch a stagecoach-driver, undid the hook securing double doors at the rear. Inside were rows and rows of hooks on which Jimmy, in time-honoured fashion, would hang the pheasants two by two, hen and cock bird making a brace. The number of birds shot in a day would not be counted individually, but as, say, one hundred brace, or one hundred and fifty two and a half brace. Half brace came into play only if the final count fell on an uneven number.

Moving along the eight stands, Jimmy cleared the ground before preparing to move on, adjusting his time so as to arrive near the next drive at the death. No need to tell this old retainer where to head for. Having done this same job over numerous years this Estate worker, Reynolds, knew the individual drives as well if not better than the other Estate worker, Reynolds, leading we brushing party around.

Pheasant drives always contained a wood, or part thereof, a large spinney, or a very rough piece of uncultivated land. Sometimes a strip of kale was sown alongside a narrow belt of trees in order to widen the drive. Usually the head keeper would suggest this be done and all tenant farmers were expected to comply, even if they didn't really want a strip of cattle feed just there.

Tenant farmers only rented the agricultural land; all game and shooting rights remained with the Estate, and were jealously guarded. At season's end a group of farmers might be invited to shoot rabbits, but feathered game and hares were strictly out of bounds to all but gentry. These Estate ground rules were cut in tablets of stone, and were learned by all those living within its bounds, even before their ABC had been mastered.

Having spoken about kale a few lines previously I must point out that this tall, heavily-leafed plant was a brusher's nightmare. However dry the day, the large leaves always held pints of water so that even the best waterproof cladding couldn't stop some of it soaking into one's clothes. It was usually the

Days Away at the Shoot

extremes of our line, which struck unlucky, and were forced to walk the kale. Jimmy and myself, who inadvertently stuck by Ernie in the centre, missed a ducking on the fifth drive, and consequently remained in a comfortable, dry state at lunch time. Our normal dinner break being at 12 o'clock, meant that our stomachs were gnawing before this late stop of about one o'clock. The cheese sandwiches, though well compressed by travelling in our coat pockets, were despatched with undue haste, and even more dismembered fruit-cake was shovelled into hungry mouths. Each member of the company collected a bottle of brown or light ale, depending on taste, from the game-cart (Jimmy's faded brown stagecoach). Never did beer taste so good, I can assure you. Freezing cold and straight from the bottle, it washed those cake crumbs down a treat. The sudden shock to my system seemed to make me light-headed for a while. It was fortunate for all concerned that no one offered me a swig from the hip flasks that seemed to appear in every gentleman's hand. I must suppose they needed some spirit to repel rising damp from water and mud shipped into the tops of "low" shoes mentioned previously. Note the word in inverted commas there. All older farm workers who wore no other footwear than boots always referred to shoes by preceding the name with that word, "low". As to its necessity, I'm not sure, as no one ever mentioned a pair of "high" shoes.

Roughly half an hour was spent standing around eating our "dinner", and the guns their "lunch", before we brushers were led away for the first of the three after-lunch drives. By the time those three were completed, making eight drives in all, light was fading as late November afternoons tend to be short, even on clear days. The overcast and threatening skies then made shooting dangerous, and a halt was called just before four o'clock. Fred Welham gathered us together for payment, and requested that we all forgather at East Walton Farm on Friday, nine o'clock sharp. With that we were dismissed and left to walk the short distance back to where bikes awaited their owners. Tired legs made hard work of the long drag up from Patch corner, leading to a slight downward incline to the base of Norwich Hill. After this very temporary reprieve, the steepness of the hill meant dismounting to push our machines for a quarter of a mile, remounting at the end of Tinkers Belt. The rest of our ride home wasn't too bad, although rain, which had threatened for much of the afternoon, began to splash on our faces for most of the way through Soigné and beyond. It was too dark to see if any progress had been made on the accursed potato hales in our absence, but we would live in hopes until the next day. Surely Charlie couldn't say, "Yoke for Little Strawberries, my fellows", on yet another morning. You want to bet? He could, and he did.

Yes, we had to go back to finish the work, but as it was nearly complete, the onerous task didn't seem so bad; after all, we had another "away-day" to look forward to.

"Did Fred Welham need you any more?" came Charlie's tentative question.

"Yes, we have to report to him at Walton tomorrow", came the answer in unison.

By half past three, with the moulding-up finished, we walked back to the farm with all the tools. Putting that precious shovel back in the carpenter's shop we sincerely hoped it wouldn't come into our hands for quite a while.

It was decided to take the overland route to East Walton, so the next morning found us cycling along the green road from White Gate corner, down the Horse Pasture, and up between Twenty-four Acres and the Hulver; then leaving Soigné land behind, we began the slow descent towards the main Lynn road. A short distance on a metalled surface brought us into the village. Meeting in the farmyard as we had done at Gayton Thorpe meant that our bikes could be left safely there.

The terrain turned out to be very different from that encountered on Wednesday when the small woods were interspersed with arable fields, and pheasants gleaned corn from stubbles, becoming fat and well feathered. Much of the day's shoot took us through large tracts of rough, marshy scrub and waterlogged woodland. The birds we put up seemed darker in colour and leaner in outline. The outlying fields seemed poor in comparison to the rich loam soils of Soigné.

Making the acquaintance of Walton Common for the first time, I recalled that on occasions fencing gangs came from Estate farms to repair and rewire its perimeters. Store cattle grazed its rough acres in summer and adders were reputed to be numerous, basking in the sunshine just waiting to sink their poisonous fangs into an unsuspecting leg. When Harry Ashby came here with his mate, "Brickie" Howard, the latter had asked Charlie for some "scrum" as an antidote for snake bite. Even if he had asked correctly for "serum" I doubt if Charlie's medicine cabinet ran to such a thing. "Keep your states tight round your legs", was the only advice the foreman could administer. I believe many a pleasant day in midsummer was spent fencing on Walton Common. I didn't see many adders basking on that chilly November day, although a very large fox rushing for cover hurtled round a thorn bush just as I came from the opposite direction, and met me head on. Both our hearts stopped with fright and surprise. I think his started working first as he sprang away with beautiful brush thrust out behind, a wonderful sight which happened so quickly I hardly had time to register it. Sections of the seemingly endless Walton Wood were splashed through, skinny pheasants were sent skywards, and slime-covered wellingtons were dragged from dank, smelly ditches. On the far side of Walton Warren the seemingly isolated Magpie Farm could be seen. Actually the farm was only isolated from Walton village, the sole direct route being a footpath skirting Walton Wood, but, if one faced the opposite way, Magpie Farm sat a bare half-mile from the busy A47 King's Lynn to Swaffham road. On the other side of Walton Wood was Summerend Farm, another smallish holding, farmed by Harry Wilson, a younger brother of our foreman, whose wife taught at East Walton school.

Having negotiated our second shoot successfully and returned to our bikes without losing a rubber boot in the treacherous mires hidden in Walton Wood, we were summoned to attend the third venue at Abbey Farm, Westacre on the following Monday. This time I found myself on more familiar ground, although much of the woodland was still low-lying, straddling the River Nar. Great care was taken to ensure no game broke away towards the neighbouring Narford Hall Estate as I believe a long-standing feud existed between the two Estates. The far wing of our brushing line pushed forward forming an arc to keep all birds looking north, instead of south towards Narford.

After a morning spent west of the village, crossing and re-crossing the Walton to Swaffham road (Narford Lane), as well as splashing around the extensive watercress beds where "Trot" Taylor spent his days in charge, we worked our way back through The Carr to take a break at the Abbey. As before, we brushers stood around to eat our food and drink the beer ration. This time the guns were invited to lunch in Abbey House with Captain Harry Birkbeck as host. As we stamped our feet to retain some of the heat gained battling through the woods, it did seem the lunch break was being extended by those in a warmer environment. But with the exception of a few, "Let's get on" growls, little was thought of it. Turn the clock on ten years and I am sure the now largely excluded hymn line, "The rich man in his castle, the poor man at his gate", would have been boiling my blood and spoiling my relative enjoyment of the day. Eventually, away we went, over the Castleacre to King's Lynn road, up past the recently redundant school (pupils were taken to East Walton by bus), to spend the afternoon session in and around The Heater, Old Bush Covert and Broom Covert, finishing at Walton Road sheds.

The next two shoots were always classed as the cream. Woods surrounding Pretoria and the large Soigné Wood being at the heart of Westacre Estate housed more pheasants by far than those already visited. As we met outside Pretoria Cottages for the next date, I would be able to eat my dinner in warm conditions and leave the gentlemen kicking their heels outside. As boys we loved standing up at our front window to watch high-flying pheasants plummeting out of the sky as the best sporting guns in our area displayed their prowess. Lead shot rattled down on hard surfaces outside, and an occasional pheasant crashed into the garden. Never yet had it been left for our oven, but quickly retrieved by keeper and dog before our covetous eyes, and well before our taste buds started to run riot. This year of course I was kept busy flushing the birds from our well-known woods, and only brother Michael occupied the large front window.

Days Away at the Shoot

The final and highest profile shoot was in and around Soigné Wood. Here the day's bag was expected to exceed any of the previous four full days' shooting. Birds, after waxing fat in the surrounding stubble fields, had withdrawn into cover as distant shots echoed across the Estate. I imagine most of the guests fell very little short of royalty on this first visit of the season, and they were always provided with first-class sport.

Jimmy and I were detailed to join the brushing gang for a second round of shoots on the days preceding Christmas, which suited us just fine for we both enjoyed the work and we were quite sad when Soigné Wood was reached for the second time. Still, two days' holiday (paid, no less) beckoned over Christmas, so all wasn't gloom and doom. A small fir tree to cut from the wood, after dark, and a fat cockerel waiting to be killed and eaten took some of the edge off all that mud and cold, wet conditions waiting for us after Christmas. Was I still glad to be a farmer's boy? At least I'd seen the world, well, been to Gayton Thorpe and East Walton, made some friends, and shared plenty of laughs, so it wasn't too bad, on dry days at any rate. With the dull days before Christmas behind me, surely the best was still to come.

Chapter 8
Back with the Thresher

With Christmas over and sugar-beet harvest completed the farm took on a new look which could best be described as "hibernatory", if such a word exists. Most cattle were now yarded and would remain so until a flush of spring grass became available once more. The prime fattening bullocks were at Elbreck Barn where Harry Ashby had a full-time job grinding mangolds and feeding his charges in time-honoured fashion; the only piece of modernisation to be added since Fred and Will Bumfrey shared the job was a small Lister petrol engine which drove the grinder. A boy was provided permanently to cart mangolds into his grinding shed and help Harry to straw down the yards. On this occasion Jimmy Lane had the job, with Violet in the shafts of his tumbril. Will still tended young stock at Soigné, and Bert Chase did a similar job on his home ground at High House. Some rough-coated cattle remained outside and were fed daily by tractor and trailer. The driver and one labourer supplied beet tops when still available, kale, mangolds, hay or barley straw.

Barney Hooks returned to his carpenter's shop, where rough carpentry work was combined with barn supervision until piecework hoeing took him out into the fields to enjoy some late spring sunshine once more. These winter tasks took up a large percentage of labour, although a gang composed of the more active employees spent their winter moving around at muck-cart, threshing, hedging, and any other heavy manual work that cropped up. Still being classed as a boy, this did not include me, so my time was spent on varying odd jobs, most of which revolved around a horse. Beauty was still my mare and we made a good team, travelling miles together in all sorts of weather conditions. Being with my horse made the work very enjoyable, although I still worried about every job, mostly without just cause.

Most of the field cultivations had ceased owing to weather conditions. The one exception was ploughing which continued from harvest end to spring. Two and three furrow trailing ploughs were used extensively, although powerlift implements were just appearing. This type of plough was attached to a tractor by arms, which lifted and dropped the implement by means of hydraulic levers operated by the driver. Fordson Major tractors came with this new innovation which certainly speeded up ploughing, but still left it as the major time consumer on our tractor scene.

As soon as harvest had been completed ploughing began on grassland — mostly one-year leys that had provided a hay crop during the summer.

Sometimes sheep had fed off a second crop, thus adding manure, which, together with grass and clover, provided a good food base for winter wheat which was the crop sown first in rotation. Wheat, roots, barley, grass had stood the test of time, although sometimes an extended rotation of wheat, spring barley, roots, barley again, and then grass was used. Norman Chase, known to us as "Brum", ploughed much of the time, although he broke off during sugar-beet harvest in order to plough out beet as required. This situation lasted until Christmas and then it was constant ploughing just as long as the land remained free from hard frost. Artie Keeley and John Bumfrey also were cast as permanent ploughmen, usually working a field together. Slowly the tractor hauled its plough across and back, turning grey stubble or weed-covered surfaces into straight, brown furrows as far as the eye could see. A black and white cloud of squawking birds followed their trail as rooks and seagulls fought over pests uncovered by the ploughshare. Ploughing was still carried out with great pride, as had been the case when team-men with horses vied against one another for the honour of master ploughman. A small ploughshare or coulter ran along the ground first, turning weeds and brash into the furrow bottom before the main share cut, and a mould-board turned over the six or so inches of topsoil. After a ploughman had passed, no rubbish must show above the ground. By travelling at a relatively slow speed, gravity took the first shallow cut downwards to the very bottom of the furrow. The vastly increased ploughing speeds that came later meant that the second cut hit much of the brash before it fell, thus leaving a large percentage sticking up above the newly-turned surface. In 1950 farmers expected to see dead straight furrows and perfectly clean surfaces when a ploughman plied his trade.

As I intimated earlier, grassland received the plough first, and then cleaner stubble fields where weed-killing, pre-ploughing cultivations were unnecessary. Many fields were so weed-infested that top surfaces were pulled around to encourage weed seed growth early. These particular fields were then ploughed around Christmas when those germinated weeds could be destroyed by turning them into a furrow bottom. Last of all came fields where root crops had been harvested or fed off by sheep. Often standing water on compacted clay ground made life difficult as rubber-tyred tractor wheels spun in an effort to get traction. The original iron wheels provided with metal spuds did a good job in these adverse conditions, whereas the new multi-purpose rubber tyres just spun on the spot. An experiment was tried whereby salt water was pumped into rear tyres in place of air, and this added weight helped to a degree. But whatever the surface conditions prevailing the aim was to finish all bulk ploughing by the end of February when, with any luck, spring cultivations could start in earnest.

By thinking about spring cultivations, I am jumping the gun. The intervening period between Christmas and March can be cruel in the extreme to both livestock and men, especially when the north-easterly wind hits Norfolk, with nothing between we East Anglians and the North Pole. It can freeze the marrow in your bones and be life-threatening if a countryman's good sense of self-preservation isn't put into practice.

The main pheasant-shooting season finished with the second Soigné Wood shoot. A few guns would walk Home Covert around the Hall on Boxing Day, with keepers providing support. After that only occasional "pot shooting" took place around isolated pit-holes when crafty cock birds of advancing age were culled. Long spurs on their legs indicated a life of several summers, and the aim was to keep the pheasant population young and virile. I have heard it jokingly suggested that the same policy ought to have been followed by the Major in connection with his Soigné staff, but Blackie Wright and his co-near pensioners vetoed the idea. Oh well, it was only a thought.

Jimmy and I were called upon once more for brushing duties, this time for hares, which were quite numerous in the large, open fields around us. It didn't turn out to be nearly as exciting as working through woods. After walking over leg-sapping clay-soil fields of anything up to half a mile in length until lunchtime, all novelty had disappeared. Some guns walked with we brushers to shoot hares attempting to run back from marksmen hidden behind a distant hedge. One animal fell to the gun near us almost at the outset of our walk down Long Elbreck. Jimmy, who was nearest, received the honour of carrying the corpse. Hanging it over his stick he trailed it down his back, with head banging against his legs with every step taken. Mud working up Jimmy's boots mingled with blood dripping from the animal's mangled head, and made a fine mess of our comrade's coat and trousers, much to the amusement of his fellow brushers. Needless to say, the poor animal would have been turned red anyway by Jimmy's language, if not by its own life-blood. A good blast of polar wind would have been very useful under those circumstances, for a frozen crust on the clay surface would have made walking much easier. I can tell you, we weren't sorry when the day ended and our services weren't required anywhere else on the Estate. Even soiling-up hales would have been preferable to hare shooting

My odd-jobbing covered all sorts of variations in work, and turned up a few amusing episodes on the way. Jimmy's work had fallen behind at Elbreck Barn owing to his one-day excursion into hare shooting, so I was detailed to deliver a load of mangolds to help him out. These feed items, as I'm sure most of you know, are large, orange roots, round in shape, consisting of about 90% water. Being susceptible to frost damage they are, or were then, stored in straw and earth-covered hales. About one yard of earth had to be removed each time a load was taken, and then loose straw shaken over the exposed face once more if frost threatened. A pitchfork was used to load, two mangolds being speared each time and then released into the tumbril by knocking the base or neck of the fork on a metal-edged side-board. Having taken up my load on the middle section of Fifty Acres, Beauty and I set off for Elbreck bullock yards. As we drove round the back Gerald and Leslie arrived at the large, double doors with a load of pea straw. Leaving them to drive into the yard to deliver their bedding, I prepared Beauty to reverse into Harry's grinding shed. Meanwhile, Dilberry and Young Laddie, to give them their working nicknames, had entered the yard, taken off the wagon rope securing their load, and were preparing to spread fresh bedding around the soiled yard. Dilberry had hauled himself up on to the load by means of the last length of rope, and began to push huge forkfuls of pea straw off the sides. For those unfamiliar with pea straw, let me explain that this brown, dust-filled material was the residue left after dried pea haulms had been threshed to obtain dried peas. As this was in the days before quick-frozen, green peas appeared on our supermarket shelves, dried peas were sold as a winter vegetable standby; they had to be soaked overnight in water treated with a special tablet of bicarbonate of soda, before they returned to something vaguely resembling an edible pea, and weren't too bad when cooked, give or take an odd dried maggot or two. Anyway, this very coarse, dusty bedding made muck when trodden in by bullocks' hooves and this is what was happening at Elbreck. Now Gerald was always on the lookout for devilment, and as Leslie walked past the load side a huge forkful of dusty straw descended on his head, by accident of course. Eventually a very red, dust-streaked face appeared and a very loud voice lambasted the ears of him above, calling Gerald all the names any ex-Army man could lay tongue to and his constant spitting and choking would allow. The miscreant doubled up with laughter at his mate's misfortune, and in all the furore failed to notice a horse and trap approaching the outside wall. We spectators, on the other hand, saw all, as the bellow from an irate Laddie was so loud that we flew to the rear door to check on its cause. Suddenly a head, topped by a trilby hat, appeared Mr. Chad-like over the wall.

"Will you wash your mouth out, my fellow", roared Charlie. "I've never heard such foul language."

Suddenly "silence reigned" — but no one got wet. Frozen statues were left gaping as Charles turned his horse and sped away up the lane, his Chapel preacher's ears still ringing with Laddie's barrack-room verbals. Which of the participants or spectators found their voice first I can't remember, but Dilberry carried the blame for his mate's embarrassment, as well he might. He really was a terror at stirring people up with his tricks, and no one was safe when he was around. After our initial laughter had subsided we all felt a bit sorry for Leslie who hardly deserved the reprimand. Having spent the war serving as a soldier, and much of that time incarcerated in a Far East prison camp, he ought to have received preferential treatment until some normality returned to his shattered life. But, to his credit, adversity seemed to bring out the best in him, as in later years he replaced Charlie as foreman when the latter retired — not that Leslie would have sought any favours, and was always one of the best men to work with, being able to laugh and joke with all and sundry.

After Leslie had shaken most of the dust out of his hair and neckband, work continued in a more orderly fashion. As dinner time was fast approaching, it was decided to build a fire in Little Elbreck pit-hole, and take our break there. These long-extinct pits were originally sources of clay, which was dug out and spread over surrounding land where, combined with lighter soil, it provided a constituent more conducive to moisture retention, so important during East Anglian relatively dry summers. Now, of course, they were dry-bottomed, with a surface covered in scrub bushes and brambles, which provided a home for wild birds and animals as well as shelter and fuel for men seeking a windbreak at mealtimes. Gerald and I took our bags and coats up first at about quarter to twelve. Collecting very thin twigs we carefully arranged them over some dry newspaper and a match was applied. By slowly adding thicker elder and thorn sticks a lovely fire was soon blazing. By the time our mates joined us at twelve everything was ready for a comfortable sit-down. Just after Harry, Leslie and Jimmy settled their sack cushions in position round the windward side of our fire a disturbance on the edge of the pit heralded an approach of two more warmth seekers. Artie Keeley and John Bumfrey, ploughing on Big Strawberries, had spotted smoke curling up from our fire and decided to join us. After sitting for several hours on a tractor seat, which was open to the elements, their frozen bone marrow was in great need of thawing out. All Soigné tractors were without cabs, although these new, mollycoddling contraptions were beginning to appear across the countryside, and not before time, as a tractor-driver's life was pretty harsh during winter months. There is no greater feeling of appreciation than sitting before a blazing wood fire on a miserable winter's day, and feeling the heat warm your face, hands and trousered legs. An occasional swirl of smoke across the eyes, as a back draught caught it, was par for the course. Hunching under our ex-Army greatcoats as a wind-break we munched sandwiches and home-made cake, with far more enjoyment than if we were in a top-class restaurant.

Harry, Leslie and Artie were top-class talkers and covered adequately for we other more silent types. Jimmy gave us yet another rendition of Charlie's exchanges with Leslie over the wall, and spiced it up with appropriate actions and a few extra observations of his own.

All too soon our allotted forty minutes had passed us by, so reluctantly we rose to scramble up the pit-side and back to work. Buttoning those thick coats around us we tried to retain as much of the heat saturated in the front of our jackets and trousers as possible. To leave the fast-dying embers of our fire took some willpower, but we knew that movement or lack of it, as the case may be, could be observed across considerable distances, especially when trees and hedges were leafless, and the give-away noise of a tractor engine firing back into life, pinpointed re-starting times to the second. It was also a well-known fact that persons in positions of wealth and power never took their meals at the same time as us mere lesser mortals, and consequently found themselves either on horseback or lurching around in an ex-Army jeep if we decided to pinch an extra ten minutes by a fire. On the other hand, an additional ten minutes had been given already by virtue of twelve-thirty being extended unofficially to twelve-forty, so really we had no complaint, especially as overall timekeeping was slack all round. Any cartoon vision of a burly, over-fed farmer standing over a skeletal worker with watch in one hand and upraised whip in the other must be instantly dispelled. Discipline was of the live and let live variety, and very rarely seriously abused. Anyway, everyone realised that Charlie and Willie were also answerable to Major Birkbeck and any of our misdemeanours reported to him by the chain of self-appointed spies dotted around the Estate would reflect badly on our two superiors. Yes, we knew there were a few "old retainers" on farm and Estate that liked to curry favour, or think they did, by passing on information about things that didn't have anything to do with them personally. This mischief-making, back-stabbing, call it what you will, had little effect really, as Major Birkbeck wasn't a man to be influenced by tittle-tattle from those who liked to think they "had the master's ear". Sometimes, of course, they ran off with specially-baited, false information, much to the amusement of those perpetrators setting up the deception. Owing to the libel laws of this country, I think it best for the known spies to remain anonymous in print, but, in practice, one just had to look out for the man who almost pulled the peak off his cap when gentry passed by, to be able to identify and label such a man as a "lickarse". Apologies to those who think the word offensive, but it was the label attached to those Estate favour-seekers.

All through our school days the highlight of the winter period was the noisy arrival of Fred Petch driving his huge traction engine, pulling a threshing tackle. As boys we followed its progress right into a field where corn stacks were due to be threshed on succeeding days. After peace was restored in Europe, Walter Desborough took over as contractor, bringing a slightly smaller and much smarter engine in from Castleacre to do the job. Recently a much less exciting tractor had replaced steam power, and now drove the drum and elevator via a small flywheel on its side – not so picturesque maybe, but much easier to drive and handle, having instant power on tap at the swing of a starting handle. The steam traction engine, such a wonderful source of power for mobile machinery, had now passed into history with most of the magnificent monsters condemned to a breaker's yard. Thankfully a few were saved and restored with a great deal of loving care, and now grace shows and fairgrounds where we all gaze in rapture, whilst trying to re-live our rose-coloured childhood memories. As for Walter, his new power tool meant a much

Back with the Thresher

later start in the morning as the need to spend time getting up steam was unnecessary, as was the Sunday afternoon cycle ride to light a fire inside the belly of his monster in readiness for work on Monday. That, I suppose, was the first nail in the coffin of threshing, which was soon destined to disappear completely. Was it such a shame that the most dusty, sweaty, lung-clogging job imaginable was set to disappear? Well, to we rat hunters whose adrenalin rose to free-flowing extremes at the very rattle of iron wheels on gritty roads, and surpassed even that when the low hum of the threshing drum went out in the frosty air, it was. One of the most important events in a country boy's calendar was wiped away for ever by the full implementation of combine harvesters, and the mass mechanisation that eventually followed in their wake.

But, before we draw a blind over this labour-intensive operation, which had employed ten or a dozen labourers for most winter days, I want to sample just once more the simple fellowship that type of gang work engendered.

Yes, the threshing tackle had arrived. Brother Michael had seen it pass Pretoria and head up the High House road, coming to rest beside an oat stack on Eighteen Acres. Michael and John Thaxton, his mate, had cycled up there to bring the information back. Oat stacks didn't stir up as much excitement as other types of grain stacks, owing to their rather low pulling power to the rat population which much preferred wheat and barley stacks as a store-house home. But, as they would be back at school anyway, it wasn't so important to them. To me the question hanging in mid-air was, would I be involved with the threshing gang? Oh, how I hoped I would be. In anxious trepidation I waited in the dark cart-shed for my orders next morning.

"Yoke for chaff-cart, Derek. Take your cart to Eighteen Acres, and burn the oat flights well out in the field. Oh, better take some more chaff bags with you as well. See whether Will has any stacked away."

Walking on air, I almost ran to the stable, hugging myself, thrilled by the fact that I had been awarded the second most dusty job possible. Of course, it wasn't really the thought of lugging great, irritation-causing bags of chaff around that set me singing, it was rat-catching fever. Chaff bags were of the large, light, hessian-type, the same sacks in which dried sugar-beet pulp came to us for cattle feed. When new they were easy and comfortable to handle, but after use, especially with prickly barley chaff, they became very scratchy, resembling the kind of unsociable material used to make the proverbial hair shirt.

Just as I prepared to leave the yard Charlie hailed me, and my heart plummeted at the thought of a change in orders.

"Just a minute, Derek", boomed Charlie. "Come to the barn door. We haven't sent the weighers or corn sacks."

So, Charlie hauled out a set of dust-covered scales, made of cast iron and wood, with central framework for corn sacks to rest against. Tiny iron wheels helped to make it just mobile, with the help of a lot of manpower. Barney Hooks and the foreman heaved the contraption up to me, and helped tie it in position. Last of all, metal weights clumped on board, as well as a bundle of stiff, patched, railway corn sacks.

At last away we sped, out and along Honeypot Lane, to the scene of action. One oat stack had been threshed out earlier in the autumn, and now we prepared to start on a second one. When I pulled into the gate my eyes took in a scene of great activity. Already thatch had been stripped from the stack roof, and cleared well away from the operation. Brorches had been collected and tied in a bundle for re-use next year. Brorches were, of course, thin nut sticks, about three feet long, which, when driven into the stack roof, held binder string pulled tightly over thatching straw to keep stack contents dry.

Many hands helped to unload the weighing machine in readiness for Blackie Wright and Walter Desborough to weigh up the oats in twelve-stone sacks. Oats, being relatively light grain, filled a standard railway sack at a much less weight than unhusked wheat, barley and rye.

Percy Barnes was sacking chaff that day, and was well prepared for the most dusty job of all with an old gaberdine mac pinned up to his coloured neckerchief. A length of binder twine held the buttonless garment tight round his middle. With trilby well pulled down, and goggles protecting his eyes, he was ready to go. On this occasion the drum was pulled up on the roadside of our stack, making sure a prevailing south-westerly wind carried much of the dust away from the majority of workers. Unfortunately, this meant Percy had to work in a passage formed by the stack on one side and machinery on the other. So, until dinner time, when hopefully the stack would be down to about four feet, thick dust filled this passage with no way to escape. Such were the environmentally unfriendly conditions of work for a chaff-sacker. Incidentally, if the wind was in the opposite direction to the drum on the other side, Percy would have copped almost as much dust blowing through from shakers and riddles. In such a no-win situation, a chaff-sacker's lot was never a happy one. Quite how Charlie's brother-in-law fell for the job in this case, I don't understand. It was usually reserved for the deaf (poor old Pat Easter used to do it), or for the current miscreant, in which case Derek Winner was surely a strong candidate. Anyway, it suited me as Percy and I had spent several harvests together, him as pitcher and myself as holgy boy, so I knew him well.

As there would be little chaff to remove for a while my mentor suggested I load the old thatching straw and remove it to my fire site in readiness for burning. Bumping well out into the middle of ploughed land, I unloaded the waste, along with two bundles of fresh straw, to get a good blaze for a start. A machine being used to bundle the feed straw tied it with binder string making a fairly loose parcel, which was quite easy to move around. Horrie Everard and Jack Curl took care of things at that end of operations.

Back with the Thresher

Breakfast break was taken quite quickly as threshing was on a type of piecework basis. One stack was threshed each day, and when finished the gang was free to go home, irrespective of the time. Usually this ranged from 2.30 to 3.30, depending on conditions. But even at the later time, half an hour was classed as a bonus and worth working towards. As soon as Percy appeared with a full bag of flights I dragged it up on to my cart and soon set off with ten or so, enough to start my conflagration. After a first, initial flare, my fire settled down to a smouldering, smoking heap, but sank down by degrees as I emptied my bags on top, returning to the stack at a speed curtailed in order to keep me looking busy if Charlie appeared on the scene. A mid-morning break enabled sacks of threshed grain to be loaded on a tractor and trailer for storing in Soigné barn. All this grain would be retained for rolling by machine, and then go as domestic stock feed.

As the stack crept downwards to eye level, the golden oat shoofs, flattened now but seemingly full of summer sunshine, seemed to radiate warmth into the cool winter air. A few rats had been feeding and despoiling precious grain, but overall prospects for a sporting afternoon looked thin. Most of the local rat population had taken up residence in and around the wheat stacks, just down the road on Honeypot. Perhaps today's bad luck would be handsomely repaid tomorrow if we moved along to thresh wheat. My day moved on steadily, and by spending ample time stoking smouldering flights, allowing the moderate wind to coax small pockets of flame around the edges, it gave a picture of full occupation, but of course the very short journey from stack to fire left me with time to kill. A fiercer fire with a few newly-threshed bundles along the fence kept us all warm for dinner break, which was also taken fairly quickly, a restart being made well within the confines of forty minutes. As the corn stack sank, the shoofs became flatter, having carried all the weight of those above. At last the semi-damp layer of barley straw, put down as a stack bottom, appeared. Its compressed cardboard surface had been cut by rat workings, and an occasional rodent fled for new cover, giving me ample opportunity to show my skill at hunting, aided by a stout nut stick. This was what threshing was about, well worth all the dust and noise.

As the stack bottom was carefully turned up, rats ran out in varying directions, hotly pursued by me and the younger members of our threshing gang. Not only was the rat public enemy number one, but more importantly his tail was worth one penny when traded in to the foreman. Naturally a huge bunch of rats' tails weren't taken to the farm, but Percy Barnes counted bodies at close of play and collected any monies due on Friday for a grand share-out amongst his workmates. Unfortunately this didn't include boys on chaff-carting, but taking part in the hunt was payment enough for me.

When all filled oat sacks had been loaded the gang mounted their bikes and set off for home. Walter Desborough and his mate hauled the drum and baler into towing order and set off the short distance to Honeypot's centre gateway. There, four wheat stacks awaited threshing on succeeding days. After one final round-up of my chaff fire I also set off for home, Beauty, with nodding head, making good progress along bumpy Honeypot Lane. Having left the empty chaff bags on my cart I felt Charlie would have to send me on the same job tomorrow, which would be wonderful.

This did indeed happen, and I felt the job would be mine for the rest of the threshing season. Wheat chaff was classed as a very useful feed additive, so there were no fires today. Instead I loaded my tumbril quite high, with Percy's help, before setting off for High House where the bags were emptied in their chaff chamber. A nice ride of about a half mile either way filled my time nicely, leaving a few minutes for rat patrol between loads. Wheat ears produce quite a quantity of chaff, so there was no necessity to kill time. Really I felt in my element, with horse and cart, plenty of cheerful company, and paid rat-hunting thrown in. Arriving home every night covered in dust meant difficult washing, owing to a complete lack of bathroom facilities or privacy, but we managed somehow with an old tin bath and soft rain water which made lathering easier.

Just one more threshing tale before this chapter ends. Threshing barley stacks near Elbreck sheds meant carting the prickly chaff into a store at the back. Jimmy was carting mangolds for Harry Ashby and had come to help me load the bags. Mid-afternoon saw the corn stack almost down to floor level when Charlie stepped on to the flattened shoofs. Presumably his quite considerable weight caused a half-grown rat to panic, and shoot up out of a hole, straight over Charlie's large, leather boot, and up his trouser leg. We two boys watched transfixed as Charlie's eyes bulged and then, with a loud bellow, he tried to grab the interloper with both hands before it reached more sensitive areas at the top of his leg. At the sight of Charlie cavorting around, watched by all pairs of eyes on the site, we two just doubled up with laughter, which became uncontrollable, no matter how hard we tried to contain it. Eventually the victim managed to squeeze all life out of his tormentor and shook it out of the trouser bottom once more. Turning on us as we fell about with mirth, he roared, "Get on with your work, my fellows; it's not that funny". But, of course, it was and still is, as my sides ache when I think about the hilarious scene. We fled to the sheds with a half-loaded cart to finish our crying with laughter round the corner. Jimmy couldn't come back at all, but eventually I managed to straighten my face and return to duty. Blackie Wright almost set me going again when he said, with poker-faced expression, "Best to tie your trouser bottoms next time, Charlie. Could have been serious". "You're right there, Master", returned our foreman, with a slight smile, "It made me sweat for a bit". Then, turning on his heel, he made for his bike and home where he could check in private whether any 'serious' damage had been done. As he moved out

Back with the Thresher

of earshot we were able to release our pent-up laughter and re-enact the performance of a stout foreman with a live rat up his trouser leg. This whole episode made me realise that our leg guards, known as "states", did more than keep trouser bottoms clean, being the best protection against unwanted livestock ever invented. Charlie would have been well advised to have kept his bicycle clips on, or to have reverted to traditional foreman's leg wear of shiny, leather buskins. These, strapped on, ankle to knee protectors, weren't worn for fashion, but apparently had very practical uses.

Chapter 9
Spring Cultivations

As January advanced into February, and the days became slightly lighter and longer, we all felt able to smell spring just around the corner. But winter still had a sting in its tail, and true to tradition the arrival of Lynn Mart, our annual fair, triggered off an Arctic blast, along with snowflakes as big as goose feathers. The large fair, situated on King's Lynn Tuesday Market Place, seemed always to have this effect in the last two weeks in February. All roads leading to Pretoria and Soigné were quickly blocked by heavy drifting. The entire labour force that could get to work was engaged in essential stock-feeding, water-provision, and thawing of repeatedly frozen pipes. Straw fires were lit under all outside taps, which had miniature skating rinks surrounding them where melted ice and spilled water froze almost instantly in sub-zero temperatures. These conditions were a stockman's nightmare, always causing my normally mild-tempered father to be virtually unapproachable, and almost murderous should he be caught up in the crossfire of a snowball fight instigated by those workmen with much less to worry about than he had..

The farm had its own wooden snow-plough which was originally pulled by horses with hooves specially roughened with nails to prevent slipping. As tractors were now in the ascendancy they had taken over road clearance, but even they were beaten where drifts were too deep. As soon as semi-normal service had been resumed by stockmen, a large gang of snow shovellers started to dig towards Pretoria, hoping in vain to meet an even larger gang of County Council temporary workers coming the other way. All the men unable to get to Soigné would have signed on with the Council for this emergency work. Tumbler Hill was notorious for its drifting facilities, and never failed to be choked with snow blown from fields, no matter which way the weather came from. Tractors, driven across snow-stripped fields, brought our essential supplies until normal transport routes could be cleared.

Shovelling snow can be a very warm job, especially if the sun shines. The reflection plays havoc with the eyeballs, especially allowing that we were working in times when sun-glasses were an unknown invention to us in darkest Norfolk. Another invention was apparently unknown also, this being a shiny shovel, which allows snow to slide off its surface, when required. Remember the rusty shovel we had at the potato hales? Well, it surfaced again and I had the damned old thing once more. Heroically we shovelled away, but as fast as we cleared a section fresh snow filled it overnight. It was like carrying water in a sieve. Then, as soon as the Mart left Lynn, and March blew in, the weather changed and spring cultivations became top priority. Tractors were snatched from stock-feeding duties to be replaced by horses. All tractor-drivers were expected to work overtime, making full use of daylight. Cultivators, rollers, tined-and disc-harrows, were pulled from field corners and long dead nettle patches. Copious amounts of thick grease were applied to any moving parts, and large hammers used to beat into submission any obstinate section that refused to respond after grease was applied.

Charlie raced from field to field, kicking the soil surface to ascertain whether it was dry and friable enough for cultivation. Artificial fertilizer, which was just taking hold, was still (for the last time, I believe) sown by men walking selected fields, broadcasting chemicals from a wooden box suspended round their necks. Most artificial fertilizer still came as powder, but granules were just becoming available, which made handling a much cleaner job. Throwing powdered chemicals into the air was not very pleasant, especially on a windy day. Norman Chase took command of the corn drill with a mate standing on the board at the rear of his machine. As driver, Norman's job was to follow the track of a marker situated on either side of his drill. This disc marker had to be set at an exact distance from the previous run to enable the machine to sow seed without any gap appearing between each drill width.

Guiding his machine into the end, Brum, as we knew him, pulled a rope leading to a mechanism on the drill, and this set it into work; a second pull at the far end lifted the drill out of work prior to circling for the return journey. Gerald Andrews spent many seasons on the drill-board, and his job entailed refilling the corn hopper from bags left at intervals along field edges, and making sure that seed corn continued to run unchecked down flexible seed pipes and into the soil as a coulter at its base made a receptive groove. In later years a combined seed and manure drill came into use. This machine had a divided hopper, and had the advantage of placing artificial fertilizer alongside seed to provide instantly available food for seedlings with limited root growth.

Gerald had a very responsible job, as there was no second chance with seeding if a mistake was made. No mistakes could be detected until the seed sprouted, and then they could come back to haunt you all through the summer. If seed failed to run cleanly a wide, brown gap showed where the drill-man's concentration had wavered. A blockage in a manure pipe became obvious when yellow-bladed plants faded amongst their lush, green companions. Likewise, a shaky hand on Brum's steering wheel gave all and sundry the chance to prattle on about "dogs' hind legs" until each row met its neighbour in late spring. I wouldn't have been able to sleep until all grain had come up and I could see it was O.K. Whether Gerald suffered in that way, I don't know, but he never seemed to show it. A joker maybe, but he always seemed to carry off any agricultural job with ease and confidence. The constant high standard of corn crops when sprouted indicated that Charlie's faith in him was well-founded.

Spring wheat came first, along with oats, both sown in fairly limited amounts. Autumn wheat and rye were already being rolled and harrowed to firm roots and encourage spread in growth. This was done just as soon as the surface was dry enough, in an effort to repair the ravages of winter. A crimped Cambridge roller and light harrows were used for this. If a very mild winter had prevailed, sheep might be run over a rye field to trim some of the lush growth and add a spattering of animal manure to the crop. As rye was usually grown on light land this dual-purpose treatment worked quite well.

Barley made up the largest part of spring sowings, Spratt Archer being the main type of seed used in an effort to get a sample to tempt the maltsters and obtain top prices. Soigné land produced some fine barley samples for Willie Thaxton to lay before the local corn barons.

Tractors didn't do all the work, even if mass mechanisation seemed to be taking control. Lighter cultivations were still carried out by horsepower in its original sense. Chain harrows were dragged over permanent pasture to pull out old, dead grass, and spread animal droppings and molehills. Every pasture had light and dark strips, showing where chain harrows had been pulled backwards and forwards – quite a good job for a lad, as walking over the grass surface was much easier than over rough, unbroken clods on arable land. The smell of disturbed soil and bruised grass drifting up into mild, spring air was very pleasant, as was dinner taken on the sunny, south aspect of a dense bramble clump. Birds, especially jackdaws, would be busy collecting hair or grass for nesting material, as well as sheep's wool for state-of-the-art lining. The short tines on rolled chains disturbed insects and pests hidden in soil or muck, giving free and easy feed to our feathered friends busily engaged in nest-building. Sometimes stock left in the field would become over-inquisitive, and annoy Beauty by pushing too close. A few hand claps, and, a token, short chase would send them away at a gallop leaving us in peace to enjoy our dinner time rest. It was always a struggle to get harrows loaded on to the tumbril, but somehow they were humped and dragged on board ready for the next pasture to be given the treatment.

Another springtime job, carried out in regard to pasture improvement, was an application of basic slag. Now the very mention of these two words, "basic slag", was enough to send shivers down the spine of every member of our workforce. The black powder, which reputedly carried every trace element vital to lush growth, covered and penetrated every inch of skin, whether exposed or not. Unloading the paper sacks initially into a dry store, re-loading for transport to the chosen pasture for sowing by hand or machine, meant a sooty complexion for days afterwards. Imagine flinging soot from a box around your neck, out into the wind, and you have a good picture of basic slag distribution. I remember Leslie Richardson sowing it with a manure drill in later years; after a few rounds the only things left white were his teeth; the rest of him could well have originated from darkest Africa. This wonderful waste product from industry stayed in fashion for several years and made chaff-sacking a "best suit job" in comparison. Treated pastures remained black, until rain washed the slag into the ground. These two jobs of chain harrow and slag-sowing show the extremes of pleasure or purgatory connected with spring treatment of permanent pasture.

Now to turn back to arable cultivations, and my involvement in that particular year. In my odd-jobbing capacity I enjoyed a roving commission. Sometimes I carted mangolds, cut kale, or ferried seed corn and artificial manure. Barney Hooks always helped me load the necessary bags at Soigné. One dinner time Charlie gave me instructions to load and deliver seed barley sacks for work "behind the belt". As usual, Barney wheeled the sixteen-stone sacks to the edge of the barn floor. Standing in my tumbril they were then at a convenient height for carrying on the back. Carefully taking the weight I staggered forward a few steps before dropping my load into one front corner.

"Your legs were a bit bowed", smiled Barney.

"I can manage alright", I puffed, whilst wondering how anyone could walk the length of a lorry or up barn steps with that kind of weight on board. If wheat had been involved I should have had two stones more to wobble with. After loading the half dozen bags I set off for the rear of Sixteen Acre Belt, just behind the farm. On reaching Little Strawberries my eyes searched for a tractor and drill, but a virgin landscape met my anxious gaze. Now what? After waiting a few minutes worry began to gnaw at my insides. What should I do with my load? Knowing from limited experience that seed sacks had to be left at regular intervals along a headland, I drew on a bit and then dropped the first one on to soggy ground under the wood. Try as I might I couldn't get the damned thing to sit upright, so I left it half sitting, half lying, on its heavy clay bed. Sweating and swearing I carried on up the wood side, leaving deep tyre ruts behind me and eventually half a dozen drunken sacks. Still no sign of Brum and his corn drill, so, turning my mare, I set off for Soigné once more. I thought Barney looked slightly surprised as I pulled up outside the carpenter's shop.

"You've been quick, Derek", he said.

"Can't hang about all afternoon", I replied, slightly puzzled by his remark, as in my opinion I hadn't been quick at all.

"How are they getting on up there?" Another slightly puzzling question.

"I didn't see anyone", my answer came, in rather a querulous voice.

"Didn't see anyone?" By now Barney had straightened up from his work, sensing that something was amiss. "Where did you go then?"

"Behind the belt and into Little Strawberries", I replied through fast drying lips and experiencing a terrible sinking feeling in the pit of my stomach. "Charlie said behind the belt."

"You're right there, but he meant Mink Belt in the fields that run down to Massingham Heath. I thought you knew where they were working."

I could have wept. A lovely long ride to the other side of High House had been mucked up and I was deep in trouble. Visions of trying to lift sixteen-stone sacks out of cloying mud flashed through my mind. I just couldn't retrieve my awful mistake. But Barney was soon coming to my rescue.

"Don't look so worried, Derek. Charlie should give his orders more clearly. I'll come back with you to pick them up and then you can nip on your way."

Barney was typical of most men at Soigné who enjoyed a laugh at some of my gaffes, but who were always ready to put things right before authority came on the scene.

It was no fun pulling those wet-bottomed sacks from the mud and lifting them back on board. Barney's shiny, carpenter's shop boots were soon covered in mud, a thing unheard of for this latter-day tradesman. But, to his eternal credit, he heaved and lifted me out of trouble, setting me on my way to Mink Belt with a very breathless, "Make haste, boy, and get going". With a hasty and equally breathless "Thanks", I turned Beauty's head towards High House, and was soon bumping along Honeypot Lane with all haste. I didn't enjoy my ride one bit owing to my churning stomach and shame-ridden guilt at making such an awful mistake. Fearing Charlie would be up there already, fuming mad if the drilling had been held up, I turned Beauty along the top of Nineteen Acres behind the belt, and pressed on to the next field, where I could see a blue tractor and red corn drill stationary at the top end. As I drew up all in a muck sweat, Brum and Gerald looked at my mud-stained person with some surprise, and even more surprise when they saw the state of the sacks.

"Where have you been?" they both queried.

"Took them to the wrong field", I mumbled, self-consciously.

Seeing my discomfort, Gerald assured me they hadn't been stopped more than two hours, which made me feel worse than ever.

"Take no notice of that lying hound", said Brum. "We've only just stopped."

Spring Cultivations

The old, familiar Andrews wheezy laughter broke out as my mate set about re-filling his machine. There had to be a leg-pull somewhere in his day, and I was the chosen victim as the choice was very limited in such an isolated spot.

After dropping off the half-emptied sack behind the drill I proceeded to unload the rest at intervals as before, but this time in the correct location. As soon as re-filling was complete, Brum hopped on his tractor and swung into action, doing his best to shoot Dilberry off the back-board in the process. Down towards Massingham Heath they went, with drill coulters rattling through stones, and Gerald intently watching that they all kept free-flowing as the seed barley was fed into the sweet-smelling earth. With less haste I returned to Soigné, hoping that Charlie wouldn't greet me with a more apposite observation than Barney on the first occasion, namely, "You've been a long time, Derek". But nothing was said, so I didn't elaborate to anyone about my slight mishearing of orders. I felt sorry for Barney's boots, which seldom lost their shine to anything worse than barley meal or sawdust.

Another little job I tried was using a set of light harrows behind the drill, covering seed before rooks came down to eat their fill. Setting off with my harrows and pole on the tumbril, and trying to remember Will's instructions on how to set them up, I made my way along the side of the Hulver to an isolated fourteen-acre field on the edge of Soigné Wood. The drill had just finished, much to my relief as I didn't want an audience present when sorting out a jigsaw of harrows and harness. After laying out my pole and attaching the harrows, I changed Beauty's harness from shaft to field equipment, fastening her chains to the pole as instructed. My efforts looked right, and seemed to work O.K. as I led her forward a few paces. So far, so good, I thought as I ran out my driving reins which enabled me to be in control whilst walking behind the harrows. Twenty past eight — shall I try one round before breakfast? Yes, let's break the ice and get started. Picking up the final piece of equipment, a hooked stick for lifting clogged harrows on the run, we set off alongside Soigné Wood. Keeping my left-hand-harrow close to the field edge, we made for the far end where the wood widens along that boundary. A sense of power flowed through me as the harrow tines skimmed along the top few inches of fine, sandy soil. An occasional small branch caught between the tines, caused a dragging action, but a quick lift at the back, using my hooked stick, released the obstruction without calling a halt. Nearing the end of my first run, and feeling full of confidence, I pulled hard on the right rein, causing Beauty to turn almost at right angles, so sharply, in fact, that after a few sideways steps, her foot went over the slackened trace chain, and I was in an awful tangle. So much for my new found self-confidence and know-it-all, cavalier feelings. If Beauty had been sharing my high-flying feelings she would have panicked as the chain sawed across her leg, but being her usual placid self, she stopped to allow me an opportunity to unhook the chain and lead her off it. After re-setting my traces, I learned the lesson of turning gradually, and by using a wider arc avoided any such trouble again.

After a quick, stand-up breakfast sandwich, I sailed up and down in fine style. The weather was perfect, cold but bright. A north wind dried the field surface so that boots and harrows remained clean, light and free-running. Surrounded by trees on three sides, with no other human being in sight, I felt king of my own domain. An open vista to the north ran away towards Gayton Thorpe as this field was on the very north-west edge of Soigné land. A few stray clouds ran shadows across the land, pheasants pecked away alongside their woodland retreat, and a couple of mad March hares tumbled around on the emerging green sward next door. The world was mine and I just loved its solitude and beauty. I felt my horse was enjoying the experience too. The task wasn't too exacting for either of us, so I pressed on with only a quick cup of cocoa taken at about 10.45. As dinner time approached I began to formulate plans for a comfortable place to take it. Should I stop early and light a fire? No, not worth it. Best to unyoke Beauty and walk the fifty yards or so into the Hulver and make use of its sunny aspect and sheltering trees to keep the cool wind at bay. It turned out to be a real sun-trap as I sprawled out on sack and coat, eating cheese sandwiches and fruit cake, appeasing a keen appetite built up over several miles of brisk walking. Beauty chewed and pulled at bare saplings around her station at the wood side. Nothing moved on this side of the wood either, although I could see the blue and red of Brum's tractor and drill stationary on the far side of Lower Thirty Acres. I think he had walked to the far side of a narrow wood to catch a sun-trap also. I dozed, Beauty chewed and rattled her harness, and the watch hands quickly moved on to 12.40, time to get up. A burst of distant sound, which followed a puff of exhaust, came to me as a tiny figure cranked his tractor and drilling began again.

"Come on, Beauty, off to work we go."

Boy and horse got started with a jangle of trace chains. Away we surged with a burst of fresh energy and eyes measuring up the land completed, and that left still to cover. "Won't finish today. Well, I might. Time will tell, just keep going." A brief visit from Charlie settled my "in the mind" argument. Casting his experienced eye over the field, he assured me I wouldn't finish the job that day.

"Leave your cart and harrows here and come back tomorrow to finish off", was his instruction. "Then drop on to the Horse Pasture. Brum will be there by that time, so you can harrow in behind him."

Spring Cultivations

After the foreman left I continued work with wings on my feet. What a grand day I'd had already, and now I had orders along similar lines for tomorrow. My harrows seemed to sing through the soil, with Beauty nodding her head at every step as if to give her approval to the whole situation.

Just after half past three I dropped off the harrows, and after tucking the shaft harness of saddle and breechings well under the tumbril to keep dry, prepared for home. By mounting a wheel I could hop on Beauty's back to ride side-saddle to the farm. We always tried to arrive there at ten to four. Any later meant a scramble to unyoke by four o'clock; earlier arrival was frowned upon by Charlie, so great care went into matching watch time and the speed of one's mount. I can tell you it isn't easy to hold back a horse whose sole intent is to get home for a feed in its stable. Dark frowns from foremen cut no ice with them.

As soon as all cereal crops had been sown, the attention centred on root crops, more especially sugar-beet, a main money-earner for the farm. As these root seedlings are susceptible to frost damage, their emergence must be very carefully timed. The required seed bed also needs much more preparation, and so intense cultivation took place on fields chosen for roots. A fine tilth finish is necessary to enable threadlike plants to get established, so all Charlie's expertise was called upon to produce this tilth. After much pulling around on Lower Fifty Acres, Charlie decided the best implement to produce the kind of finish he needed prior to drilling was a light, flat roller; the only one available was horse-drawn, and I was given the job. The roller was attached under a wooden frame, pulled by a horse working in shafts. This time I was able to ride by making a sack seat on the cross members of the frame. Driving with long reins I set off along the straight dividing-line between the unfenced sections of this large field. Quite why this field was usually divided into three parts, whilst others of the same size or bigger carried just one right through crop, I don't know. It may have been because both light and heavy soil types made up its structure. Anyway, I began work on the lighter end, which ran down to Half Moon Belt and the rough road to Rats Hall. A large tree-filled pit-hole sat in the middle, and would play havoc with my attempts to keep a straight line of work so essential in the eyes of those seasoned campaigners passing along the road. Remember, in those days no one kept their eyes on the road for approaching traffic, they all took stock of crops and work in adjoining fields. Also, they travelled at speeds conducive to this kind of observation, being either on bike or horseback. Try as I might, I lost my line after the first end or so. Taking less than a full roller width here, and an over-full width there, seemed to make things worse, so by the time I reached the aforementioned pit-hole my line was non-existent, anyway.

Spring Cultivations

I bumped along on my none too comfortable seat, with the roller rattling over small flint stones, pressing them down into fairly soft earth. A light dust came up from the drying surface, which was ideal for the type of work being done. Sometimes I walked beside the roller to stretch my legs that became stiff suspended in mid-air, there being no way I could ride with legs supported. Again, it was an enjoyable job, and dinner time came in a surprisingly short time. Using the pit as shelter, I flung down on the sunny edge, after securely tying Beauty to prevent her over-eager attempts to reach some succulent spring growth taking her down the steep side, roller and all.

A horse's life was much easier now that the tractor had taken on most of the heavier work such as ploughing and bindering. In this transitional period between horse power and mechanisation the horse did many useful tasks where tractor use could be described as "taking a sledge hammer to crack a nut". My job today could be a prime example. A heavy tractor pulling a light roller would have left tracks of over-compressed soil, whereas horses' hooves left very little compaction behind. Speed of operation hadn't really entered the equation, so a job of work remained for a boy as he went through an unofficial apprenticeship. Nowadays, of course, the huge machines used in farm cultivations leave only one deep set of tracks per acre, or is it per hectare, as they pull or carry implements almost three miles wide — a slight exaggeration, I know, but agriculture today was a world unknown and unimagined by me or anyone else on the day I rode up and down Lower Fifty Acres on a one-horse, light, flat roller. I had a job, pure fresh air, and a wonderful live workmate with feelings and a heart-warming response to a kind word and a pat on her neck. If profit per £1 invested had been the yardstick then, I would have been a statistic in Government unemployment figures, and Beauty would have filled dog food tins on a supermarket shelf. If only we could have seen the "wonderful" future being planned out for our beautiful countryside and simplistic living. A modern-day Robert Kett, or Wat Tyler, would receive much support if they decided to lead we peasants to London with the one object of wiping the financial square mile off the face of this earth for ever. But could we find again the real world and a real life? I fear we lived it for a while and then lost it for ever in the lemming-like charge for progress. Can I complain? Not when I helped to lead that charge, although the progressive changes I fought for would be chicken feed compared with those forced upon many through head-in-the-sand stagnation that existed in our agricultural world of the fifties.

As one field after another received its cultivations and crops for the summer, the frenetic activity slowly subsided, and became concentrated on the few fields late in disposing of the previous year's crops. As cattle were either sold as fatstock or turned out to grass, the dreaded season of muck-cart came

Spring Cultivations

round once more. At least when it came I wasn't incarcerated in a south-facing bullock yard, hauling trodden muck on to carts with strengthening April and early-May sunshine raising the temperature to heady heights. My job, along with Jimmy's, was to collect the loaded tumbril from Elbreck Yard, drive it on to waste ground behind and unload. Half the load would slide off when our tumbril tipped, but then half had to be thrown up to give a nice high pile. Being out in fresh air, with thorn bushes breaking into leaf, and crushed nettle growth underfoot, helped to dispel the rich manure smell, but it did cling to clothes. Personally, I quite liked the scent, but others, including my mother, tended to throw your precious boots and states outside before you could comfortably divest yourself of them. The hands also changed colour as brown liquid worked its way up the fork shaft or covered securing pins in the cart tail-board. Washing facilities were at a minimum, so slightly marinated sandwiches became the norm. At least my brown bread didn't show my finger marks, but sometimes the taste left much to be desired. I think it assisted in longevity as Grandad Bumfrey passed the 90 year mark, and quite a few local men worked on into their eighties. Occasionally an affliction, called locally "the back door trot", meant a few quick trips to a nearby pit-hole, but all in all we were a pretty healthy lot.

As the fickle month of May progressed, all eyes were turned on beet crop growth. Hand hoes were taken down, new blades riveted on by Wally Lloyd or Walter High, all in readiness for piecework on chopping-out and singling sugar-beet and mangolds. Like yarded cattle fretting to get out to grass, men also fretted to leave muck yards for open fields where there was a chance to earn a little over the basic wage for a few weeks. At last the order went out, "Bring your hoes on Monday morning. We'll start on the Nurseries". Saturday, half-day, seemed like the end of school term. Very little muck was moved, and at 11.30 forks were meticulously cleaned, states rolled up, and carts emptied. The forks were then placed in my care, with instructions to store them in Will's stable. Jimmy and I made our way back to Soigné, me in front riding Traveller, with Beauty in shafts tied behind. As we had been sent off fairly early, I tried hard to restrict my horse's speed so as not to arrive before the allotted time. But Traveller had a hard mouth, and no amount of pulling held him back from the promise of a weekend out on the pasture.

So the summer season was about to start, and with it new jobs. The farmyard would become almost deserted as work became field-orientated, with few men coming for daily orders, except for we boys, Jimmy and myself.

Chapter 10
Summer Jobs for Us Boys

The cart-shed was silent, except for a couple of house sparrows squabbling under the tiles. Tractors across the yard would soon burst into life and speed off to their allotted tasks, although some would remain silent for the next few weeks as their drivers joined the hoeing gang. Jimmy and I stood waiting for orders as Charlie came rolling round the corner. We were the only two considered too young for piecework hoeing. It would be odd jobs for us, as usual, with no chance of any extra money until hay time and harvest.

What a transformation had come over everything as the sun climbed higher daily, and warm air came at last to Norfolk. The spring had been cold after the promise of early March when a short spell of balmy weather lulled us into thinking that winter had gone for good. A long run of north-easterly winds had sent everyone back into Army coats and thick jerseys. But at last warm sunshine restored life to our bone marrow. Biking up to Soigné through fresh morning air, with the promise of a "shirt sleeve" day to come, was a pleasure. Roadside verges leapt into life with cow parsley, or hemlock as we called it, growing at the rate of a foot per day. Hedges and trees were thick and green, whilst every field was dressed over all in its own shade of green depending on which crop grew in its rich and carefully prepared soil. Slight disturbances of the bankside growth showed where the current schoolboys had discovered a bird's nest. Tar barrels and sand heaps indicated that Bert Pitcher and his road-patching gang would be along to effect repairs some time during the summer. The smell of hot tar was synonymous with high summer, either from the boiling tar pot or melting road surfaces. A much greater effort was needed at twenty minutes to one when I had to haul myself up from a grassy bank where dozing after dinner was a must. The smell of bruised grasses and the drone of insects pulled my eyelids towards each other, whilst the warm sunshine sealed them together when they met. What bliss to stretch my legs and watch steel-cleated heels scrape lines in the dusty soil. No need to creep into the blacksmith's shop or light a fire in a pit-hole at mealtimes now. Flop down at twelve and enjoy forty minutes of complete rest before work started again — well, perhaps not every day, as a few Arctic days crept back in from the North Pole during late May and early June. When this happened we worked under our thick Army coats in freezing drizzle and wished we were a few short miles inland where blue skies gave sunshine all day.

Summer Jobs for Us Boys

One job that took up quite a large amount of my time was keeping the cattle and sheep supplied with water. Some pastures didn't have piped water, or, if the pipes were there the galvanised coating had disintegrated allowing rust to build up and block the passage of water. This meant carting water to keep tanks topped up whilst cattle occupied that particular field. Most other tanks were fitted with battered, metal ballcocks, and these either jammed when water was required, or dribbled continuously giving an overflowing tank with a muddy patch for several yards around it. This of course supplied the necessary mud for swallows and house martins to construct their neat nests, but did nothing to conserve water when wind failed to turn the sails above the water bore.

The, sheep on the other hand, moved from field to field all over the farm, and so had no piped water. During cooler months sufficient moisture came from grazing wet foliage and juicy roots, but hot, very dry weather meant the water-cart had to be called for.

Now, the stock water-cart consisted of a large, rust-coloured, round tank, set lengthwise on a wooden framework which, in turn, rode on a set of ex-lorry rear wheels. A hole in the top was covered by a thick, wet sack, which cut down too much splashing. A very heavy metal ball counterbalanced the bung at the back where water was discharged. This wonderful contraption had to be operated from above in order to avoid a real soaking when opening or closing. By standing on the frame, with legs well back, I bent forward to reach a piece of wire attached to the aforementioned ball. A hefty heave brought it up with a loud clang as it hit against the tank. Out shot a fountain of water straight into a tank, if the angle had been worked out correctly. As most drinking troughs were long and narrow, by backing on to the tank end, one could hit the target on most occasions. When sufficient water had been run in, the ball was dropped back into place, causing a sideways spray of water to whip out, soaking any unsuspecting onlooker if standing too close. I'm not sure who was responsible for the quaint design used there, but I've a suspicion that Barney Hooks had a hand in it. He always looked a bit guilty if anyone squelched into the blacksmith's shop swearing about the design and suggesting where the person responsible for it should put the iron ball. Beauty always stood still when I was hanging over the back, but on one occasion I had Traveller instead of her, and halfway through the operation he decided to jerk forward, and sent me and the weighted stopcock downwards. A good spray from the closing bung and one leg in a half-filled water tank did nothing for my good humour. I spent a fair time standing in the hot sunshine, with steaming trousers and shirt, giving a good impression of a sea bird with wings outstretched drying my feathers. Barney was out hoeing, so he didn't have to listen to me venting my spleen on the unknown designer.

Visiting the sheep meant meeting up with Charlie Andrews, the shepherd. He always had something amusing to recount, and never failed to give me a message for Will which was intended to put his back up when he returned to see to the horses. Most of these messages were conveniently forgotten, but sometimes Will would ask what squit Charlie Lop had been talking, so I passed on some information, and then received back a wisecrack to pass on when next visiting the shepherd. This friendly banter went on all the years I worked at Soigné, and more so when Charlie relinquished the sheep to become cowman at the farm.

By the latter part of May the lambs were becoming quite well grown. They still drank from mother, hence the need for water, as animals cannot make milk without taking in water. The lambs also fed off the best feed by virtue of the fact they had the run of next day's fold a day early. By squeezing their fat little bodies through a special hurdle designed to let them past but not their larger mothers, they fed undisturbed. As they squeezed back a loud bleating ensued as lamb and milk-supplying mother sought to become reunited. It was a lovely scene, so different from the sodden, muddy conditions of a few months back when we passed them by on our way to pull swedes. Now the heat threw back from the land, larks sang way up in the blue sky, the sheepdog panted, and the smell of sheep dip and dung seemed to blend itself into a feeling of peace and wellbeing around Charlie and myself as we leaned on the sheep net and gazed out over the undulating expanse of Ash Tree Shift shimmering before us. The dark mass of Soigné Wood gave a cool, shady line along the south side, whilst Half Moon Plantation baked away to the north hiding Rats Hall as it nestled in a hollow below Donkey Hill. The clink of hoe blades against flint stones came from Fifty Acres where sugar-beet were being chopped out by the piecework gang. On that side of the fence no one stood looking at the scenery as time was money with them, but we two on day work had time to stand and stare whilst putting the world to rights. I suppose Charlie, who worked alone for most of his time, was glad of someone to chat with when the opportunity arose.

Leaving the old, brown water-cart half-empty and propped up on legs, I unhooked Beauty and prepared to make my way to Rats Hall where a near-empty domestic water-cart awaited the weekly refill. Half walking, half sliding, we negotiated the short but very steep Donkey Hill, and made our way to the barn. Being well used to the procedure now, I soon yoked up and made my way back along Waterpit Lane, and on to the hard road. All the hoeing gang had gathered beside the hedge for a drink, and were chatting with Bob Chapman, the young keeper who lived in a lonely cottage called "The New Buildings". Derek Winner — who else — had managed to part Bob and his twelve-bore gun on some pretext or other, and was hatching some mischief. Suddenly a trilby hat sailed up into the air and was sent spinning sideways as a

Summer Jobs for Us Boys

discharge of lead shot went through the crown. Beauty left the road with all four feet, and I almost left her back. More by luck than anything else I held on to her, and we continued on our way at a much faster speed than before. With a great deal of swearing the hat's owner retrieved his battered headgear, and Bob took charge of the gun. The incident caused much merriment, especially amongst the younger members of the gang. Life was never dull when Derek was around, and we all missed him when he volunteered to join the Navy shortly afterwards. Charlie Wilson's parting observation was, "Put you in charge of a ship and you'll start World War 3". I'm sure the poor foreman slept more peacefully with Derek on the other side of the world. Not only him, I would suggest that the entire village saw his departure as a mixed blessing, although a bright spark of life went with him, and our lives didn't contain too many of them.

May I just recall one more amusing incident that happened in the spring of that year. It was Tuesday, and Charlie had gone to Lynn Market as usual, leaving we younger element working around the farm buildings. Some of us had the job of re-bagging artificial manure in a disused stable. Quite a number of paper sacks split in store and were left when re-loading took place. Whilst engaged in this not too exciting occupation, one of our number found an old-fashioned bath chair hidden away at the back. I believe Dick Welham suffered a leg injury at one time and had used this "blast from the past" to get around. Dragging the rusting contraption outside, we examined its possibilities. A handle across the back enabled it to be pushed, and its passenger steered by means of another handle leading back from the single front wheel. We took turns in riding up and down outside the stable with the machine gaining speed with each succeeding lap. When Derek Winner tried his hand at steering, the propelling party set off down the slope, round the corner, and out into full view of the road. Our passenger fought manfully to control the Heath Robinson steering mechanism in order to stay on the road. Suddenly the warning went up, "Look out, he's about". Charlie was approaching from the opposite direction. Pushing power stopped suddenly as we turned and took to our heels back to work. Derek, robbed of his power, carried on for a few more yards before taking to the grass verge. Not being designed for rough ground travel, the bath chair overturned, flinging its passenger out only a short distance from the slimy, green-surfaced pond. Who was the most surprised, Charlie or Derek, I don't know, but I've no doubt the former had a job to keep a straight face whilst demanding an explanation. That was the last trip the old bath chair made as its flimsy wheels were buckled beyond repair. I expect it ended up in the pit-hole behind the farm where all our rubbish was tipped when Charlie had a purge around the buildings. Its old cane body would soon have rotted, but a buckled wheel may still poke out of a nettle-patch as a silent reminder of the days when Soigné

Farm echoed to the laughter of exuberant youth. The six men who work both Soigné and Abbey Farms today can seldom meet as a gang and enjoy the laughs we did. I expect there were smiles between Charlie and his wife when he recounted some of the antics he came across. Thank goodness both Willie Thaxton and Charlie Wilson had very convenient "blind eyes" when the situation demanded. The only "sack" anyone had on that farm was the one to sit upon at meal times.

Kept on one of the side-pastures were two colts, almost four years old and only partially broken in. They had in fact been abandoned half way through training as the call for heavy horses was in steep decline. On one of his tours of the farm the Major enquired why these two healthy animals were eating grass without giving back any work.

"Get them broken in to work, Thaxton."

"Yes sir, yes sir, I'll get Will on it at once", was Willie's automatic answer, without giving any real thought to the order. Passing the order down the chain of command, Charlie spoke to Uncle Will about it.

"I know what you will say", Charlie prepared his case before putting the order, "but the Major wants those two colts broken for work."

"They're too old now", was Will's reply. "We shall be wasting our time."

"That's what I said, my fellow, but Willie says we've got to try."

And so I became assistant horse-breaker to my uncle for a short time early that summer. We rounded up the pair of high-kicking, freedom-loving Suffolk colts, and drove them into the horse yard. By stealth, Will managed to get a halter on them, and spent hours getting them used to being handled, dodging rearing front hooves and keeping well clear of those lethal rear feet. I don't think I really thought much about danger, and loved every minute of it. Eventually I held a long lead rope whilst Will attempted to drive them on long reins. My, the sweat ran as we stumbled over the dry, crusty and uneven, strawed surface. Some limited progress was made, enough anyway to allow us to attempt field work with them. The only fallow field available was ten acres of poor, sandy land, alongside Stowborough Heath, on the edge of Soigné Wood. In the morning we took one colt up there and spent the time pulling a log of wood or a heavy harrow round and round the field in an effort to tire the animal into a more docile frame of mind. Every time he stopped for a breather, on we had to push him. In the end it was us who broke first after walking for what appeared to be miles through ankle-deep dust. In the afternoon we came back with colt number two for a repeat performance, under scorching hot conditions. Each step of training took considerable time, going from rope halter to bit and bridle, then a collar – what a performance to get it over a flinging head – followed by trace harness and chains. Finally the day came for putting them in shafts. The flat roller was the implement used, and we managed quite well in the first session. After dinner the luck left us, and a near fatality occurred. Having backed our fractious animal between the shafts, Will set about fastening his chains. Suddenly, without warning, he reared up, almost wrenching my arms out of their sockets as I pulled the rope on his head.

As his forefeet descended, one missed Will's head by a whisker and somehow became wedged over the shaft. It was like a scene from a Wild West rodeo as we fought to hold him. Clouds of dust flew as he pulled the rope and me all over the place. Luckily in the ensuing fracas his leg disentangled itself from the shaft without smashing the woodwork. I shall never forget that split second as a huge hoof appeared to be descending on Will's head. The one thing that pleased and surprised me was that I felt no fear at all. I was ready to go on and show this horse that I was the boss and eventually convince him there was nothing to fear. Alas, just as Will felt we were achieving limited success, a halt was called to the job. The novelty had worn off as far as the management was concerned, and hay harvest beckoned requiring all hands to the work. The colts were turned out once more, and eventually were sold as surplus to requirement. Will swore quietly over all his wasted efforts. For me, it was an experience I was never called upon to repeat, but which gave me yet another glimpse of centuries-old skills about to be lost for ever. Well, not quite, as the dedicated heavy-horse breeders still persevere in producing fully trained animals for shows and very limited haulage work. The abandonment of colt training meant that Gipsy was the last example of Will Bumfrey's expert horse-breaking, and what a wonderful animal she was. My dreams of helping to produce two working companions like her never came to fruition, but that's life. At least I did my best and enjoyed the experience.

For some days now the chatter of grass cutters could be heard at Pretoria as the thick, red clover and ryegrass one-year ley was cut on Pretoria Breck. This field lay to the left of the Westacre to High House road, running northwards from behind our cottages. The sweet smell of newly-mown grass drifted into our gardens and with it came a promise of long, hot days, so necessary to good quality hay. After wilting in the warm sunshine for a few days, the heavy crop was turned by a tractor-drawn hay tedder to allow the underside a chance to lose its sap. Charlie strode the field, picking up handfuls here and there, twisting and smelling his samples. Great care had to be taken with hay, as carting too early or too late can both lead to disaster. Green hay will heat in the stack, causing a fire, whilst over-dried grass loses most of its feed value. On this occasion Charlie was helped by a fine, dry spell of weather, which is unusual to say the least. A heavy thunderstorm or a spell of dull, wet weather can upset the best-laid plans and destroy a full year's work by producing mouldy hay.

As soon as it was decreed ready, the tractor-drawn horse-rake pulled the hay into long rows. Now came we horse men into the field to play our part in these operations. Aboard our tumbril was a wooden implement consisting of long teeth attached to a back frame with two wooden handles. Gipsy, dressed in trace harness, was fastened to the front, with me on her broad back on a sack seat and my legs stuck down each side outside the trace chains. My instruction was to steer a course as near as possible to a row of rakings, and proceed across the field. Will then steered his implement under the row, which pushed up a large heap as we went. When the hay had built up to the limit of Gipsy's pulling power, Will lifted his handle slightly, causing the teeth to bite into the ground and turn completely over the top, leaving an untidy heap behind. This procedure continued up and down the rows, with me having a wonderful time in front — in contrast to the sweat-and dust-covered Will at the back. This operation was soon to be superseded by the buckrake which was mounted on a tractor; it made heaps by reversing along a row until the required amount was collected, and then easing forward leaving its load behind. Anyway, that was to follow in the next season.

The object of collecting the hay into these large heaps was soon obvious as a group of men appeared, armed with pitchforks. Splitting into pairs, they soon rounded each heap by building a very neat haycock, so constructed that should any rain fall it would run off the gently-sloping sides. Soon the field was thickly dotted with dome-shaped cocks. As well as waterproofing the hay, these haycocks allowed an extra drying period of a gentle nature, which held the nutrients whilst ensuring there would be no risk of heating in the stack.

About a week after the initial work on Pretoria Breck, Jimmy and I were ordered to join the carting gang as loaders. Now here was a tummy-rumbling situation if ever there was one. Me loading hay! What did I know about loading — or Jimmy either for that matter — but he seemed unperturbed by the prospect? We were given a very short-handled pitchfork each and sent on our way. The stack was to be built inside the middle gateway where a load of barley straw was already being spread out evenly over the 12yds. x 6yds. stack area measured out on the previous day by the foreman. An elevator was being unfolded over the bottom by the stackers who were led by Blackie Wright and his right-hand-man, Barney Hooks. The crop was to be loaded on to trailers, two large brown ones and a smaller green one. Each trailer had large slatted ends and open sides. These slatted ends called "ladders" slotted into holes front and rear, and were very heavy and awkward to manipulate. This wasn't a problem to us as the trailers were made up ready for use on this occasion.

Mounting the first trailer we rode out behind Georgie Wright, who pulled his tractor alongside the first haycock to be loaded. Percy Barnes and Harry Ashby were the pitchers, one being right-handed and one left. This meant they were able to pitch as a team from opposite sides of the cock. Percy pitched to me at the front, and Harry to Jimmy at the back. Once more it seemed I was to have Percy as my instructor.

"Do you know how to load, Derek?"

"No idea Percy."

"Right then, I will show you. Remember, always keep your arse behind you."

Well, this was a baffling instruction as I had always kept mine in that general direction. What he meant was always draw your forkful towards you, then put one foot to hold it until the next binds it in.

"Place the first forkful tight to the front ladder, just sticking out over the edge. Tuck the next one on to the edge of it, and work down the trailer."

Having done one side, I was instructed to repeat it on the other, before filling the middle to hold the load together.

Slowly our load rose as George moved us on from cock to cock. Finally we were told to fill the middle well, before that first load went off to the stack and we leapt down on to an empty trailer-bed and began to repeat the operation with Bob Clarke driving the second tractor.

"Remember you two", said Harry with a familiar twinkle in his eyes, "If you load down it will cost you a gallon of beer".

Well, the first few loads looked for all the world as if the gallon was about to be bought as they drunkenly made slow progress to the stack. Experience told our drivers to pull in with the worst of the list leaning towards the elevator so that if and when the side went down it would be in or beside the machine. Luckily the modern elevator, driven by a small petrol engine, was much lower than its horse-driven predecessor, so pitching was mainly downhill. Somehow the two drivers got our shaggy heaps to the stack without mishap, but we both endured plenty of good-natured banter.

Slowly our pitchers' tuition paid off and our efforts began to look more like loads and less like heaps on wheels. Pride slowly took hold as we worked hard at the art, and eventually watched some very decent loads making their way to the stack before a halt was called for dinner. The sun was high in the sky and sweat poured off us as hard work, combined with nervous energy, took its toll.

Midway through the morning Willie Thaxton arrived with a stone bottle containing a gallon of mild beer. This traditional hay making beer ration was very welcome. The work was taken on piecework, at a set price for clearing an acre plus a gallon of beer per day to be shared amongst the gang of eight men. Four men worked out in the field, who on this occasion consisted of Percy Barnes and Harry Ashby pitching, with Jimmy Lane and yours truly loading. Blackie Wright was chief stacker and "lord" with his backer, Barney Hooks, and with Horrie Everard and Jack Curl on the stack. To return to the beer ration, by the time the bottle came out into the field it was unanimously agreed to be more than half empty. It was also agreed to lay the blame for over-indulgence on Blackie as he was reputed to be the best beer swiller in Castleacre, especially if the drink was free. He was Jack Eagle's best customer at The Ostrich where, according to him, he could wheedle a pint out of any unsuspecting visitor who called in, especially if they worked at Soigné. As luck would have it Percy was teetotal, so having three only to share we got a pint each. How good that beer tasted, certainly on a par with the bottle issued on cold brushing days. Harry was quite certain we boys would load down after filling our bellies with beer, but the liquid refreshment had no detrimental effect on our work.

At dinner time we took our sacks and bags across the road into the cool of a shady wood. Huge beech trees made a very welcome canopy of shade, and their trunks some comfortable back-rests. As I had brought my dinner with me, being unaware of my work destination that morning, I elected to stay with my gang instead of biking the short distance home. Anyway, I had a longer rest that way, and I felt in need of it. Handling loose hay is hard work, as well as hot and dusty. Moist, honey sandwiches went down well that day as I lay resting my semi-tortured body. My muscles hadn't yet hardened into heavy manual work, so I suffered quite a bit from fatigue. But in no way must weakness be shown. The work-hardened backs and arms round about me belonged to professional labouring men, who knew how to pace themselves at a speed which would carry them through the day, the week and the year of various manual tasks which were all hard, with some harder and more physically demanding than others. Peace, perfect peace, as we sat chewing away at our varied simple fare.

"Hie up, there", a voice broke the silence. It was my father freewheeling down the road and home to dinner.

"All right there, Fred", a voice returned the greeting before a reverential hush descended once more, broken only by a rustle of greaseproof paper and pouring of drink from a flask. Outstretched legs were dappled by broken sunlight filtering through leafy branches high above, and a few flies circled round our heads on near silent wings. A few more would have gathered had we been using horses, but the modern tractor had very little appeal to the common fly. Even Blackie and Harry, usually full of chatter, seemed to want a respect shown to the silence and sat almost dozing over their dinner. No one moved, as their watch-hands met and passed 12.40, hoping that Blackie would doze on for a bit longer. But Mr. Wright, like his predecessor George Hall, had an inbuilt alarm system, which passed a message to his brain saying, "No work, no money". With only one extra minute or so gained, up rose our lord and back to work he led his troops. The sun seemed to have gained even more strength whilst we had slumbered in the shade. The dry hay reflected this heat, forcing Percy to hang a red neckerchief down over his neck from under a wide-brimmed trilby.

"You look like the Sheikh of Araby", quipped Harry, but his mate didn't care who he looked like as long as it helped him to stay reasonably cool. This additional piece of equipment also kept irritating hayseeds from rubbing his neck around a wet shirt collar. Percy dressed for the job in hand, and not to be a fashion plate.

The long, hot afternoon wore on. The stack grew slowly as the patch of cleared land increased. We were all ready to down tools at four o'clock, and I was soon indoors having a good wash to rid me of all the dust and hayseeds. There was still no bathroom, of course, only a bowl of soft rainwater on the scullery table. Some dirt came off in the water and some on the towel, but I felt refreshed afterwards and ready for a cooked tea and a game of cricket with the boys afterwards. First my sodden shirts had to be hung out to dry for we didn't have clean shirts every day. Clothes washing was kept to a minimum at all times as water had to be carried in and carried out again. Lack of taps and drains tended to keep our clothes-changing within strict bounds. I know that by modern standards we would be classed as dirty, but everyone had to do their best under prevailing conditions, and we were both clean and respectable.

At least we put patches on our trousers and avoided looking like tramps in purposely-torn jeans and ragged woollies. We lived in a real world where clothes were a necessity and not just a fashion fad.

The weather remained fine and very warm as we slowly swallowed up the haycocks. One stack was completed and a second started at the top gateway where Pretoria Breck bordered the Forty Acres. Somehow Jimmy and I kept our precious record of not losing part of a load as they crept towards the stack. Our two tractor-drivers, George very tall and thin, Bob short and well-proportioned, worked wonders in saving us embarrassment by skilfully avoiding furrows which might upset a precarious balance. Whether the much talked about custom of beer being bought for the gang if a load fell off was ever operated, I don't know, but we had no intention of putting it to the test. Obviously it was no joke pitching a load twice if it did end up on the ground, so we tried hard not to make additional work. It would have been an even greater catastrophe if a stack side slid out. If this looked likely, as occasionally happened, a thick, wooden stack pole would be put in to shore it up as settling took place. I cannot remember a complete collapse, although quite a few stack poles were in place before the hay and harvest stacks were completed.

As hay-time drew to a close, our eyes turned towards the corn harvest. Acres of barley began to tuck their horned heads downwards, and the breeze caused waves to flow across the ripening grain. But, before work began on this main harvest, we had our holidays to look forward to.

Chapter 11
Harvest — Still My Heaven

Most farm workers took their limited annual holidays either between hay time and harvest or immediately after the corn harvest, before sugar-beeting began. Charlie Wilson left the scene in July, which meant that Will Bumfrey, as head team-man, took over the reins for a fortnight. It was traditional for a head horseman to replace the foreman in his absence, and Will carried the responsibility very well. I was never sure whether it was advantageous to have an uncle as foreman or not. I certainly didn't get any special privileges. On the contrary, my standards were expected to be impeccable, but orders came with much more explanation, eliminating silly mistakes such as my seed corn debacle in the "behind the belt" misunderstanding with Charlie. Sometimes I missed my uncle's fortnight of power by virtue of the fact that we also took our holidays in late July. Our before or after harvest holiday depended mainly on whether Geoffrey Thaxton could take over milking at High House to relieve my dad. Whichever option came up, we always went over to Briston where my mother's parents gave us a warm welcome and a lovely holiday.

Grandad Eke was, by this time, in his late seventies, but still active enough to crop his fairly large garden and tend to the outside chores — except for the Rhode Island Red fowls which came under the jurisdiction of the lady of the house. Walter Eke had modelled himself a wonderful retirement schedule, despite having left the railway on a pension of ten shillings a week. Work in the morning, and then a seasonable choice — either a snooze by the kitchen fire with his book sagging on his lap, or retiring to his warm, sweet-smelling, wooden shed where, in company with his two cats, he would smoke a pipe before slipping into the land of Nod. An unwritten decree banned all noisy games during siesta time when old-fashioned, countryside peace settled over No. 1, Tithe Barn Cottages. Being deaf, I don't think he would have heard too much of our noise anyway. We could hear his snoring as we slipped out of the gate and away for a walk or a sit by the clear, running beck, just below Henry Williamson's farm.

Most of our fortnight was spent going by train to Sheringham, Cromer or Yarmouth, where the sea air was clean and bracing. The steam trains rattled us out of Melton Constable in the morning and back home in the evening, when a setting sun cast our long shadows in front as we tramped home from the station. Granny Eke, although younger than our Grandad, was past the walk

Harvest — Still My Heaven

and a long day out. Still very interested in our doings, she plied us with questions over supper as to whom we had seen at the station, or whether various shops were still open at Sheringham. Having lived all her life in and around Briston, she knew everyone and they knew and respected her.

Hours were spent walking the roads and lanes, catching up with crops and farmers along the way. We played cricket in the rough loke, where no two tennis balls kept the same course, and pitch-halfpenny — Granny saved her halfpennies for weeks so that we had plenty — was played round by the shed most mornings. Dad seemed to cream off most of the profit which meant Michael and myself had to raid Granny's coin store quite often.

Fresh cockles for breakfast with cats in close attendance, herrings and kippers all from the local fishmonger who called twice a week, raspberries from the canes, brown eggs, crusty bread delivered from the local bakers, home-made jam and cakes to follow — Granny's larder produced them all to give us unforgettable treats on a wonderful holiday.

All too soon the fortnight was over and we loaded all our luggage and dog into the local taxi which conveyed us to the top of Melton station steps. Down on to the platform we went, with Waggs doing more puffing than any of the engines which soon whisked us away to Massingham where Frank Clarke's car completed our trip back to Pretoria and another year's work. Holidays taken away from home were still uncommon, so we were the exception rather than the rule. How lucky we were to have so many lovely holidays at Briston both during the war and quite a few more after, although National Service and the passing of Grandfather Eke meant that only one more would be enjoyed by all of us together.

Returning to work after a holiday is usually pretty grim, but to receive a dreaded order, "Yoke for muck-cart", on the first morning is a bit beyond the pale. Joining Jimmy at Will's stable, we prepared the horses and set off for Elbreck Yards, a site we left so readily at the end of May. Wading through docks and fat hen grown almost head high in the intervening three months, we opened up our muck heap once more. There was not much excitement in making the short trip back and forth to fetch a full load from the double yard gates on the front. A sight of half-rotted pea straw brings back a memory of Charlie lambasting Young Laddie for his language after he'd received (Laddie, that is) a large, dusty forkful of the stuff on his head. Jimmy set us laughing with his interpretation of Charlie's hell and damnation Chapel tones after having his ears assaulted by foul language. Our heap grew as the four-foot deep, well-trodden farmyard manure was forked out of the yard on to tumbrils by hand, and unloaded in a like manner. This full employment theory was alright, but monotonous all the same. I often dreamed of being an engine-driver at Melton Constable, but my Uncle Fred would have told me that the six or seven apprenticeship years as engine cleaner would have been doubly monotonous. But dreaming helps us to get through monotony without going mad, so thank the Lord for dreams.

All around, the fields of cereal were changing colour and ripening rapidly. At High House, combines were being serviced by Artie Keeley, Bob Clarke and Harry Boughen, the latter coming up from Westacre Abbey Farm as the combines still covered both acreages, as required. Frank Clarke, Bob's father and farm mechanic, supervised these operations. A slight hitch occurred when Artie, forgetting his large machine steered from the back, swung the wheel round too early and almost took the barn corner out. Needless to say the combine came off worst and needed quite a few large hammer blows to restore its tin-covered rear end to a semi-rectangular shape. Artie also received a deal of leg-pulling as Geoff and Ted Thaxton were present and set a tall story circulating that had the barn almost completely demolished. It was common practice that minor mishaps grew like fishermen's tales, especially if Geoffrey was involved in the telling.

John Bumfrey was also preparing the eight-foot-cut Massey Harris binder for action. Canvases removed for out-of-season storage were refitted, grease nipples pumped full of their thick lubricant, and the knotter cleaned and threaded. Already the rye crop on the far end of Waterpit, in front of Rats Hall cottages, was fit and ready for cutting. This tall cereal was grown more for its long straw, which was used for thatching than the small, grit-like grain. After cutting and standing on the shock, this crop would be threshed straight away to supply straw for after-harvest stack thatching. Oh how I wished I would get the job of riding on the binder, but I knew from past experience that a younger boy would get it as soon as school finished. John Thaxton took over until his lazily dangling foot caught in a drive chain revolving at the back and he was sidelined with a slightly chewed toe. I don't think poor John got much sympathy from his bailiff grandfather who tore him off a strip for not keeping his feet on the footrests provided. My Uncle was more upset than either grandson or grandparent, and John, being made of tough stuff, was soon back in his seat. There wasn't much compensation for industrial injury then, and all John received was a bent ear for being so careless.

With the onset of bindering and combining, came after-tea-sport, when nut sticks were collected from shed corners, and rabbits pursued for the pot. Rye wasn't very conducive to rabbit cover, being so tall with a clean bottom and very little hide. It was impossible to strike into the corn and get a kill as, by the time a stick descended through five feet of straw, the victim had shot away up the drill space to safety. Nevertheless we gathered around their rapidly shrinking cover until they were forced to run across to a hedgerow. Then a banshee-like howl would go up, and half a dozen savages set off in pursuit of one terrified animal. Mostly the rabbit made for cover down the hill, disappearing into a large, grassy area in front of Rats Hall cottages. After another fruitless chase, we would trudge back to the corn edge and patrol slowly either way until another tentative head peeped out in readiness for a dash to safety. Then, allowing the rabbit to leave its standing cover and creep in amongst the lying shoofs, we would beckon our mates and set off in hot pursuit once more, yelling our heads off in an effort to disorientate the quarry. Occasionally Brer Rabbit would stop and hide under a shoof. Having marked the spot, the first person on the scene would crash down on top, frantically fishing underneath to find fur. What a triumph to have caught a rabbit dinner. I have known the time when, running at high speed, I've taken my eye off the shoof marked and fallen on the wrong one. Imagine the red-faced shame as the rabbit flew out from under the next shoof in line, leaving yours truly grounded and too winded to give chase. Not so those "hounds" running up behind, who, with an ironic cheer, would set off and perversely catch "my" rabbit. That's the way "sod's law" works.

An evening in the harvest field was quite a social occasion as we young bloods paraded our hunting prowess. Dilberry was there — he had a catapult as well as a stick. The first weapon could be useful to hit a sitting target, although tough rye stalks would probably deflect the round stone missile before the target was reached. Brother Michael and myself had come from Pretoria, along with Jimmy Lane, and Gerry and Colin Deasley. As school term hadn't quite finished, John Thaxton was free to join us as well His binder seat job was filled temporarily by Uncle Ted Thaxton (or "Titch", as we called him) until school ended and John could take up his holiday work. Harry Ashby and Nobbie Easter strolled over from their homes at Rats Hall to join all this activity, the like of which was rarely seen in this secluded spot.

As the sun slowly sank towards Heron Hill and shadows grew longer, the patch of standing rye shrank before the relentless attack by John Bumfrey and his binder. With sails sweeping cut corn back on to the revolving canvas carrying it into rapidly working packers, the binder tossed out neatly tied shoofs which bounced on hard ground, but then lay in straight lines on all four sides of the field. If the binder string broke, Ted would bang loudly on a metal safety cover and the tractor would stop, and the men dismount in order to re-thread the needle and knotter. Then, collecting up any loose shoofs and placing them on the canvas for re-tying, away they went with a roar from John's tractor and a burst of renewed noise from the intricate binder mechanism. A haze of dust surrounded the two workmen, making their clothes and faces turn grey as the day progressed. By about 8.30 the last swathe of corn disappeared up the canvas, and a final shoof was spat out, helped on its way by the revolving tines which turned once as soon as the knotter had secured the binder string around each shoof. By activating a lever on the tractor, John shut off his power-take-off shaft, rendering the binder suddenly silent. Almost reverently, the tractor, relieved of its labour, drew its load down the wide path left at one corner of the field, with the binder making a small clicking sound always associated with out-of-gear binders. Drawing into the corner where oil and grease drums rubbed shoulders with paper sacks of binder string bearing their familiar red star logo, John stopped and dismounted and prepared to silence his machine for the night. As was his idea, he turned the machine from TVO on to petrol and allowed the carburettor to fill with easy-start fuel. This gave him a first time firing of engine next morning at the initial turn of his starting handle. With a final cough the tractor engine stopped and almost total silence stole over the peaceful field. Where a crop of standing rye had been that morning, row upon row of neat sheaves lay, head to tail, almost touching, silently demonstrating a very good crop. For a moment nothing moved until Ted, breaking the spell, unrolled a canvas sheet and drew it over his machine. Soon the growl of John's motor bike with Ted on behind, died in the distance, leaving the harvest field to gathering dusk, a few pecking pheasants, and a last lingering look by Harry Ashby as he closed his back door and prepared for the night. Rats Hall wrapped itself once more in silence, leaving its displaced wildlife to make new homes for themselves, whilst resting itself in readiness for more activity on the morrow.

Muck-carting the next morning came as quite an anticlimax after racing around in the harvest field. Of course, now that the first field had been cut, the special smell of harvest was in the air, although slightly masked by the steamy stink of hot muck. At about ten o'clock Charlie arrived to direct our labours to the field of freshly-cut rye. Jimmy and I were to stable the horses and then join the rest of our gang on Lower Waterpit. The task before us was to shock the crop, thus allowing a few extra days' drying and ripening before the threshing tackle arrived. So off we went in high spirits, boys and horses, back to Soigné. Bumping along Waterpit Lane on our bikes we caught up with the others just as they prepared to move out into the field. At Percy's suggestion I partnered him, whilst Jimmy teamed up with his bullock-feeding buddy, Harry Ashby. Moving in the opposite direction to that taken by the binder a day previously, and taking two rows each, we moved off across the field. Closely watching my mentor, I picked up one shoof, tucked it under my arm with head forward and butt end two-thirds out behind, then did likewise from the second row. Then, walking towards the centre of our four-row section, we met, and lesson number one began. Percy turned round to look back the way we had come and plonked his two shoofs down on their butts, leaving a gap between, then pushed their heads together at the top.

"Come on, Derek, remember, bang their arses well into the stubble then knock their heads together. They will stand then for a month."

Facing him I tried to follow his advice without making such a neat job as he did. The pattern was repeated to give eight shoofs to the shock. The near-vertical stalks allowed any rain-water to run to ground whilst the ears dried

Harvest — Still My Heaven

easily in sun and wind. A shock, being open-ended, let any air movement straight through for both drying and prevention of wind resistance when a gale might blow them over As each new shock was started, Percy religiously turned to look back, sometimes shuffling to one side before planting his initial markers. I later learned that it was in order to keep a straight line for those crooked rows, oft-spoken of as "dogs' hind legs", were taboo in any farming job be it ploughing, drilling or harvest. A straight line also helped the holgy boy or tractor-driver at carting time. My arms soon became sore on the underside where rough stalks scratched my soft skin. It took me some time to realise the reason Percy had his shirt sleeves unusually buttoned down. After suffering discomfort when salt-sweat smarted in my scratches, I followed the new fashion and unrolled mine also. The other plague connected with shocking up, thistles, wasn't evident in this tall rye crop. Thistles could be the very devil when cut and tied with grain. Grabbing a handful of thistles hidden on the shoof underside often meant an evening spent with a sewing needle and sharp eyesight trying to prise out the painful spines.

After the first round was completed, the men, who had taken the longer outside rows, turned right over so that they gained this time by taking the shorter ones. Obviously, as the binder had worked from the field edge round and round to the middle, each succeeding row became shorter. Percy and myself worked in the middle of the gang so our row lengths were pretty constant. On one or two occasions I had to nip back to pick up an odd shoof of mine that had slumped sideways, but most of my efforts remained upright, at least until we left for home.

Dinner was taken under the shade of Half Moon Belt. Most of us dragged a couple of shoofs to make a backrest. I enjoyed the dry, dusty, yet slightly aromatic smell given off from freshly-tied shoofs. Even the binder twine used had its own particular smell, which even now takes me back to boyhood harvests whenever I handle it. Lying back and gazing across towards Rats Hall reminded me of my dinner in the same spot last October when on my first assignment to collect their water-cart. I'd moved on quite considerably in the intervening nine months and now felt one of the gang. Pulling a piece of yellow bedstraw, I smelled its "hot day" scent. Pink bindweed crept out towards the path and small, brown butterflies flitted from one horn-shaped flower to another. Flies buzzed, and Blackie snored on as Dilberry tried to wake him by tickling his face with a long cock's foot grass seed head. It seemed as if everyone's cares and troubles had been banished in exchange for half an hour's perfect peace of mind and body.

By a quarter to four the field was finished. Every shoof had been set up in regimental lines without a dog's hind leg in sight. Bags were shouldered, bikes mounted, and a flotilla of workmen set off for home. We younger elements made plans to meet later, on Twenty-two Acres where the binder would be cutting the first field of oats. It was debatable whether a finish would be made that day, but we had seen action there well before we left Elbreck, which was only one field away. The field in question was landlocked, lying between Long Elbreck to the west and Eighteen Acres to the east. Honeypot, now a green sea of potato tops, bordered its southern edge and Little Ashbreck lay to the north. By biking up the High House road and leaving our machines inside the Eighteen Acres gateway behind the remnants of last year's oat straw stack, we were able to walk along the headland, and in that way. It looked as though John and Ted had enjoyed a trouble-free day as the standing corn was well away from the hedge when we arrived just after six. But the luck failed to hold when a broken packer stopped the work until Frank Clarke came with a new part to set the machinery clattering again. Only a few more rounds were possible before damp began to rise as the sun set in a blaze of glory promising another fine day tomorrow. Even a small amount of damp on binder canvases caused them to shrink and burst a strap, so a halt was called for the day, leaving a square of standing oats from which every rabbit would sneak under cover of darkness. The square of corn would be cut tomorrow morning without even one rabbit remaining to give sport for any boy who had skipped school to be there. Freewheeling down the hill towards Pretoria we wondered if the combines on Twenty-four Acres had completed the barley. Perhaps we would give them a visit the next evening and try our luck there.

So for a week we did some muck-carting, some shocking up, and spent our evenings hunting rabbits. The sport wasn't quite so good behind the combines. For one thing, they spewed out a continuous line of threshed straw, which, unlike individual shoofs, provided our quarry with a ready-made hiding place under which they could move without our eagle eyes detecting them. Also the drivers tended to cut out sections of crop instead of proceeding round and round, as did the binder. These wretched sections often had ends only four or five rows from a hedge or wood, enabling rabbits to scoot the short distance before we could give chase, let alone catch them. Yes, modern machines that cut at the front and not at the side, had a lot to answer for. It was apparent to me the inventor of a combine harvester never chased rabbits in the summer or caught stack-bound rats in the winter. Schoolboy and youthful country sporting activities were set to be ruined forever by this labour-saving, grain-devouring predator that prowled our harvest fields from the late forties onwards.

Oats of course needed to stand on the shock over three Sundays at least to allow their heavily-covered grains to fully ripen and the thick, leafy straw to dry out. So they were left for a while and real harvesting started on the seed barley crop.

Seed barley wasn't cut by combine, but tied, stacked and threshed during late autumn or early winter. Two harvesting gangs were employed against the original three used before combines appeared on our scene. One gang worked with wagons pulled by horses, the other being mechanised with tractor and trailers. Jimmy and I loaded on wagons which was more difficult than trailers owing to the reduced width and lack of vertical ladders front and back. Wagon ladders, or "lethers" as Barney Hooks would insist on calling them — much to our amusement — were really horizontal extensions which clipped on to sideboards, allowing about one-third more length. Remembering to keep our "arses behind us", we loaded by hand this time as the use of even the short-handled pitchfork was out, owing to the close proximity of one's fellow loader. As it was we spent the first morning stepping back into each other at frequent intervals. First the wagon buck was filled with shoofs lying in an orderly fashion, butts towards the front and reversed in Jimmy's half; then followed a row right round the sides, again butt outwards with one-third length over the respective rails. A gap was left for the pitchers, on one side if shocked corn was being carted, and either side front and back if thrown-in shoofs were being pitched. After having spent one season loading hay we soon mastered corn-carting, which tended to be easier as long as we remembered to load shoofs knot down, and work our way methodically round the load. This systematic loading meant the unloader at the elevator could reverse the procedure and easily pick off the shoofs and place them on to his machine conveying them to his mates on the stack. As the shoofs dropped off the elevator end one man, called the feeder, passed them butt end first to a second man, the backer, who delivered them to the stacker, who built them into the walls. This system was adopted when the far ends of a stack were being worked on. The middle parts of the walls, being nearer to the source of shoofs, used only two of the men, the third one, usually the backer, filled up the middle, working back from the sides, still keeping a set pattern of butt outwards and ears towards the centre. Every shoof was handled and laid in position, and only a little loose corn was ever left untouched under the elevator end. Each operation was thought out and designed to help the next person in the work-line, thus making hard, continuous, manual labour as easy as was possible — well, most of the time at any rate, although there were occasions when a shoof trailed a long piece of binder string from its knot. This happened when the knotter knife on the binder had failed to carry out its allotted task, causing a loose shoof on the next occasion the fork turned its bundle on to the floor. This trailing string could be cunningly tied to a wagon strut by a devious-minded loader who then watched for his opposite number to pull and tug at this stubborn shoof. Having to stop, find a knife to cut the string, and then start up again did nothing to improve the temper of the stackman or help our paypackets when on piecework. But these tricks had to be played for boys will be boys, some older than others, as the following tale shows.

Harvest — Still My Heaven

Ernie Deasley, the gamekeeper, had worked on the farm before taking up keepering at the retirement of Clem Softley. He and Diddie Frost lived next door to one another at numbers 4 and 5, Pretoria Cottages. When they worked together on the stack, neither of them had a watch and so were for ever asking someone else the time. As this seemed to happen every quarter of an hour, a plot was hatched to give a wrong watch-reading. A barley stack was being constructed on Lightning Breck, just at the top of Pretoria Hill, and as usual, these two comedians kept asking Charlie Andrews, the shepherd, roped into harvest work, "What's the time, Charlie?" "Quarter to four", lied Charlie, keeping a straight face. As the afternoon was very warm, the field gang decided to come in for a drink around about ten to three. This action coincided with Charlie's advanced time-check, so Ernie and Diddie thought fourses were about to be taken at four o'clock. Descending the ladder they leapt on their bikes and set off for home, watched open-mouthed by the pitchers as they drank from their cold tea bottles.

"What's wrong with them two?" they asked Charlie.

Unable to reply and laugh at the same time, Charlie almost burst with mirth. Meanwhile our intrepid heroes flung their bikes down in the passage between their houses and marched round to the back doors. Their respective wives, who were having an afternoon gossip over the fence, gaped at their menfolk.

"What are you doing home?" they finally struggled out.

"Come for our teas of course; haven't you got it ready?"

"What for?" May Deasley fired back, stung by the inference that she had been gossiping instead of preparing tea for Ernie. "It's only three o'clock".

"Course it isn't", said Ernest. "They've all stopped up the road. Charlie Lop told us it was fourses time."

"If you two don't believe us, then come in and look at the clock."

Both women marched indoors, followed by their respective husbands. After inspecting separate timepieces on separate mantle shelves they reappeared.

"Well, I'm damned", said Diddie. "His watch must have gained or something. We'd better go back and tell them."

Still unaware they had been duped, bikes were remounted and the slow haul back up Pretoria Hill began. It wasn't until they cleared the narrow belt of fir trees alongside Frank Clarke's house and saw a trailer being loaded out in the field that the penny dropped. Then a torrent of uncomplimentary verbals poured out, aimed at the frantically working figure of Charlie Andrews.

"The rotten bugger, playing a trick like that. Could have got us the sack if anyone saw us."

Thrusting their bikes into the hedge and grabbing pitchforks they hurried to the stack where already a loaded trailer stood waiting and a huge heap of shoofs lay under the elevator mouth where one lone stackman had been unable to clear the decks.

Charlie, with a poker face, enquired where they had been. Had they been taken short, or been promised something special if they went home to their wives in the afternoon?

"You rotten sod, you Lop, you did that on purpose. We shall have to work like hell to clear this lot."

"I said to Charlie Wilson when he came, we can't carry them two if they keep taking the afternoon off. You ought to cut their money."

Of course, the last piece of fabrication led to even more swearing at their tormentor who coughed and wheezed his way through the waiting trailer load as fast as he could to add to their confusion and heap of shoofs on the stack. That little episode raised quite a bit of leg-pulling as it made its rounds of the farm. It even led to Diddie carrying an old alarm clock in his bag to keep a check on Charlie's watch just in case it "gained" an hour at any time during the rest of harvest. Quite what was said to the two womenfolk when our neighbours returned for tea at the appropriate time, I don't know. Maybe they had to eat humble pie and admit how easily they had been taken in. It would have been nice to listen in as a fly on the wall.

Working in gangs gave plenty of opportunities for tricks and leg-pulls, which helped to pass days of heavy, manual work in a less tedious manner. Laughing was a good salve for aching limbs and joints on Soigné Farm during most of the years I worked there, and almost all joined in, no matter whether it was for or against them.

Poor old Charlie Wilson took quite a lot of stick, much of it brought on himself. When the gang moved on to Twenty-five Acres, a stack was set out by Charlie inside the White Gate corner. As the road turned at right angles here, telephone wires on poles had been taken across the field corner on their way to connect Soigné to the rest of our world. Ernie and Co worked on and the stack rose skywards until someone caught the end of a pitchfork handle on an obstruction. As there shouldn't have been anything between those stackers and the sky, all stopped to investigate this strange occurrence. There, just above their heads, stretched four telephone wires right across the stack from corner to corner.

"Oh, Lord", said Ernie. "We can't stack them in. I know, I'll just ring Charlie and ask him what he wants done."

So, hooking his fork against the wires, he had an imaginary conversation with the foreman, much to the amusement of his mates. Charlie was not so cheerful when he arrived, and after much head scratching and useless input of ideas from Ernie, it was decided to re-build alongside clear of the offending wires.

"My fellows, fancy me making that mistake", said Charlie. "Those blessed wires have been there long enough" — and they had. I expect Charles was concentrating on his sermon for Sunday when he strode out the stack bottom. If only he had cast his eyes up to Heaven for inspiration he would have spotted those wires and saved himself a rather embarrassing situation, and his men a lot of extra work. Perhaps it was worth it for all the laughter generated as soon as Charles departed for home, swaying his bike from side to side, as was his peculiar habit on those traffic-free roads of 1950.

Chapter 12
More Harvest on Farm and Garden

Harvest work meant packing my bag with three meals and enough drink to last me from 7 a.m. to 7 p.m., unless of course our work was very close to Pretoria. The food didn't cause many headaches as rationing was pretty well over, and with a good store of home-made jams, heather honey brought back from Briston, and our own lettuces, a variety of nice, moist sandwiches could be made up. Cucumbers and tomatoes were bought from George Wright, the head gardener, who sold them on behalf of Major Birkbeck in whose greenhouses they were grown. The first of our Bramley Seedling apples were by this time just cookable, so juicy apple turnovers made a welcome second course. Drink, on the other hand, caused more of a problem. Most older men relied on a couple of bottles containing cold, black tea which they declared was the best thirst-quencher available. For my part, having crazed my mother to make me a bottle when working as holgy boy and found it tasted foul, I took one container of milky tea for starters and then cold, lemon drink to be consumed later when my other with milk content would have curdled. Juicy, summer apples from a tiny tree opposite our shed, and Malabella plums, helped to keep me from dehydrating during a long, hot, dusty day.

I must admit my diet did help to attract wasps whose nests in the hedge banks were now becoming quite active and causing quite a mealtime nuisance. A couple of shallots were always carried in our dinner bags for fast application to any stings. A cut shallot face rubbed over a wasp sting brings almost instant relief, and stops swelling and discomfort. Wasps seem to take a furious dislike to some unfortunate people, stinging them at the least provocation, but I can't remember ever being stung at work. My shallots dried in the bag, except when used to salve brother Michael's many war wounds as he received his share of stings and mine as well. Wasp nests were destroyed by using a white, chemical powder, which required water to be poured on it after it had been placed outside the nest entrance. On one occasion my father and Charlie Wilson went to poison a nest, but found they had set out without water.

"Put the powder down, Fred, and then stand back, my fellow", said Charles.

When the powder was in place, and assistant Fred had withdrawn a few yards, Charlie proceeded to urinate upon the chemical, much to my dad's surprise and suppressed mirth, as his imagination worked overtime conjuring up visions of rotund Charlie fighting off a wasp swarm intent upon attacking the source of his water fountain. As it happened, the water carrier withdrew before the enemy realised the situation, but the scenario could have rivalled or even surpassed the occasion previously described when a rat ran up our foreman's trouser leg. At any rate, the tale lost nothing in the telling when Dad came home.

As I indicated earlier, our horse-drawn wagons began work on a seed barley crop whilst the mechanised gang went to Rats Hall where Walter Desborough set up his threshing tackle amongst the rye shocks. The very necessary, long thatching straw became a reality, and loads were soon on their way to the haystacks, which had remained with roofs open to the weather since their formation in late June and early July. Georgie Wright and Leslie Richardson would have the job of carting this straw, at the rate of a load per stack, and delivering it to all hay and corn stacks constructed. They were also responsible for supplying a load of the last year's barley straw for stack bottoms, required before each new structure was started.

Barley shocks appeared to be in miniature compared with rye, wheat and oats. Most of the shocks were picked up by the simple method of placing a pitchfork into each end and lifting the whole bodily on to the wagon. It was barley shoofs, which contained most thistles and, having no gloves, our hands suffered as a consequence. Owing to the fact that barley straw was usually very ripe and dry when cut, most fields were carted straight behind the binder when shoofs still lay on the ground. To make room for a horse and wagon to run without trampling shoofs, two binder rows were thrown into one before carting began. Once more we all set off round the field in a similar manner to shocking, but this time each man had his own individual row to throw in to the adjoining one using his pitchfork. Very occasionally we disturbed a rabbit, which was up and away before we realised it and made a successful dash to the hedge. Rats also shot out of the long-standing shocks of wheat where a comfortable home, with good food supply, had been set up. A quick slash with a pitchfork usually turned our public enemy number one belly-side up where he lay twitching his life away.

After a week or so of continuous hot, sunny weather, a few silent prayers were sent up for a drop of rain to give us all a rest. The smell of rain on the warm soil and straw seemed lovely when prayed for, but not so good when shoofs were soaked for days on end, causing grain to grow in the ear. Wet harvests were a nightmare with shocks having to be laid out to dry bottoms, and then re-shocked on fresh ground. Laying shoofs were turned over for quicker drying, only to have them soaked again by a sudden downpour before carting could begin. Barley and oats had to be bone dry before being stacked as their soft straw flattened immediately when weight came on them from above. The best scenario one could expect then was shoofs resembling compressed cardboard, and containing mouldy grain, at threshing time. On

More Harvest on Farm or Garden 121

the other hand, the worst could result in over-heating and a stack fire. Wheat, on the other hand, with its very stiff straw, allowed air to enter the stack, and as long as threshing was delayed until springtime the grain would be hard and dry. So this meant that on very damp mornings, or after rain, we moved all the equipment to a wheat field and worked there until the barley dried out. Then off we would go once more to either barley or oats, until the weather decided to take a hand once more. All these moves and time wasting had to be borne by the piecework gang, so obviously every move meant a loss of earning power. Therefore, you see why a prayer for rain was always silently uttered, for the saying of, "More rain, more rest", didn't really apply to piecework.

A very wet morning meant reporting to the farm when day work would be recommenced, which, in turn, meant muck-carting for we lesser labouring men. Then prayers were quickly offered up for sunshine to return. In and out of steamy old bullock yards we went on all the slack periods during spring and summer. Elbreck, Soigné, High House and even Field Barn were there to be cleared out in readiness for next winter's stock to be yarded. But these venues were considered a holiday posting compared with the sows' yard and pigsties. Bullock muck smells of roses compared with that of pigs, especially when one's fork went into a heap outside the sties and a long-dead, sucking-piglet came out on the tines. That kind of smell made me spit, I can tell you. Dick Welham, who had buried it there, wasn't flavour of the month, you can bet. Contagious animal diseases should have been rife with the kind of hygienic conditions prevailing, but thanks to some tough stock, nothing too serious broke out. The only thing impressed upon us was to be careful not to clear muck to the very bottom of the sows' yard as erysipelas germs lurked there and would attack the pigs if up-turned. As to the authenticity of this theory I cannot comment, but any excuse not to dig deep in pig manure was latched upon and adhered to, to the letter.

Come back sunshine and let's get out into those open harvest fields again was now the universal wish. Anyone who had silently prayed for rain a few days previously had learned his lesson, and was more than ready to take up his pitchfork and a longer working day.

Gerry Deasley was our driver bringing out empty wagons and returning the full ones to the stack. Gerry did not gel naturally with horses, having his heart set on being a tractor-driver as soon as he was old enough and the opportunity arose. Having a permanent problem with eyesight didn't help him draw the correct line with his empty conveyance when pulling up alongside our load to enable we loaders to slide off into the empty wagon. On several occasions, by taking too tight a turn from behind us, he managed to catch his front ladder in the corner of Jimmy's rear load almost pulling it out before hauling his horse to a stop. The next occasion might mean over-compensation, and a jump of three feet for us to relocate. It wasn't Gerry's fault; he was a mechanically-minded lad caught up in the very last web of the horse age. Much hilarity often ensued, causing our mate to get very flustered and embarrassed. Gerry was a good friend and neighbour, being much more at home behind a tractor wheel when his opportunity came a short time later.

On the other hand, I was never more at home than when I was using horses. After any break and a fresh wagon was required, I always rode our horse to the point of work. The warm feel of a horse's back, and the click and rattle of a wooden wagon were life blood to me. Gipsy, Beauty, and Traveller were in shafts, with Violet, as Gerry's trace horse, helping to pull heavy loads to the elevator. When changing field locations I always put my bike up into a wagon in order to take the horse along the road. Walking up the left-hand shaft to plonk my sack across a broad, brown back behind the saddle was second nature to me. Gerry could have his noisy old tractor; give me my horse every time.

Whilst our two gangs, or companies as they were called, pitched and stacked the shoof corn, combines cut crops of barley on both Soigné and Abbey Farms. At first the operation was far from well organised or very mechanised. Although the threshed grain poured into a hopper on each combine side, which was designed to disgorge its contents whilst on the move, no open, tipping trailers were used at this early stage. Instead each combine drew up beside a large, flat-bed trailer in the field corner where a gang of men held sacks under the spout for filling and weighing. These sacks were then tied and transferred to Geoff's lorry, which conveyed them to Swaffham or North Elmham for dressing and drying if excess water content made this treatment necessary. It was a slow, labour-intensive way of handling what should have been bulk grain in all its stages of harvesting. A few years were to elapse before this obvious system came into being.

At this juncture, the back-up team required for combining was as large as that needed for the age-old system of shoof-carting — another example of maintaining full employment and a much sweeter one than unrelenting muck-cart, designed, I must add, for a higher class of citizen than the first example. It was becoming blatantly obvious to some of us that only persons from certain backgrounds qualified for what we called "seat" jobs, whilst others were destined to remain labourers forever and a day if they lived that long. It wasn't envy that I felt, as the mechanical side of farming didn't appeal to me at all. It was a feeling of unfairness against the men who would work manually, that rose up in me whenever we worked next door to the combines, and saw more men than sacks jostling for position on the stationary trailer, whilst we worked our guts out to earn our pittance in fine weather and for sod all if it rained. I now realise that a tiny seed of resentment had taken root against men in privileged positions who were content to abuse those who knew how to work hard in order to carry others who hadn't much intention of doing so. This tiny

More Harvest on Farm or Garden

seed was destined to grow into a large, deep-rooted plant over several years until it caused me to choose between my principles and my roots.

These seemingly minor observations did little to mar my enjoyment of real harvest work. The few growls of discontent from the older men only partially entered my still-resting brain as I worked my first harvest as a full-time farm worker. There was no spectre of school at the end of this harvest as in previous years. I could stay on working with my mates into autumn with no academic problems or fears to cloud the horizon.

After a few corn stacks had been erected, Horrie Everard and Jack Curl went off with their long, orange thatching ladder to commence protecting stack roofs from the weather. Commencing on haystacks, now well settled after a couple of months, they would follow we carters until all stacks were thatched. Jack drew the long, rye straw to make bundles which, I believe, were called "yelms". The straw was first dampened, then carried on the back, with a sack protecting between, up the ladder where Horrie bedded it into position and secured it by means of binder string and sharpened nut brorches driven into the stack roof. This layer of rye straw protected the valuable grain from rain until threshing took place four or five months later. The thatchers wore thick, leather kneelers to protect their knees and trousers from wear on the ladder. Horrie had a special rake to comb down his thatch, which was relatively basic but very effective. With the increased use of balers for hay, and combined straw, stacks became fewer and the thatching trade died when Horrie finally retired.

At the end of the corn harvest our mechanised gang went on carting bales from behind the combines. All their loose straw had been baled up and left out in rows. These close-compacted bales of about three feet in length were quite easily lifted on a pitchfork.

Meanwhile, Percy and I went carting rakings. These rakings were the result of all loose corn stalks being tractor-raked into rows after the initial carting had been carried out. It was a dusty job, but as we were on day work and not pushed along, it was quite a pleasant end to my happy harvest season. This "raking corn" was made into a small stack at the end of a full-sized one, and known as a "five-foot wash house". Threshed on Saturday, half-day, the resulting grain went off to the keepers for pheasant feed. Almost as many small flint stones came out of a "wash house" as good grain, but this tradition of rakings went on until shoof corn became a thing of the past. I suppose the pheasants could glean for themselves when combines cut off as many heads as they gathered from weather-affected and partially-layed crops.

Over-ripe barley stalks were prone to dropping their heads to almost ground level, which resulted in the oscillating knife cutting them back on to the ground, instead of the canvas. Early combines had wide, wooden sails, which pushed corn stalks back on to the revolving canvas. The twelve-foot cut was divided into two sections, which conveyed the cut grain towards a central canvas, which took the two streams up into a mobile threshing drum. Separated grain ran into a large tank on one side which had a long spout protruding for emptying when required, either on the move or stationary. The straw poured out behind in a continuous stream, except when poor quality straw was broadcast by using a revolving, three-bladed fan. This second-quality straw was then either burned or ploughed in. This was the exception rather than the rule, as most straw was baled for use as cattle feed or bedding, part of the raw materials in the making of muck to keep us busy at slack times, and to return essential nutrients to the land.

As the last of the fields were cut and cleared, acre upon acre of stubble shone golden in September sunshine. Tractor cultivators sailed up and down scuffling the top inches in order to encourage weed seed growth as soon as rain fell. Whereas the threshing drum shook out millions of weed seeds in a heap underneath, enabling them to be destroyed, the combines returned them to the ground over a wide area. As crop spraying was in its infancy, combines brought serious problems in weed control when cultivation systems changed. With tractor power came deeper ploughs turning more brash and weeds into the furrow bottom. Turned in also was nutrient-rich topsoil which was replaced by chalk and clay. This, in turn, meant the need for heavier dressings of up-and-coming chemical fertiliser, and so began a cycle of events, which saw the demise of the real farmer who used, and worked with, nature. His replacement soon became spoon-fed by the industrial chemist, and money-making, fertiliser merchants. Now, at last, the wheel has turned full circle and organic fertilisers are coming back. Maybe I could make a comeback also if my muck fork and states are still at the back of the shed.

Early September days were still warm enough to make the sugar-beet leaves wilt in mid-afternoon. A few yellowing specks showed up across the green expanse. This indication of sugar being sent down to the roots meant the advent of sugar-beeting wasn't too far distant. This wouldn't concern me for this season as the age of eighteen was generally accepted to be the threshold from boy to man. Gerald had passed this milestone and would be setting out with the men on this very demanding work. Again there would be horses and tractors sharing the task of hauling beet off the fields to a convenient roadside clamp

Dry September evenings were valuable for getting ready for winter which would close in upon us all too quickly. It wasn't only inclement weather that curtailed outside winter activity; more often than not it was lack of light. Having no electricity to fall back on, a lantern or natural moonlight were our only sources of power outside the back door. Battery torches were available to guide with a single beam, but were uneconomic for work. So you can see it was essential to get as much work done for ourselves whilst the light evenings lasted, especially as my father worked as cowman at weekends.

More Harvest on Farm or Garden

The many rows of late potatoes were there to be dug. If a damp season had caused the dreaded potato blight to strike the crop, then tops were cut off before the virus reached tubers sending them rotten. Strangely, we never owned a flat-tined fork for potato digging, but favoured the normal round-tined muck fork. Carefully scraping away soil between each rootstock to ascertain whether a tuber lay just below the surface, the fork was then pushed down and the root lifted. By shaking gently, the potatoes separated out to lie on the surface. To pierce a tuber with a fork tine was considered a crime without equal. To do it on two roots running was a hanging offence on a par with sheep stealing in earlier decades. This job could be enjoyable if large, clean potatoes lay out drying before you, but, if only seed-sized and chicken boilers were the reward for a season's work, then spirits sank below boot top level. Across all the gardens could be seen the bent backs of men digging and lifting their crops, with only a faint chink of steel against stone breaking the silence. After a short time a less-dedicated back would straighten and work-relieving banter would begin.

"How's your crop, Fred?"

"About three tearters to the seck, I reckon."

"I see Arthur's growing his specially for chickens again this year. He'll need buy half a dozen more hins to eat that lot."

The bluff, over-red face of Arthur Futter rose up to declare that the tenant of No. 4 must have forgotten to set seed, as only "stuns and quicks were turning up".

Certainly the constant cropping of potatoes on the same plot of land tended to spread disease, as did the continued use of home-grown seed. Partial rotation was possible, but having potatoes as a main crop meant over-growing had to take place. This is why our stack bottoms came in handy, as a change of soil was then possible. Majestic, the popular white potato, suited our soil best, although scab was a common scourge. King Edward, the pink-eyed pride of the potato world then, needed a richer soil to be successful. Aran Pilot and Home Guard were grown as early and second-early varieties.

As the evening progressed and light began to fade, wives and offspring would appear to pick up the dug crop. Three pickings were required, eating potatoes being sacked up first, then seed-sized for next year, and finally the marbles for chicken feed. Boiled for mixing with barley meal, these last tiddlers made a lovely steaming mash for laying hens. Every last tuber was gleaned, with only an occasional one left hidden to re-appear as a "self-sown" in the spring. Strangely, these rogue plants were never affected by a late frost, whereas the soft shoots of a potato planted in line would be burned and blackened as soon as the sun came up. Nature can be cussedly awkward at times. "It's all sent to try us", was a favourite expression of Uncle Will's, and usually we were "well and truly tried". Only a complete cessation of daylight would halt my father and force him to clean his already shining fork and hang it on its appointed nail in the shed. Then, carefully scraping his boots across the inverted spade blade stuck in the bank near the door, he would click the shed lock in its hasp and staple. All other gardens were empty and their labourers resting indoors before Fred Bumfrey finally left the scene of his labours to join us in the soft lamplight behind drawn curtains, after hanging his cap (he never went outside without it) on its nail in the scullery wall.

There was just one thing I missed out from the potato-digging scene, although I'm sure it's been mentioned previously in the garden-digging chapter. If the harvesting took place prior to the removal of Dick Barton, Special Agent, from our sound waves, all forks would have been grounded between 6.45 and 7 p.m. as everyone listened to the latest episode. After Dick, Jock and Snowy were laid to rest by the BBC there was no excuse to stop as The Archers never held any drawing power to us when work was there to be done. The only other broadcast likely to pull Dad off the garden was a heavyweight boxing match. I remember once when Bruce Woodcock, the British champion, fought, the accumulator ran down and the reception faded. Leaping up and grabbing his jacket and cap, Freddie set off on his bike to the Hall where Hubert Watts recharged these very necessary accessories on radio sets. But by the time a sweating boxing enthusiast connected up the new "cumalator", a much tougher and better-fed American had knocked our champion out, or at least beaten him into submission.

"Well, I'm blowed", gasped a breathless husband and father.

"You didn't think the fight would last long enough for you to bike to the Hall and back, did you? Then you are a bigger fool than I took you for, Fred Bumfrey" — this from the lady of the house who usually knew best, especially after an event. To have biked half a mile uphill with one hand on the handlebar and the other balancing a heavy, glass, acid-filled accumulator, then the reverse journey hanging on to a none too efficient brake, was bad enough. To have missed the fight and have your foolishness confirmed by a woman, to boot, was unbearable. Like Bruce Woodcock, my dad was magnanimous in defeat. Picking his cap off the nail, he set off for the garden with a quiet, "Well the 'cumulator needed changing, so that's one job done for tomorrow". Freddie never wasted time in arguments, his garden always required urgent attention if friction raised its head in the home.

Early that September Willie Thaxton caught Dad when he entered the dairy to collect his milk pails. "Fred, the Major wondered if you could clear those fallen boughs under the trees on the Park. He thinks it makes the place look untidy".

Clumps of trees, mostly oak, ash and elm, dotted the Park around Westacre High House, or the Hall as we knew it. Winter winds and the heavy snow had broken large boughs off these trees leaving them lying or half fallen underneath.

More Harvest on Farm or Garden

"Borrow a wagon or trailer to cart the wood home, Fred. Must try to keep everyone happy you know."

Without further bidding we set off after tea the same day, equipped with saw, chopper and lengths of baler twine. Hanging our jackets on a convenient branch, we trimmed off the brushwood before proceeding to cut manageable lengths of thicker wood. Michael packed brushwood into a faggot to be tied with string. Waggs, our half-bred spaniel bitch, sat by, quietly puffing in a most well behaved manner, as was her habit when Dad was present. With we boys she ran riot and was deaf to any shouted reprimands, returning only when she felt like it, and usually with her long ears full of tangled burrs.

Moving from tree to tree we kept on working until fading light suggested we call it a day. The evening had been peaceful, except for any noise made by our own exertions. The only motor vehicle on the private road had been the Major's grey Opel as he and his faithful black dog made their way slowly homewards after an evening touring the Estate. The only drawback to our enjoyment had been the midges congregating under the trees where cattle droppings seemed to encourage them. Our ears had made them a communal supper from which the small amount of tobacco smoke from Dad's eighth-of-an-inch of hand-rolled cigarette had hardly discouraged them. Father and sons were at peace with themselves and the world as they followed the road, which entered the dark tunnel made by overhanging trees, before eventually emerging on Pretoria corner. Pale light from oil lamps illuminated most of the downstairs windows as we made our way up to No. 6. Tools were put away in the shed before we sat down to a drink of cocoa as a nightcap, everyone satisfied that a good day's work had been done.

After three or four nights of preparation our load of firewood was ready for collection. A very disappointed Beauty was kept back in the stable on Saturday in readiness for me to take a wagon on to the Park at four o'clock to meet my father when milking was complete. Michael and I rattled up the Hall drive and away across the grass until the farthest stack of prepared wood was reached. After parking his bike just inside Anmer Gate, Dad walked across to help load up. Michael rode Beauty from tree to tree until all our thick wood and faggots had been loaded. Looking back we could see tracks cut by the iron-shod wagon wheels zigzagging across the soft grass. I must say it looked much tidier now that the fallen branches were cleared. It seemed as if someone cared for the heart of the Estate. Back down through the wood, and up alongside our garden fence, faggots over one corner and thick wood further along, tomorrow morning would see it all standing around the Dr. Harvey apple tree to await log-sawing for winter months. At least an hour every Sunday morning was spent at the sawing-horse — outside if dry, and in the shed if wet. Rain never stopped play, and only warm, summer weather, with limited indoor fires, halted the ritual, and even then some wood was needed for cooking on the range. Every season saw my father carrying his saws to Harry Reynolds for sharpening. Harry was apprenticed to a firm at Swaffham, and had qualified as a tradesman carpenter. Living at home in No. 2, Pretoria, with his parents, he was one of the very few residents who worked off the Estate. A quiet and reserved man, he disregarded overtures for him to work for the Estate, and retained his independence, preferring to cycle the seven miles each way to work until the purchase of a small motor car eased this burden a few years later.

Chapter 13
Autumn Mud and Mangolds

The one thing crucial to a manual worker was good health. Often to maintain this high level of health meant having access to a doctor at all times. To this end my Grandfather Eke, a lifelong subscriber, had made me a member of the Oddfellows Friendly Society which meant free medical attention on the payment of a small monthly fee. This sensible action helped my parents financially throughout my delicate childhood when the doctor was, by dire necessity, a regular visitor to No. 6, Pretoria Cottages. With the advent of the National Health Service in 1948 the clubs, as we called them, were by degrees superseded. An adult club member also drew a small sum of money during sickness, which made the difference between survival and starvation for many, as employers seldom paid for sick leave.

The working man was always at his most vulnerable when ill health entered the delicate equation between agricultural worker and farmer. Living in tied cottages meant not only losing your wages over a prolonged period of illness, but, in many cases, your family home as well. Let me hasten to add that this kind of situation did not apply to the Westacre Estate we knew, whilst the men in charge remained, but changes could have taken place and then who knows what the position would have been. A lifetime of hard knocks and survival fights had taught my Grandfather Bumfrey, and through him his family, to protect themselves as much as possible from unexpected employer tantrums. All were lifelong members of the National Union of Agricultural Workers, and their monthly publication, called "The Landworker", had its place beside the Daily Herald in our quiet, but fiercely loyal Labour household. Grandad had rubbed shoulders with Will Edwards, the Methodist preacher and Union leader, over in North Norfolk, at early Union gatherings. He himself had squeezed a farmer in a gate until the terrified employer agreed to pay wages owing. He had seen his wife with only cabbage or swede to boil for a family of children. It was his hard background and strong, determined character that eventually fired in me the urge to try to win better wages and conditions for fellow workers — but it was a very shy person who had to pluck up courage even to ask Horrie Everard if I could join the Union. From that day in late 1949 I remained a Union member for all my employed working life, and was always proud to be so, especially in the N.U.A.W. Horrie collected the subscriptions around the farm, not as a shop-steward, for we didn't have one of them, but to make sure those who were too busy or idle to bike to Westacre once a month in order to attend the meeting held in our Reading Room, stayed members. On Soigné Farm the Union existed as a helpmate in time of trouble, otherwise the giant slept whilst its members were content to enjoy a free and easy working existence, but with only the minimum return in pay. It suited the majority who were heading for retirement, so the few younger elements were pushed into the background until the hardest work was there to be done, and then it was a slightly different story, but again, not on the wages front.

After a full year at work, these situations were just beginning to make themselves known in my brain, which was very slowly coming out of hibernation and starting to function once more as it adjusted to my new environment. But, in the main, I was blissfully ignorant of farm politics, and the only blot on my far-distant horizon was the fact that agricultural worker exemption from National Service was under review, and it was very likely that I would fall fifteen days short of the final exclusion date, 31 December, 1950. Jimmy Lane, who was a bit older than me, went to Swaffham to register, as was required under the law. When asked which service he would prefer to serve in, he replied, with his usual cheeky grin, "The Salvation Army". Needless to say, the recruiting sergeant, lacking any sense of humour, suggested Jimmy would need to do a lot of praying if he was his drill instructor, and slammed James down to serve in the Army. My other friend, Gerald Andrews, fell well inside the exclusion dates, and as Jimmy left soon afterwards I never knew if he was called up. If he was, I sincerely hope he didn't meet up with the old, sourpuss, recruiting sergeant at basic training camp. I could just imagine Jimmy's short legs lapping the parade ground, with heavy rifle above his head. There wasn't much to laugh about when defending King and country, well, not for the first fortnight at any rate. But that experience for me was still to come, and as I knew nothing of the joys awaiting me in that field, I remained blissfully ignorant.

October's arrival completed the calendar for my first agricultural year, and I had experience of quite a number of varied jobs. During early October I did some beet driving, bringing filled tumbrils off Big Ashbreck to Will who was haling on the wide, roadside verge opposite Massingham Heath. Again we were able to enjoy the real peace of the countryside. An occasional motor vehicle passing along the narrow road was almost a novelty in its rarity. Tuesday morning saw the bus going to Lynn, with dim faces peering out of steamy windows. The return journey in the afternoon reminded us we were in the last hour of work. Crushed bracken gave off its own particular smell, and its fan-shaped fronds, now turning golden brown, were the only token left of the old heathland which had stretched almost to Massingham from time immemorial until it was cleared and cultivated during World War 2.

The potato crop on Honeypot had long since lost its green foliage with the haulms lying brown and half-rotten across the potato ridges. No longer were

Autumn Mud and Mangolds

the Land Army girls there to call upon for picking; their organisation had been disbanded. Instead a company of local women had been enlisted and assembled on a cold, wet, late October morning to begin work. I had arrived with my tumbril load of baskets, and John Bumfrey was there with the potato harvester. We all huddled under leafless trees in the large, wooded pit-hole at the top of our field. The rain dripped upon us, giving the most miserable scene you can imagine. Hardly any of the ladies had substantial wet weather gear; one even had a pre-school age child with her. John and I managed to get a fire started, although our sodden fuel made life difficult. As the flames gathered hold, John made mother and child as comfortable as possible in front of his fire. He was very concerned about the child who looked frozen and ready to cry. The cold wind whipped through the sparse cover, and, I can tell you, the toddler wasn't the only one of us unhappy and cold. When the rain eased, John made a token start, shaking a few rows of potatoes out of their muddy bed. Squelching along, dragging heavy, waterlogged baskets, was no picnic, and everyone was glad to get home to a hot meal and warm fire. As the week progressed, and weather improved, the work began to get easier. We haled the tubers alongside the road hedge, and as the clamps lengthened I began to have nightmares on the subject of moulding over them with my old, rusty shovel, as we did on Little Strawberries the previous year. My first year's experience allowed me to measure out the sections to be picked, and explain the method of moving round one stretch each time our digger went past. I felt quite an old hand, and enjoyed my senior status until one or two pickers started to complain about this and that, with me caught up in the crossfire. Still, it was quite enjoyable really, and once more I was sorry when the thirty-five-acre field had been cleared. Unfortunately, no trip to help on Abbey Farm came up this time, but, as often in life, one door closes and another opens. The shooting season was round again, and Gerry Deasley and myself were instructed to meet up with the head keeper, Fred Welham, at the first shoot over in Gayton Thorpe.

Our format was the same as in previous years, so we will not labour through it again, but suffice to say I enjoyed every minute of it, well, perhaps not the soaking wet kale crop, but Gerry seemed to hate everything to do with it. It think it fair to say our comrade was unhappy with every job that fell short of being a tractor-driver, which, I'm very glad to say, he eventually became.

On one occasion we were soaked to the skin on the way to the shoot, and returned home to dry out. Fred Welham threatened to refuse our labours the next time, only to be told by Charlie Wilson that he either had us two or nobody at all. Eventually Fred had to climb down, but we lost our day's pay, which was a severe financial blow. The shoot came first, and soaking wet bodies risking pneumonia came a very poor second in his dictatorial eyes, but times they were a-changing, the serfs were on the march. Luckily for us though there was no love lost between Charlie and the Major's head keeper, so we were shielded by our foreman's bulk. Fred growled at us when we arrived for the next shoot, issuing threats of dismissal should we fail to turn up on any future occasion. Rather red-faced, we set off with the rest of the beaters, muttering to each other and calling our esteemed head gamekeeper a miserable old sod. Anyway, by tradition, no one allowed himself to like under-keepers, let alone a head one. Pre-war gamekeepers and policemen were to be treated as lepers and left well alone. By 1950 we got on well with the lesser keepers, but the policemen and Fred Welham still held the stigma of law enforcers representing the rich against the poor, the "haves" and "have nots". As we fell well within the second bracket, everyone present was on our side, albeit silently.

Most of the local brushes with the law centred round bikes, their lights, or the lack thereof. When my parents lived at High House they cycled to Castleacre one Saturday afternoon. Parking her "sit up and beg" bike outside Joplin's grocery shop, mother entered, and as luck would have it, started a long "mardle" with Mrs. Joplin. They were both good talkers, so it went on a bit. Waiting outside, my father saw the local bobby approaching. He stopped and examined the parked bike.

"There's no reflector on the back of this bike", he remarked.

"Oh, no", said Freddie. "Perhaps it worked loose and fell off."

"You don't know whose it is, by any chance, do you?"

"No", lied a sweating husband. "It was here when I came. She must have gone off down the village to the other shops."

Hoping upon hope his wife wouldn't come out Freddie was like a cat on hot bricks.

Eventually P.C. Plod gathered himself to move away.

"If she comes back tell her she's breaking the law."

"Yes, I'll do that. Perhaps she saw it loose and put it in her bag."

As soon as the burly figure disappeared under the ancient arch straddling the street, Dad shot into the shop, whipped his still gossiping wife outside, and sped off with her in the direction of home. Breaking the law by having no reflector was one thing, but perverting the course of justice by lying to a policeman was rather more serious. Just think, my parents could have been transported to Australia before I even saw the light of day. Of course Dad got no sympathy from Mum for the lie, and was called a silly fool, but that wasn't an uncommon occurrence. It was much less painful than paying a fine, I suppose.

Going back to Dad's single days when he lived at Baconsthorpe, I will recount a tale he often told us. Freddie and John Gee, his mate, prepared to cycle the four or so miles to Holt. It was a dark night, and neither had lights on the rear of their machines. John set off, but for some reason his mate fiddled with something before following a few hundred yards behind. Suddenly

Autumn Mud and Mangolds

Freddie saw the large figure of a policeman shoot out of a darkened gateway and pursue John along the road.

A deep voice behind John said, "Where's your back light?"

Thinking it was mate Freddie fooling about, John yelled back, "Up my backside, can't you see the wick hanging out?"

"Tell that to the magistrate, John Gee", said the law enforcer as he drew level.

Poor John was flabbergasted and tried to explain his mistake. But the tale of a mate biking behind held little credence as no mate was in evidence. The so-called friend had melted into the darkness quietly, wheeling his machine, now without lights, away from the scene of crime.

"Some bloody mate you turned out to be", complained the heavily fined John Gee.

"No sense in us both paying up, was there, so I hooked off home", came the reply.

But eventually it ended in a good laugh and they remained friends long after the Bumfrey family moved across Norfolk to Westacre Estate.

I don't think we crossed swords with the keepers after Charlie Welham allegedly shot our pet cat at High House. Very few farm employees dabbled in poaching, as the fear of losing job and home loaded the dice too heavily against them. I've no doubt the stewpot occasionally held a "two-legged rabbit" with "larks' eyes" (fat globules) on the gravy. I remember Charlie Wilson telling Dad how he had accepted a lift in an employee's cart, and as they bumped along a cock pheasant slowly slid out from under a pile of sacks in the bottom.

"My fellow, was I glad to get down from that cart. We could have both got the sack."

But no action was taken by the foreman, apart from a warning, as was the case when Willie Thaxtor drove up behind his bullock feeder who had pheasant tail feathers poking out of a hole in his dinner bag. As the man in question was about to pass Fred Welham's house, a quick warning was issued and the feathers tucked in out of sight. One couldn't afford to lose good men for the sake of a pheasant, but any blatantly obvious taking of game was frowned upon, and the culprit warned as to future conduct.

As the short November days slipped past, with brushing for Gerry and myself every other day, a fresh nightmare raised its head on the intervening days. Sugar-beet had been harvested on Middle Thirty Acres, and a clamp made inside the gate beside the green road leading off to Westacre. Every morning a lorry belonging to Sommerfeld and Thomas came at about 6.30 to load beet for Lynn factory. The driver was expected to load it himself, and this was, without doubt, a daunting task. Most men did just that as it was a contract job. But the particular driver allocated to Soigné was a wily fellow, and found Charlie a soft touch. By telling our foreman he would be unable to load and convey the two loads allocated daily without help, he talked Gerry and myself into a job we hated. Charlie himself was in a cleft stick situation, as it was crucial the allocated loads got into the factory before severe frost ruined the crop. So off we two went, armed with heavy beet forks. These forks were shovel-shaped with knobs on the tine ends to prevent stabbing the beet. Anyone who has tried to scoop up beet from a muddy clamp-base and then fling them up on to a high-sided lorry will know how hard and soul-destroying it is. We sweated and swore our way through an hour and a half until Cyril decreed his lorry full, and proceeded to tie a net over the load. On dry days it was hard work, but on wet ones, shovelling away in a heavy, ex-Army greatcoat was murderous, especially so for Gerry who had to work in the middle and received lashings of mud off the forks on either side, Cyril being left-handed and myself right. But the worst time was after the lorry had dragged its load off towards King's Lynn and we were left to freeze as our sodden shirts quickly cooled on our backs. A fire in the nearby pit-hole helped to dry us off, but it still remained a very uncomfortable feeling and did nothing to ease the aching muscles of our backs.

In the mornings it was dark when we passed the beet hale just before seven, and we pedalled "hell for leather" towards the farm.

"Tell Charlie I'm here", a voice would yell, but of reply there was none.

"Did you notice if the lorry was there?" was Charlie's opening gambit.

"Never saw him", came the reply, in unison.

"My fellow, he is late this morning. You had better go up there and wait for him.

So much for purging your soul by lying.

Even if the foreman decided that perhaps our beet allocation had been cut, owing to production problems at the factory, and prepared to send us on another job, the dratted lorry would drive into the yard to look for us.

"Any help this morning, Charlie? Must get the two loads in today."

Hauling ourselves up into the cab we would ride off the short distance to White Gate corner.

"Didn't you see me or hear me shout when you went past?"

"No, must have been someone else you shouted to and they forgot to tell Charlie."

More lies and more soul-purging, and still no escape from this hell on earth situation. What good fun it was to be a farmer's boy, I don't think! But, as on many previous occasions, we didn't know when we were well off, for as soon as the shooting season finished we were at it five days a week instead of two, with three loads allocated per day instead of two. By now we were working on a clamp situated inside Lower Fifty Acres gateway. I could dream of my halcyon days of flat rolling when the world was bright and fair as we huddled around a fire of fir boughs in the slightly sunken road to Rats Hall, between loads. At least we had a rest period even if conditions for it were uncomfortable.

Autumn Mud and Mangolds 135

All good and bad things have to come to an end eventually, and at last the final load of beet disappeared up the road to Long Plantation and our nightmare ended, for me at any rate. Next season I would be sugar-beeting with the gang, not realising that in actual fact December 1951 would see me square bashing at Hednesford R.A.F. Camp in conditions much worse than those encountered on Waterpit corner. At least my mud-sodden boots didn't have to be shiny in readiness for Charlie's inspection next morning, or uncreased trousers incur two hours spud-peeling at night.

When the Lane family moved away from Pretoria I took over Jimmy's job supplying mangolds to the bullocks housed at Elbreck. Every morning I picked up a load of mangolds from a hale on the Hulver, where surplus roots had been grown, then proceeded with Beauty to Elbreck sheds. There, Harry Ashby would be filling and carrying skeps of sliced roots all round the wall-bings. Leaving my mare backed into the grinding house I then began filling the skeps, by means of a beet fork, and setting them ready for Harry to dispense. This speeded things up, especially as the bullock feeder had no need to straddle over the three feet board placed in the doorway to prevent over-eager bullocks entering the feed house as serve yourself policies were not encouraged in those days. If, for any reason, I was a bit late arriving, Harry would be quite snappy about it, which made me feel uncomfortable, especially as I was helping him to do his work. Often I felt myself rushing along in the morning, with stomach churning, when anyone else would have turned collecting a load of mangolds into a leisurely, pre-breakfast stroll. If Harry was especially sarcastic on my arrival I felt like telling him to fill his own skeps, but I never had the courage to do so. Nevertheless, it was quite a nice job, and Harry usually became his jovial self when the bullocks were fed by breakfast time. I was pretty well my own boss collecting straw bedding from the nearby stack, chaff from the store at the back, then mangolds as and when required. A small Lister petrol engine drove the root cutter, with me dropping whole mangolds in its hopper, and Harry shovelling the slices from underneath. A heap was made behind the aforementioned board near the door leading into the yard. Chaff, either wheat or barley, was mixed with the juicy root slices which had a rather sweet smell as they heated slightly, prior to the afternoon feed.

There was no form of heating to warm us after our exertions, but we were dry overhead and on very wet days I restricted my journeys to the bare minimum, and Charlie never interfered as long as the work was done. The south-facing yards gave an early prelude to spring when mid-winter sunshine became trapped there to add its slight warmth to the heat rising from the trodden muck below. On days like this, which were all too few, I sat on a bale amongst cud-chewing fatstock and ate my dinner, the overfed animals being too lazy to be obtrusively inquisitive. I never felt it was unfeeling of me to enjoy beef sandwiches, even if my companions were destined for the butcher's shop.

As spring cultivations came round once more it became a case of all hands to the pumps. As the fattest of our bullocks were siphoned off and loaded on lorries for Lynn market, my job became more part-time. Other tasks had to be fitted in, which again seemed to upset Harry's temper, with me feeling the brunt of it when Charlie sent me off at short notice. Eventually, of course, all the fattened stock went off to market, and Harry once more joined the manual labour pool in outside work, and I ceased to travel to Elbreck every morning.

One of the most exciting jobs that came up occasionally in spring and summer was driving cattle from one pasture to another. A company of men would be sent up to High House to meet up with my father and Willie Thaxton in the farmyard. We would then be posted at strategic points along the proposed route, in order to prevent the animals running off course. Some of we younger elements would then slowly walk round the herd of young stock or cows with calves, gently easing them towards the gate. The one thing to be avoided was sudden movement or noise, which, in turn, might cause a stampede. My dad was an expert in this work, and we all took our lead from him. On one occasion they were moving suckler cows and small calves from the park, across the farmyard, and along a rough, green lane to Codlings pasture. Everything was proceeding with stealth and caution, allowing the leading matrons to sniff and blow at each unfamiliar object and then pass on to the next. As the leaders passed the old granary, a wooden building set on staddle stones, one of their number ambled slightly in the wrong direction. This minor deviation, for some unknown reason, set off a time bomb in the form of the tiny figure of Diddie Frost, who hurtled out from under the raised building, yelling and shouting like a dervish. The effect on the cows was electrifying and they turned tail, barging the following herd, and set off at full speed down the farm drive. Men in heavy boots set near Olympic-speed records as they tore down an adjoining pasture to get in front of the runaways before they reached the public road. Cows roared and calves cried, as the mêlée continued. Eventually some semblance of order was restored, but it was impossible to get the charges past that black building again. After a couple of abortive attempts, it was decided to return them to their original pasture for a few days, and then try again. I shall not even attempt to record the names Fred and Willie used to describe Diddie. Luckily, most of the hot language was drowned by the terrible din coming from the distressed cattle. It was this part of the upset which infuriated my father. Willie wasn't best pleased as his well-laid plans for an easy transfer had been thwarted, and Charlie certainly wasn't overjoyed at the waste of man hours. To the boys it was an unexpected rodeo set up without any help from them; in fact, they were heroes of the hour as their fleetness of foot prevented any stock reaching the public road. As for

Autumn Mud and Mangolds

Diddie Frost, well, let's just say that he was never sent on cattle moving work again. In fact, he didn't go near High House for quite a time, and kept a low profile at No. 4, Pretoria, if the tenant at No. 6 was outside. This event happened before I joined ranks at Soigné, but the graphic description given by Dad, after he had cooled down, has stuck with me and always brought a smile on the occasions when we urged cattle past the old High House granary.

Of course, cattle-droving was a common occurrence before World War 2. In those days all roadside fields were fenced and gated, and with very little traffic, just one man in front and a couple behind, sufficed to move the beasts. Dad used to help drive store cattle from Westacre to Wootton marshes in the spring, and presumably back again in autumn when the marshes flooded once more. That would have been a distance of twelve to fourteen miles, I suppose.

Charlie Andrews moved his sheep along the road with help from his dog. After they had passed, the road and banks were covered with particles of mud, manure and wool, and a whiff of sheep stayed in the air for some time. Looking down on the flock from the bank, we viewed a solid block of sheep moving rhythmically along the road, baa-ing softly as they went. It was a sight we, as children, always rushed to the gate to see. The other sight and sound attached to sheep we watched going by was a long line of wheeled iron hurdles being pulled either by horse or tractor. Inevitably one or two wheels were missing, causing the dragging axles to shower sparks when in contact with a flinty road surface. Their approach could be heard for miles, so we were always up on the gate or hedge bank to see the procession pass our house. These farming manoeuvres were the highlights of local children's days, and not to be missed. Any unusual noise approaching on the road drew children to a vantage-point — I know it did we boys when at home. The highlight was unquestionably the threshing tackle hauled by its mighty traction engine. The replacement tractor of latter days took away some of the attraction, but even then all eyes followed its progress up Pretoria Hill. A tractor pulling Cambridge rolls in tandem made quite a loud noise equalling the iron hurdles mentioned earlier. A wagon load of straw, or in fact any wheeled farm vehicle, was worth a quick peep. On one occasion a runaway horse caused quite a stir as Traveller decided to take Dilberry and Derek Winner back to Soigné at a rather faster pace than they would have liked. The spectacle resembled chariot racing at its best as the charging horse and empty tumbril, empty that is except for the two unwilling charioteers, careered up the hill with Dilberry yelling "Whoa", and hanging on for dear life. As luck would have it, the errant Traveller ran out of steam and fright before reaching the White Gate corner when the cart would have overturned, with very serious results there was no doubt. Runaway horses were part of farming life at that time, and usually occurred without good reason. The same horse repeated his stupid antics when I had him out, but fortunately he left me behind and I soon caught up with him again, after he had wrapped the cart round a gatepost by cutting the corner too sharply. No damage seemed to have been suffered by horse, cart or gatepost, so we returned to work with Traveller as quiet as a lamb thereafter. No one ever discovered why the silly old fool should be quiet for six months, and then run off for no apparent reason. I liked him and used him quite a lot when the quieter Beauty was allocated to younger, less-experienced workers. But, as I have stressed before, horses never frightened me, and a little bit of playing up made the adrenalin flow to brighten the day.

Chapter 14
Taking to the Beet Field

One of the late winter and early spring jobs I liked was clearing up stack bottoms. After threshing there was plenty of old, waste straw left lying about, and this often remained to get wet and soggy before anything was done about it. Setting off with fork, shovel to clear up weed seeds dropped under the drum, and a horse and cart, promised a couple of days of freedom for me. Sometimes I had a mate, but quite often it was a one-man-job. A nice, long ride, such as down to the heath road, was ideal, but not always the case. Any combustible material had to be carted well clear of the straw stack before a fire was started. Being a non-smoker, my matchbox, carried in the bottom of my dinner bag, was usually well flattened, as were the few pages of newspaper stored there. Once a small fire had gathered some heart, damper straw was gently sprinkled over the top, causing a wonderful smoke blanket to drift across the open fields. All the weed seeds and saturated straw were loaded, then driven to and tipped down the side of a nearby pit-hole. Great care had to be taken when reversing to the pit edge for fear of losing cart and horse over the side. These sides were usually scrub-covered, and not too steep, but I don't think Charlie would have been too pleased to see a tumbril half way down them. There was always the chance of a rat chase, and on one occasion, a stoat shot off across the ground to disappear into cover before my eyes blinked twice. Stoats and weasels were classed as serious vermin by the keepers, and worth a shilling each if caught. Being so very fast and elusive, those shillings took some earning, and mine disappeared before I drew breath for the chase. Breakfast and dinner were taken in the pit-hole where a fire could be built at leisure and kept topped up all morning with a plentiful supply of dead wood always available, especially in the more isolated parts of the farm where workers only visited occasionally. Fields behind High House and along the heath road were my favourites, and I was left to my own devices far from the foreman's eye. The quiet and solitude were enjoyable, as long as I had my horse to talk to and no difficult human companion needing constant conversation. Even wet and dreary days had their compensations at meal times for there is nothing more comforting than letting the warmth from a good fire soak into one's trouser legs. A previously-cold face soon glows and numb fingers tingle when outstretched towards the life-giving blaze. Large droplets of water dripping from overhanging trees hiss loudly as they hit the flames. Boots and trouser bottoms steam, and life is wonderful for half an hour whilst sitting crouched under a thick greatcoat tent. A smoky, toasted sandwich, made with the help of a forked stick cut from a nearby bush, tasted delicious, even when the wretched bread opened up to drop your cheese into the fire where it sizzled agonisingly just out of reach.

Spring moved on into summer, and the hoeing season came round once more. This time I had to take up my "long hoe", as we called the tool used to chop out and single root crops. I wasn't considered old enough to join the main hoeing gang, but was put to practise on short rows, or "scutes", where constant speed, coupled with expertise, wasn't essential. As I plodded away on day-work I found that hand and eye co-ordination began to develop, giving me hope for the day when I could join the piecework gang. At that time the men chopped out beet as a gang, under the leadership of the "lord". Blackie Wright had taken over this post when George Hall left to become a working foreman in Leicestershire. The "lord" set the speed of work, and each man took a separate row and followed his lead. They would all hoe right-handed until their leader decided it was time to change hand in order to rest certain muscles by hoeing left-handed. So one by one the change was made, and no member worked quicker or slower than Blackie. Thus, alternate hands were used all day, enabling this constant speed of work to be maintained. By the time I returned from National Service and graduated to qualified hoeman, a different system had been adopted, but more of that later.

Towards the end of June my work had taken me to a large stack bottom planted with swedes on Twenty-four Acres. A cold, damp, out-of-season day found me shivering with cold and aching in every joint. I managed to stick it out until four o'clock, then dragged my weary body homewards. Being too ill to work next day I remained in bed. A visit from the doctor confirmed I was suffering from a severe bout of chicken pox. Having been bypassed on several occasions when this childhood ailment broke out at school, I now found myself floored for three weeks and not enjoying the experience at all. No one else in our vicinity had the affliction, so where I picked it up was a mystery. By the time I returned to work my hoe was out of season, and hay time, or "haselling", was well advanced.

After a fortnight's holiday with our grandparents at Briston, which incidentally was the last as a complete family, harvest was approaching rapidly. It had been evident that Grandad Eke had aged considerably in the past year, and was no longer able to work his garden up to the high standard he set himself. Before the next July came round he had passed on, and I myself was a corporal policeman in the R.A.F. So our family holidays came to an end as all things do with the passage of time, but the memories live on — simple pleasures enjoyed by simple people who were happy to live uncomplicated lives and be grateful for small mercies which bred contentment for all of us. We had wonderful grandparents, lovely parents and aunts and uncles, who cared for us, and made our lives as happy as they possibly could. All the Ekes and Bumfreys loved children so that we felt, and in fact were, part of a big, caring family. It was no wonder I felt bereft when the time came for me to go off for National Service.

Harvest again followed a similar pattern, with binders and combines sharing the work. My partner on the wagons this time was Gerry Deasley, as Jimmy had departed to pastures new.

It was very rare that fresh crops were introduced into the Soigné rotation. Peas, in a dried form, have been mentioned and when first grown on the Nurseries prompted us to re-name it "The Pea Field". I recall flax being grown on arable sections of the Park towards the War end. A special machine came to pull the crop and bind it ready for transportation to special "retching" pools where it lay in water until outer-stem layers rotted to reveal precious linen threads. Carrots were once left to seed over a second year, then cut and stacked for threshing. This was the large stack on Twenty-five Acres, which burned down when Charlie Wilson fired a wheat-straw stack in close proximity. This year mustard had been sown on Fourteen Acres where, the previous year, my light harrows had followed the corn drill. When mustard ripens it becomes very brittle and spiny, closely resembling the modern rape seed crop. These days combines cope very efficiently with this type of crop, but in 1951 a binder cut and bound the mustard, and of course it had to be carted, stacked and threshed. Every effort was made not to tread the small, yellow seeds out of their brittle pods, and to this end we stood on the wagon floor loading around ourselves before placing a few shoofs loosely in the middle to hold the sides together. Old binder canvases were placed above the straw stack bottom to catch the mustard seed dislodged by stackmen's boots. All loose seed on wagon bottoms was bagged at the end of our day, this being stored in the barn until threshing took place. This rough collection was then shot into the drum, so that special riddles could clean and sort it through. All in all the careful handling produced a much slower operation than normal grain-carting, but I suppose a higher price per acre had been negotiated for this crop. Without doubt this mustard was grown under contract for Colmans of Norwich whose mustard products are still world famous.

During routine grain harvesting a nice, wet-break job was to fetch the wagons on to the pig pasture for sweeping out. All the loose grain dropped in the wagon bed would be scraped out on to the pasture where the old sows fought and squealed over their feast. Then each wagon wheel was jacked up and removed for Barney to administer thick, yellow grease on the exposed axle. Finally a dab with the greasy stick where the front carriage turned under its body, and I would be away to the field for another one. Barney Hooks had succeeded George Hall as technical advisor on wagon maintenance and was the only man, apart from George, whom I saw with a carpenter's pencil behind his ear, a sure sign of a tradesman if proof were needed. Barney used technical terms as well for he called axles "eclsters", and ladders "lethers", so he must have been a cut above we labouring men. I had undergone woodwork lessons at school for five years, but I would never have taken the liberty of lifting that greasing stick. One had to remember the unwritten pecking order at all times as farming at Soigné peeped tentatively into the twentieth century. The ride backwards and forwards to the damp harvest field more than satisfied me, so I left the complicated jobs to those more qualified to do them. And that's why I never left the bottom rung of the farming ladder in ten whole years.

On one occasion Charlie gave me the job of undertaker. Armed with spade, shovel and pickaxe, I set out for the bottom corner of Soigné Wood. With me went a tumbril carrying the carcass of a huge, black sow which had succumbed to an unspecified disease and needed cloak and dagger burial. Traveller wasn't at all pleased with his load on that morning, and snorted all the way to the cemetery with ears laid back in a most "I'll run away any minute" manner. Tying my uneasy companion securely to a sapling, I staked out a clear patch in the floor of the wood, and commenced digging, quite pleased with myself at finding the earth fairly loose. Needless to say, my luck ran out just as soon as my spade scooped up old bones, and I realised that a previous undertaker had used the site before me. Nothing for it but to begin again on virgin ground where tree roots and compacted earth made my task much more difficult. A break for breakfast in the vicinity of a partly-putrefying, black mountain of pork was of little relief, and I soon pressed on with the task in hand. Boy, was I thankful when my backed-up cart shot the corpse into its freshly-dug grave, and the earth was trodden down level once more. I did some spitting I can tell you, and my hands and clothes seemed to carry the smell for days. Traveller sped back towards the farm, and I didn't object to speeding with him. It took a while for wind and rain to rid that tumbril of its reeking, dead pig smell.

One of the first things I bought after saving some of my meagre wages, was a new bike. Choosing a dark-green Sunbeam model from a catalogue supplied by Godfrey Hannant of Castleacre, I eagerly awaited its arrival. Godfrey was both deformed and partially disabled, but he had set up a cycle sales and repair business in a shed alongside his brother Fred's garage. This new bike was my pride and joy, which meant a thorough cleaning every Sunday morning. All the mud collected during the week had to be removed and the whole machine shone up into pristine condition – outside the shed on fine days and inside when wet, I never missed. This dedicated cycle cleaning didn't allow me to miss the hour on the crosscut saw though, for that chore was written on tablets of stone. As soon as Freddie took down his sack-wrapped saw, cleaning rags were discarded, and station taken up alongside the sawing-horse. My heavy, Zugg working boots were also cleaned thoroughly before blacking or dubbin was liberally applied. The church bells might ring in Westacre village, but at

Pretoria the commandments stated, "Thou shalt clean your boots and bike before or after helping thy father saw wood", that was if you were the eldest son of a Bumfrey. The turn of a younger son was soon to come when King and country took first claim on eldest son's time — National Service loomed large. Brother Michael was destined to don the mantle of assistant sawyer before the year's end.

It must be remembered that our tied house still had no modern services. All drinking water had to be carried from the pump situated at the hill bottom. This pump itself was far from new and often had to be primed with the aid of a jug left filled by the previous water seeker. Washing, both bodily and clothes, used soft rain-water collected in tanks at front and back whenever possible. All water carried indoors conversely had to be carried out again by bucket and emptied either on to our vegetable garden, if semi-clean, or on to the muck-hole if dirty. Our bucket toilet, adjacent to the shed, needed emptying weekly into a freshly dug hole in the garden, this operation being carried out at dusk to avoid polluting the atmosphere when neighbours were outside. Squares of the aforementioned Daily Herald newspaper hung on a string beside the wooden box seat. Cinder ash from the fires was spread along paths to bind the top layer together, but this pulled up badly on the feet when frost began to thaw out. Tins and bottles were barrowed down to be tipped into a dry ditch inside Home Coverts, or Pretoria Wood as we called it. All these antiquated systems of hygiene and waste disposal began to aggravate my progressive-minded mother who had experienced running water and flush toilets twenty-five years previously when working in London. Dad, on the other hand, saw nothing wrong in the age-old methods he had known all his life. The very thought of electricity was as alien to him as outer space, despite the fact he had used electric milking machines at Baconsthorpe prior to 1927.

A slight altercation between Mrs. Bumfrey and the Estate powers cropped up a year or so earlier when a fouled pipe prevented water flowing from the Hall bore into the holding tank under our communal pump. Far inferior water was transported from Soigné to be shot into the tank via a manhole cover situated in George Wright's chicken run. The muck and chicken excrement which went in with the water seemed of little consequence to the hierarchy, but Mrs. B. objected strongly to giving her family contaminated water. After a furious row with Charlie and Willie she eventually took an unheard of step by approaching Major Birkbeck in person. He was not at all amused by this affront, but the pipe was quickly located and cleared so that clean water flowed to Pretoria once more.

Friction began to rise again when large cracks appeared across the top of our long-serving kitchen range. This range, situated in the living room, as no proper kitchen existed at Pretoria, was dual-purpose in that saucepans boiled on the top and baking took place in its side oven. It was our only real form of heat supply, apart from a small, open fire with metal bars across in the scullery. My father acquainted Willie Thaxton with the situation, and he in due course passed the problem on to the Estate office. It seemed to take an awfully long time for each person in the chain of command to pass the buck to another, and this did nothing to improve Mother's temper when she viewed the flames of her fire flickering through the widening fissures in the black-leaded stove top. Daily, my father's ears were bent with enquiries as to progress, until he asked his superior once more, with slightly more urgency in his tone. Eventually Mr. Cameron, the Estate manager, called to examine the stove. After much head-scratching and a fair bit of flannel he decided that a new stove was out of the question, as it would be setting a precedent. If we had a new stove everyone on the Estate would be crying out for a new one as well. I am pretty sure the new Estate manager quickly gathered that his theory had a considerable number of flaws in it, or at least he had tried it out on the wrong person. I thought he was lucky to retreat without having the saucepan of boiling potatoes thrown at his head. My dad, who had just come in for dinner, tried to calm things down and as usual said the wrong thing, and was lucky not to get his head bitten off as well. As it was, he had strict orders to instruct Willie Thaxton to advertise for a new cowman as we were looking for another situation where the employer at least gave us adequate cooking and heating facilities. Poor William was thunderstruck.

"Don't do that, Fred, no need for that. Leave this to me. Tell your wife not to worry", and off he went to the telephone.

Ted Green, the building foreman, arrived next day with a catalogue and a new model was measured for and ordered. The poor old range readily fell to pieces on removal, and its replacement looked splendid in situ. But handsome is, as handsome does. It was a devil to light, the far side of the room was like an ice house, and the oven wouldn't bake a rice pudding in a fortnight. So much for progress and modern science. If only they had still made those cast-iron, black-leaded, antiquated, but very practical and efficient ranges. I learned a lesson in life then – and my Rayburn is behind me now, working perfectly. Thanks Mother, I owe you a lot. Just imagine the Estate manager's reaction if we had suggested a high-class Rayburn cooker to solve our problems. Cardiac arrest would have been a likely result, for both him and Captain Harry Birkbeck who was trying to come to grips with a rather tired and very rundown Estate.

Highly charged and full-blooded these altercations may have been, but they rarely resulted in bad feelings on either side, and both adversaries would pass the time of day with one another in a most civilised manner when next they met. For this, great credit must be given all round, for my mother could be a most painful thorn in anyone's side when she had the bit between her teeth. Her determination and ability to think fast on her feet made her a formidable

Taking to the Beet Field

opponent, asking neither favour nor quarter in a battle of wills. These previous minor skirmishes only helped to feed the fire of her desire to have electricity and mains water installed for all tenants. After prodding and carping over the next three or four years, her efforts were eventually rewarded, and semi-civilisation came to us at last.

One or two other moves towards progress slowly came into being. As petrol rationing and wartime privations dropped away, bus services perked up. Bert Eves and Billy Carter continued to run their Tuesday Market-day bus past Pretoria to King's Lynn. "Teddy" Bear ran a bus service through the village to Lynn on Thursday, with Jack Eagle servicing from Castleacre to Lynn on Saturday. A new service ran past Pretoria to Lynn on Saturday afternoon, as did a bus from Westacre to Swaffham. Many of the coaches still had the utility, wooden-slatted seats, which left one's nether regions numb and deeply indented after twelve miles or so over war-worn roads. These buses were often over-subscribed, with passengers standing on most trips. Being a gentleman and giving up one's seat to a lady wasn't too difficult after riding a few miles on wooden slats. To stand down on the step inside the sliding door was an honour not to be missed as opening and closing it made one feel a good step up on the social scale. Jack Eagle or his brother, Squiffy, would come straight from the pigsties or cow sheds — we knew this by the excrement adhering to their trouser bottoms — and hop into the driving seat. I don't suppose anyone had public service vehicle licences then; possibly they had never even taken a driving test as these niceties went by the board during war years. We passengers had great faith in these men who shot our fare money into rough jacket pockets, along with hayseeds and binder string. Always ready with a laugh and cheerful word, they waited if you were late, and dropped you off at your gate if at all possible. They carried news from one village to the next, and knew everybody just as everybody knew them.

The cheerful Billy Harrison left Joplin's grocery delivery van and opened a fish and chip shop in Castleacre. We renewed old acquaintance when we were in that village for a haircut at Joplin's hairdressers. This "room in a house" shop was run by George Joplin who spent most of his time waving scissors around whilst talking to customers, and Eric Barnes, his assistant, who, despite his crippled feet, did most of the work. We always hoped to get in Eric's chair because the throughput was much faster. A seat in the proprietor's chair could mean a stay of half the afternoon whilst George held an animated conversation on world events with a potential customer who, in reality, had only come into the salon to pass an afternoon away. Sometimes one felt like leaving with only half one's head de-thatched. With a cloth cap worn on most occasions, whether for work or pleasure, I'm sure no one would have noticed. The Norfolk man's custom of always wearing headgear was just beginning to break down, but I still adhered to this old-fashioned style until my two years away from home broke the mould. My Dad and Uncles Will and John never went out without their caps, having a working and a best one. The fact of having near-bald heads may have contributed to their fashion. My own hair was as thick as a mat so no such problems worried me.

Another character in Castleacre was Reggie Eggleton, part-time postman and boot repairer. Reggie, like many others, had seen hard days when his mother was forced to take in white washing from large houses. Having heavy sheets hung around a handful of fire to dry had filled the small boy with a hatred for moneyed gentry. He often recounted the story of those sheets, ending with, "I felt like kicking the buggers over, but I knew my mother would larrup me". His fast-talking and often vitriolic propaganda against the stinking (his word, not mine) rich sowed a very tiny seed of discontent into my mind. Riding back home past the Hall I began to measure my lot against the life-style of "my master", as Reggie termed Major Birkbeck. This part-time postman delivered mail to Westacre High House as, for some reason, it came within the Castleacre postal area. I don't know if the butler who saw to these things pocketed Reggie's Christmas box, but the little pro-communist was always like a wasp on heat when giving vent to the shortcomings of "your bloody master". Even if I didn't agree with all the boot repairer came out with, I enjoyed his leaping around, and jack-in-the-box gesticulations, eagerly awaiting the time he would swallow a mouthful of tacks.

Private cars were still thin on the ground. Frank Clarke drove one, which doubled up as the local taxi. Major Birkbeck had his grey Opel for personal use around the Estate, and a more opulent model in which Watts, his chauffeur, drove him to the railway station for banking business. Hubert himself had a small car, as did Dick Welham. His baby was a soft-top Austin Seven, known to us all as the "Flying Flea". Willie Thaxton meandered around in old CBY 22, and Charlie Wilson was just venturing into the motor age, not heeding the warning to "keep death off the road". Charlie was a danger to life and limb, even on a bike. The only other cars in our small community at this juncture, were used by the tenants of Soigné Farm house, and Harry Reynolds, the carpenter. Car ownership amongst the peasants wasn't so very far away, but we will come to that later. Uncle John Bumfrey had always been a motor cycle man, as was Nobbie Easter at Rats Hall. Harry Ashby, also at Rats Hall, took his small car out towards Gayton, so we rarely saw him at the wheel.

As soon as harvest work was finished I caught the Saturday afternoon bus to Swaffham in order to purchase a sugar-beeting hook from Plowright's, the ironmongers. This half-sickle-type hook had a pointed nose on the end for piercing and picking up beet prior to severing the top. A broken section of carborundum stone for sharpening came from our shed, so that saved some expense. Old cycling leggings could also be commandeered to keep water and mud off the legs when knocking beet on damp days. Beet leaves, like kale, hold

Taking to the Beet Field

more water than one can imagine and manage, when handled, to tip it all down one's front and legs at the least provocation. Uncle Will advised the purchase of thick, rubber gloves, which he obtained from his favourite Lynn shop, the Army and Navy Surplus Stores. These were an abject failure when first used on a hot September afternoon, but came into their own when early November frosts made conditions unfavourable to bare hands.

Late September saw me as one of the sugar-beeting gang engaged in piecework. Blackie Wright was "Lord", or ganger, and he put me under the watchful eye and guiding hand of Horrie Everard. One afternoon my mentor and I were set on knocking beet whilst the rest of the gang were topping. Under the system used then, the sugar-beet were ploughed out and left in their individual rows. The ploughshare lifting them left a fair amount of soil adhering to the root, and this had to be removed before carting took place. Each person engaged in "knocking" pulled beet from two adjacent rows, banged them together to shake off the clay soil, and then placed them neatly in one single row. Putting two rows into one made gaps between for cart or trailer wheels to run when topping took place. On this particular afternoon the sun shone brightly, and with late summer warmth I considered it too hot for thick, rubber gloves, and having discarded them, proceeded to snatch at the fleshy-stemmed beet leaves as I pulled and knocked my way across Long Elbreck. The soil was heavy, that is containing a high clay content, and this property helped to hold it more firmly on the roots. The sun baked it, and also baked me as I struggled to keep up with my companion whose age was fast approaching sixty. The more I struggled and sweated the further behind I became. Flesh from the beet leaf stalks worked its way under my nails until I felt part of some Chinese torture. To his credit, Horrie eased his back at the row end, then worked towards me to help finish my row. The pain in my lower back made me feel sick, sweat ran into my eyes, and my tongue felt swollen from lack of moisture. Phew! If this was piecework labouring, then to hell with it! Roll on call-up time and let's get into the R.A.F. But eventually muscles settled into the tortuous, back-bending routine required for sugar-beeting. Knocking was still hell, but at least I could keep up fairly well by mid-October, and the weather wasn't so warm then. As the days became shorter and the weather wetter, mud spattered us but helped to clean beet without quite so much knocking. As November came and my calling-up date of the 28th approached, I began to wish for a permanent job at sugar-beeting. Lurid and exaggerated tales of Army life from Blackie, who had served in World War 1, did nothing to calm my fears. His descriptions of female camp followers left nothing to one's imagination, but needed a big pinch of salt to swallow. He usually ended with, "Ent that right, Percy?" His workmate would wink and reply, "If you say so, I suppose".

As I gathered up my working gear on the last night everyone wished me luck. I had spent the murky, damp November afternoon topping beet with Blackie, Barney, and Horrie for company. Whilst taking a breather on the end, Blackie had put forward his opinion that after seeing something of the world over the next two years I wouldn't want to return to Soigné.

"You won't want to come back to this, boy", had been the gist of it.

"Why not, you all did after life in the Army", I said. "We were glad to, after the trenches, and besides there was no other work", all three voiced together. "You have a good education and can get a good job. You'll realise that when you get this mud off your boots".

But I thought differently because I had tunnel vision as regards work, and just wouldn't see any other job for me. Home life was good, and living on an estate as we did, there was very little choice of work within seven or twelve miles. Swaffham, being the nearer town, provided hardly any industrial work at that time, although King's Lynn had openings if one looked for them and was prepared to cover a twenty-four mile round trip each day with non-existent public transport to help out.

There was no other thought in my head as I bid a rather tearful farewell to my family but to return to Soigné just as soon as my National Service was over. Devoid of ambition and paranoid about the lack of ability to learn of anything remotely mechanical, I was destined to be anchored in the past even more so than those three World War 1 veterans left behind to finish the beet harvest.

When real horsepower ruled the roost c1938. Left to right: John Bumfrey, Albert Richardson, W. Miller and Aubrey Simmons.

At the horse drawn harvest. Left to right: S. Hilton, Jeffereey Rye, Will Bumfrey, Basil Chase and Cyril Goose. Note the high horse driven elevator.

Is anyone going to open the gate . . .

. . . and let me get home for my tea?

Gamekeepers outside no. 1 Pretoria Cottages. Jimmy Reynolds is on the Gamecart. Left to right: Victor Williamson, Ernie Deasley (Pretoria), Clem Reynolds (Gayton Thorpe), Sid Spooner (Buildings), Bob Chapman (Westacre) and Derek Earl (East Walton).

Will Hinksman in the pheasant rearing pens on Soigné Horse Pasture, late 1950s.

The sitting yard at East Walton late 1950s, Colin Deasley and Roy Kingsley.

"Happy" Jack Legge, Colin Deasley with Will Hinksman the new head keeper.

The Soigne water tank where I filled the Rats Hall water-cart.

Hand shearing at Abbey Farm with Horrie Everard in the centre and Leslie Richardson smiling, at the back.

East Walton School with Westacre children mid 1950's. Back Row: Susan Cameron, Noel Nichols, Robert Large, Colin Johnson. Bernard Nichols, Paul Buckenham, ? Batterbee, Chrissy Smith and Pat Blower. 3rd row: Jenny Nichols, Janet Johnson. Judith Goose, ?, Ann Large, Madge Smith, Pamela Meachin, Mary Abel, Vivien Meachin, ? Brewster, Jennifer Bly and Pamela Lloyd. 2nd row sitting: Janet Easter, Helen Petch, Ann Abel, Brewster ?, Rosie Blower, Diane Easter and Sheila Bly. Front row: Gerald Jackson, Dennis Batterbee, Trevor Armiger, Johnny Overson. W. Boone and Robert Thaxton.

Pupils at East Walton School with Westacre children 1954. Back row: Colin Shackcloth, Barry Jackson, Roger Taylor, Michael Bumfrey, John Thaxton, Gordon Parnell, Terry Eagle, Colin Deasley and Tony Large. 3rd row: Sylvia Williamson, Pearl Lane, Beryl Barnett, Joan Nichols, Ann Nichols, Joice Baine, Dorothy Wilkin, Elaine Doughty. Daphne Futter. Madeline Overton, Glenda Futter, Angela Smith and Pat Nichols. 2nd row: Linda Nichols, Angela Wilson, ? Johnson, Janet Meek, Margaret Sweeting, ? Frost (twin), Valerie Jackson, Maureen Frost, Pamela Meachin, ? Frost (twin), ?, Lizzie Adcock, ? and Ann Large. Front row: Robert Large, Noel Nichols, Tony Abel, Russell Williamson, Colin Futter, Paul Buckenham, Hubert Wilkin, Colin Johnson, Bernard Nichols and Jeremy Cameron.

Westacre W.I. party held in the village hall 1951. Seated 2nd and 3rd from left are Mrs Andrews and Mrs Richardson, sat on the floor, first and second are Eileen Softley and Ethel Meachin.

East Walton Cricket team 1950s. Back row: Vic Barrett, Charlie Howard, Curly Shackcloth, Fred Petch jnr, Bob Fuller and Frank Petch. Front Row: Eric Shackcloth, Alan Green, Maurice (Moke) Petch and Alfred Skeet.

Looking across the river to Westacre from the rectory corner.

Maypole Dancing at the village fete c1950.

Westacre Bowls Club presentation 1950s. Left to right: Jack Bly, Bill Taylor, Jack Wilson, Fred Brewster, Joe Bly, Tom Able, Cyril Goose, ?, Harold Plummer, Reg Meachin, Bob Dawson, Spencer Bly and ?.

The end of an era at Westacre School 1949. Back row: ?, Terry Eagle, Michael Bumfrey, John Thaxton, Roger Taylor and ?. Middle row: Jean Andrews, Madeline Overton, Janet Meek, June Eagle and ?. Front row: Colin Deasley, Tony Large, Derek Grimes, Tony Abel and Oliver Dix.

Methodist Chapel Sunday School mid 1950s. Back row: Mrs Ivy Wilson, her son Jack, Terry Eagle and Miss Eva Wilson. Centre row: Madeline Overton, Shirley Sweeting and June Eagle. Front row: Margaret Sweeting, Vivien and Pamela Meachin, Angela Wilson and Angela Smith.

Methodist Sunday School, Cup year 1953.

Westacre School House, a private residence since the school closed, the children were taken by coach to East Walton.

"The Wooden Hut", overlooking the green. It housed our workmate Horrie Everard for many years.

The "lads" on a day out c1950. Left to right: Gerald Andrews, Bob Clarke, Leslie Richardson, George Wright, Ted Dack and John Bumfrey.

Michael Bumfrey, Dick Bland, Colin Deasley and a friend at Butlins.

The popular East Walton School mistress Ena Wilson with new husband Harry on their Wedding day.

Filey 1955, the author (left) with Gerry Deasley on a Butlins "fun bike".

R.A.F. service at Feltwell. Looking serious on the left (with Sgt.) and Cpl. "Chicko" Martin.

In the centre looking less serious (without Sgt.) and Cpls. Swann and Martin.

Cpl. Ron Atkinson on the motorbike I came to love, push and fall off at various times.

Round towered Gayton Thorpe church where my Uncle Stanley and Granny Bumfrey lay at rest.

Maurice Petch, the scourge of Westacre batsmen with his wife at their son's wedding. He looks fit enough to bowl a mean ball even today!

Entrance to Westacre village. Note the narrow sunken road between the steep banks.

Soigné Cottages with the original cow pasture in the foreground and the horse pasture beyond.

The muddy horse pond where our wheel chair chariot almost ended up complete with passenger.

Foreman Charlie Wilson's House from whence he strode each morning to give us orders.

Leslie and Derek — two old workmates.

Our old house, No. 6 Pretoria Cottages, my fathers neatly trimmed hedges look to be a feature of the past.

> **PART TWO**
> **November 1951 — November 1958**

Chapter 15
National Service

Sitting in the corner seat of a train which was taking me out of my local environment for the first time was not my idea of heaven. Usually any contact with the railway gave me untold pleasure for my mother's family had been steeped in oil and steam over many years at Melton Constable. All my previous rail journeys had either taken me to Briston where a warm, grandparents' welcome awaited me, or to the delights of bracing Sheringham or Cromer for the day. But this particular journey had an unknown ending scheduled to be at the R.A.F. Camp, Padgate, somewhere in Lancashire. Being well-versed in gardening I knew that to transplant a seedling, one carefully lifted the root with as much surrounding soil as possible to avoid any damage to its tiny rootlets. I felt as if life had ripped me straight out of my soil and stripped my roots away in the process. Although I didn't know it at the time, I was destined never to settle back into that native soil in the same happy and contented way I had enjoyed prior to this momentous day. 28 November, 1951, was the watershed of my life, shaking me out of a time-warp and unceremoniously pitching me into the real world for which I was woefully unprepared, hence my feelings of utter dejection as I sat gazing out of the window at a dull, wet Norfolk countryside. After changing trains at King's Lynn the scenery also changed to show me huge expanses of flat, cheerless fenland, grey and characterless under a lowering November sky. Small gangs of sugar-beeters knocked and topped, never pausing as our train sped past — only intent on clearing the acres, as piecework was the order of the fen worker's life. Time was money for "Fen Tigers" or "Lincolnshire Yellow Bellies", depending on which part of the Fens one was in. Oh, how I envied them their mud and backache. If only I had been born fifteen days earlier I would have remained exempt from National Service and all this worry and upheaval. Another uneventful day on Long Elbreck, listening to the oft-repeated tales from Blackie, which I knew by heart, would have been wonderful. There was no spirit of adventure in my soul that day, or any other come to that, as I remember. To think that a muddy sugar-beet field would be considered all I asked from life makes me cringe as I write. If ever a chip flew off the Bumfrey block, it was me.

The bleak November day never brightened, but eventually the Fens were left behind, to be replaced by dry stone walls instead of fences as Yorkshire came and went. Each stop supplied a few more anxious-looking youths all bound for the joys of Padgate Camp, but showing no signs of excitement at this opportunity of serving their country. By the time our train crossed the Pennines into Lancashire a motley crew of would-be airmen sporting an even wider selection of luggage and accents had gathered in adjoining carriages. Just to prove to me that the world outside Westacre was full of crooks and conmen (my mother's final words of wisdom), two card-sharps appeared to entice us into a game for money. A few worldly lads joined in and quickly lost what little cash they had and the prestige they hoped to build up. We bumpkins may have lost face by refusing the challenge but we kept our money.

After a week at Padgate, during which time I lost my personal identity to become a number — namely 2540928 — lost my hair, civilian clothes and freedom, we entrained once more en route to Hednesford Camp in Staffordshire. Situated adjacent to Cannock Chase, a coniferous wasteland if ever there was one, we were subjected to weeks of rigorous training designed by a devil's advocate and intended to turn us into useful members of His Majesty's Royal Air Force. There was no opportunity for me to think of life at Soigné Farm as I ran, marched, worked, cleaned, sweated, froze and almost slept on my feet. If I imagined I was fit when it all started, then it was a superman who left for more of the same — only worse — at Netheravon Police Training Camp. Yes, true to tradition, the R.A.F. had ignored all my preferences and in its superior wisdom decreed I was to be an R.A.F. policeman.

A very short leave at Christmas and another break between training camps gave me a chance to get home. On each occasion everybody, without exception, met me with the same words, "When do you go back?" Perhaps they were trying to tell me something. My mother very kindly likened me to a frightened rabbit with eyes almost popping out of its head. Well, after being harried for weeks by the corporal, sergeant, warrant officer and anyone else who cared to join in, it was no wonder.

Having no leanings towards leadership, it was understandable for me to quake at the thought of becoming an acting-corporal policeman. The very idea of taking airmen to task and charging them for minor misdemeanours frightened me to death. I daren't even think about being the armed guard on a bank run where thousands of pounds were involved. So why not fail the next written exam, thus becoming a reject destined for a less stressful job such as cookhouse orderly where I might even graduate to carting swill to the pigs which were kept on most stations? Alas, it seemed I was destined for greater things for, despite attempting to make a mess of all questions, I finished in pole position with 76%. I gathered that all my mates, who also wanted to fail, were much cleverer at the job than I was. So the die was cast and 2540928 Acting-Corporal Bumfrey D. received a posting to R.A.F. Feltwell, a pilot-training station just inside the Norfolk county border, on the very edge of the Fens where black soil predominated and blew around in a most awesome fashion in dry, spring conditions. The airfield resembled a typical pre-war station with grass landing strips over which the tiny training aircraft bumped and lurched so violently that one expected wings to fall off at any moment. During the summer, contractors cut and made hay on the perimeter land, so I felt partially in contact with the farming fraternity once more. Gang-mowers whirred continuously around the camp, and gardeners attended neatly-kept flower beds, especially around Nos. 1 and 2, Officers Mess, for all the trainee pilots were officer cadets and, as such, had their own mess facilities, and their officer status meant a salute from we common airmen every time we met. The security was very low-key, and the only real problems came from American airmen who escorted members of the W.R.A.F. back to camp and then, becoming over-amorous, refused to let their lady friends book in before curfew time. A quick call to the American Air Force police produced a vehicle from which poured a posse of enormous, uniformed Tarzans. Using their chair-leg truncheons liberally, and without provocation, they soon saw that the amorous servicemen were quickly separated from their girls and bundled unceremoniously into the truck. Usually the U.S.A.F. personnel came from Lakenheath or Mildenhall and attracted many of our female colleagues with their money and smooth talk. After the rapid disposal of the American allies our task became easier as the drink-generated defiance of camp rules quickly evaporated and a queue of muzzy-headed, tearful girls waited at the guardroom to book in and subsequently face the charge of being absent from camp after 23.00 hours. This charge usually carried a punishment of 14 days' confinement to camp, although persistent offenders could get 28 days, depending upon the temper of the W.R.A.F. officer sitting in judgement. Although escorting broken-hearted females back to their barrack block at midnight might not have been as exciting as muck-cart on a wet day, it had its educational side. Many a sorry tale came forth on breath laden with gin-and-orange fumes highlighting a side of life very different from that lived at Westacre. But, despite the sob stories poured into our sympathetic ears we knew the tellers would not be going "Yankee-bashing" for the next fortnight, but would be reporting to us at 18.00 hours every evening for two hours' "jankers". The time spent peeling spuds or onions in the cookhouse certainly dampened their ardour, but did very little permanent damage to their courting for, as soon as the fortnight was up, they were away once more. Unfortunately, eventually the ultimate price had to be paid and it was with a certain amount of sadness we issued a one-way travel warrant, which meant a discharge from service on medical grounds. The modern fashion of one-parent families had begun, but in a much more hostile world, for the disgrace of illegitimacy was still very much the order of the day. Having spent so much time at the guardroom window these girls were, in a strange way, our friends, and we knew them far better than those many service ladies who kept to the rules.

Being all National Service lads, with just one exception, we never troubled trouble unless it troubled us. Often accused by our superiors of not producing enough "janker wallahs" to do the dirty jobs around camp, we had occasionally to issue charge forms to cover ourselves. Usually we let it be known that a purge was to take place on long hair and scruffy uniforms which allowed those with brains to tidy up. Those full of bravado or lack of common sense were caught in our net and soon joined the two hour shift of "volunteer" labour in the cookhouse. A good number of workers here helped to keep us in with the cooks who made sure their appreciation was reflected in our out of hours meals. It was no wonder my weight increased by two stones in double quick time after consuming huge fry-ups at the end of each shift and drinking endless cups of very stewed tea in between.

All in all, life was very pleasant with no real pressures at work and a good crowd of mates to help pass hours of leisure time. But, despite living the life of Riley at the Government's expense, shame we didn't get paid much in wages, we National Service lads diligently crossed off the days to our demob. I personally couldn't wait to get away from this lord's life with janker wallah servants and elevated status, thanks to those two acting-corporal stripes combined with a red and black armband and white, webbing belt. Yes, an R.A.F. policeman's lot should have been a happy one if only we had avoided brainwashing ourselves from day one. Suggestions that we ought to consider signing on as regular servicemen were greeted with hoots of derision. Visions of returning to Soigné Farm were like the picture of an oasis to a desert traveller. There were times in the future when I realised they were only a mirage and sighed for the R.A.F.

I'm pleased to record there was little if any animosity between we law enforcers and the airmen at large. Frequent visits to The Cock public house, the most popular of three hostelries in Feltwell village, meant we could mix freely and everyone knew our eyes were blind and our ears deaf when not on duty. Demob. parties were open invitations for us to enjoy free drink with the sure knowledge our mates on the gate would put us in a safe place to sober up. One special mate, Ron Atkinson, had an old motor cycle, which needed a push to start on most occasions. As repayment for my propulsion from behind he ferried me around, which was a big improvement on years of pedal power. Before the advent of Ron's motor cycle I biked home periodically to get washing done and renew supplies of home-made cake. As previously mentioned, Feltwell sat on the very edge of the black-soiled fenland, but one soon saw a totally different scene as on the other side Norfolk breckland began in earnest with large tracts of coniferous trees or open heathland. Meeting up with the main road at Brandon I pedalled homewards through Mundford, Hilborough and Swaffham, before enjoying a lovely downhill swoop into Westacre village. A final grind up Tumbler Hill brought Pretoria into sight, and a warm welcome at No. 6. At first my comfortable and reliable Sunbeam cycle served me well, but in the second year at Feltwell I purchased a "jack's the lad" racing bike from a hard-up AC2 "erk" and used that. The hard saddle, and gears, which worked when they felt like it, did little to aid my speed or comfort my ride. In fact the old saying that pride comes before a fall caused me to lose faith in the machine and sell it on at a loss. Having made friends with an elderly man, who kept a small shop and farmed a few acres, we often cycled into the village on warm afternoons in order to buy ice-cream. A couple of moveable, metal signs stood on a loose-gravel forecourt, and on this particular afternoon the proprietor himself stood smoking a pipe and enjoying the sun. Leading my squadron in to land, I decided a showy sliding stop was called for and proceeded to display my prowess with a speedy approach, then brakes full on giving sharp deceleration, intending to end up inches from the pipe-smoking spectator. The loose surface proved my undoing, for as I slid sideways with locked wheels my machine took on a life of its own and ploughed into the signs before depositing me on top in a cloud of dust. My slightly more sane companions drew up, and after surveying the scene of mass destruction, hauled the signs and mangled bike apart whilst I shook dust from my best blue trousers and gingerly tested limbs for multiple fractures. As luck would have it, only the obligatory gravel rash marked my hands, and after picking my cap from under the hedge where it had taken cover, I tried hard to recover breath and composure befitting an acting-corporal in Her Majesty's Royal Air Force Police. Being a good, country shopkeeper, our ancient friend sold me plasters and gave me some good advice quite free of charge: "Get rid of that damned bike before it gets rid of you." Needless to say, I reverted to using my more reliable but not so dashing Sunbeam after that disaster.

Prior to the coming of a police sergeant to oversee the guardroom, we had spent an easy life under the senior corporal. As cycling around camp was very necessary, we used the only R.A.F. bike available — a very old but serviceable machine on the guardroom inventory. As it was in constant demand and had to be shared by six or seven people, one often had to walk. How pleased we were when the sergeant informed us of his plan to request another machine, that is until it arrived — a brand new cycle and greatly admired by a deputation of corporals. Imagine our faces when the sergeant pulled rank on us by declaring it was to be kept for his sole use. Back to sharing the old one, but not for long.

After spending the evening at our local hostelry we off-duty policemen took a short cut through to the camp dance. As we walked along the gravel roadway my spinning head suddenly decided to go haywire with the result that I sprawled headlong lacerating my hands both front and back, along with my face down one side. Hauled up by my companions in a great deal more sober state than when I went down, I was half dragged, half carried into the light outside the dance hall. I must have looked a right mess for they whipped me off to sick quarters where the duty orderly cleaned and patched me up.

"What caused this accident? I must enter it on my report."

A hasty council of war was convened and suddenly I had a brilliant idea, or as it turned out, was it another drink-induced brainstorm?

"I fell off the police bike when the wheel suddenly locked."

What could be simpler than to concoct a tale to cover the orderly, and more importantly to pacify our sergeant?

Arriving for duty next morning, patched and bruised and looking a sorry sight, I repeated our well-rehearsed version of my near fatal cycle crash, hoping my superior wouldn't examine the bike. What luck, he didn't even think of it. He just said, "That's it, I knew that old bike wasn't safe. Poor Bumff", (I'd inherited Grandad Bumfrey's nickname) "he could have been killed. Put the damned old thing in the store and lock it up. I forbid anyone to ride it again".

A stunned silence met this uncompromising announcement and my wonderful idea sank without trace. As my comrades walked the camp thereafter I could feel they somehow bore me a grudge, although they never actually mentioned it. Just in passing can I mention that we never used our civilian bikes on camp as this class of machine had a strange habit of disappearing unless kept under lock and key. So you see, the poor old police bike had a Sunbeam for company in its enforced retirement and I am pretty sure my mates would have loved to shove me in the store as well.

What else of note happened in my two-year absence from the farming scene? Well, I had the measles and spent several delirious days in sick quarters missing the terrible gales, which caused widespread flooding along the East Anglian coast. Kept in quarantine, I was the only airman on the camp to go down with the disease. The nurses were good to me and never once used blunt needles or cold hands to get revenge for the "late back to camp" charges I had put them on. Still, it's an ill wind (excuse the pun) which blows nobody any good, and after crossing Norfolk by train, which took almost a whole day, I arrived at Briston to spend ten days' well-earned sick leave at Granny Eke's homely cottage.

I spoke earlier of Ron Atkinson's motor cycle, a two-stroke, which left a dense cloud of blue smoke for the first half mile after starting. We always tried to park at the top of a rise, which enabled the pusher, usually yours truly, to get up speed before Ron slapped it into gear. On one occasion my mate offered to take me home and as we lived half way up Pretoria hill, I hoped we could restart without me having to demean myself as a lowly bike pusher. After enjoying a good tea we prepared to set off back to camp. Using our feet to begin freewheeling towards the corner, I made one fatal mistake. In turning to give a royal wave to the assembled company of neighbours I let go of Ron's greatcoat belt, and this lack of security coincided with the driver letting in his clutch. Off went the bike and so did I; after a couple of initial bumps on the rear mudguard, I found myself spread-eagled in the road, wearing a halo of blue exhaust smoke and a silly grin, but mine wasn't as wide as those worn by Arthur Futter and Ernie Deasley who doubled up with laughter. How the mighty had fallen as I had hoped to cut a dash with my first taste of mechanised travel. To cap it all, Ron, realising his pillion passenger had left early, turned the bike on the corner and then stalled the damned thing. After pushing him half way to Shortrow Pit without a spark of life we had to clean and dry the plug before finally chugging off to Feltwell with every ear at Pretoria listening to our engine dying in the distance a good half an hour after leaving No. 6. Pushing a man and machine over that distance whilst wearing an R.A.F. greatcoat and a badly crushed ego was no fun. My trusty Sunbeam brought me home for the subsequent visits.

Being short of money and often free from duty during the day fired me with the idea of chopping-out sugar-beet on the land farmed by our shopkeeper acquaintance. After half a day belting iron-hard ground with a borrowed hoe I felt yet another of my brilliant ideas had backfired. I also discovered just how soft my muscles and hands had become whilst pen-pushing. Rather than lose face I carried on for a day or so, and then pleaded extra daytime duties as a way of extricating myself from the job. This experience sent a warning message of what to expect when demob. came in November and the tail end of sugar-beeting awaited me at Soigné. I had visions of emulating Frank Clarke who rented a very small field from the Estate, and after planting it with beet, spent a whole Saturday knocking and topping his crop in readiness for transport to Lynn factory. Being unused to this type of intense physical labour, Frank became so stiff on Sunday that he was unable to move from his sofa where he lay prostrate for the whole of the Sabbath. I believe he went into partnership with Artie Keeley for future ventures and left the manual side to him. They rented one field which ran between the road to Pretoria and a narrow, sunken lane just below Tumbler Hill, and a second piece of land in the village above the original eight Council houses where Council bungalows stand now. Quite why these tiny pockets of land were not incorporated into Harry Mills' smallholding rented from the Estate, along with The Stag public house, I fail to understand. It would have saved Frank all his pain, but we would have missed out on a good laugh, as his son, Bob, told the tale later.

In the second year at Feltwell I found that my visits to Westacre became less frequent as camp life took over. Having a large percentage of Scots people with us seemed to make R.A.F. living far more permanent. Lads from north of the border had neither time nor money to return home for short leaves, so everyone made a life where they were. I was very much involved with them. The days on my calendar were not crossed off with quite the same enthusiasm as previously, and by the time November 1953 approached I found my remaining days had taken on a much more valuable aspect. It wasn't the R.A.F. career prospects which appealed to me, but the comradeship and social life I knew would end with my service. Last but not least, was the fear and in fact certain knowledge that my current friendship with a member of the W.R.A.F. would fizzle and fade when demob. came. Observations and experience gained at the guardroom window told me that very few courtships survived after one member re-entered civilian life. As it turned out my fears were fully justified and after one visit to Pretoria and a few meetings in her home town of King's Lynn our ways parted. She had no liking for the non-modernised living of Soigné Farm staff, and I didn't care enough to break away at that time — how different from my own parents when my mother left service in London to bury herself across that pasture at High House after marrying my father — well, different on the female side, but not the male side, for my father could see no other life save the Birkbeck Estate, and was quite satisfied with a Spartan existence far from civilisation as the world was beginning to know it. I too thought along those lines, but time eventually told a different story, though not before I had spent a few more years at Soigné.

One memory of that 1953 summer stands out in my mind and that was connected with sport. Len Hutton, after bearing the brunt of Australian fast bowling for many lean years had been appointed as the first professional cricket captain of England. Despite having to fight four "backs to the wall" drawn games, he managed to gain victory over Lindsey Hassett's Australians at The Oval and so clinch The Ashes series. Bill Edrich, our Norfolk-born hero, and Denis Compton were at the wicket when the winning hit was made which sent the avid listeners in our guardroom billet into raptures of delight. I believe the notorious bodyline tour of 1933 was the last time this feat had been achieved, and how our batsmen suffered at the hands of retaliatory Aussie fast bowling during the intervening years. Broken bones and cracked heads were commonplace as Ray Lindwall and Keith Miller unleashed a battery of lethal deliveries safe in the knowledge that they in turn only had to face a fast-medium English attack led by the wily, but not intimidating, Alec Bedser. But slowly the worm was turning as at that time a tearaway young fast bowler Freddie Trueman was playing for the R.A.F. Caring nothing for cricket etiquette, we still lived in the strict world of gentlemen and players; the fiery Fred had many early brushes with authority, but eventually emerged to strike up a formidable partnership with Brian Statham. The Wars of the Roses forgotten, the Yorkshire, Lancashire pair gave us the power to retain those Ashes, so dourly won during that summer. No one dared kick sand in our faces for the next few years. Beer flowed freely at Feltwell to celebrate, and after having been repeatedly whipped by those cocky Australians our victory was well worthy of celebration.

Just one more sporting memory takes me back to the Hednesford Training Camp, and a visit to the Wolves ground at Molineux. Seeing in the flesh two of the most famous teams of the early fifties was something to remember. Bert Williams in goal for Wolves, along with Billy Wright, Johnny Hancock, Jimmy Mullen and Stan Cullis also performing for the home team was something to write home about. Coupled with the legendary Jackie Milburn and the Robledo brothers in black and white stripes for Newcastle, this was football far-removed from our usual diet of Division Three South standard served up at Carrow Road. These names, previously only heard on radio or read of in the paper, were real men very capable of serving up skills in the mud of a typical January day. Foul-mouthed sergeants, soaking wet feet on route marches, hours of onion peeling — these slight hindrances in life were forgotten as I stood on the open terraces of a football heaven to watch these legends play. It was the only game I managed to attend whilst in the Midlands, but it was a never-to-be-forgotten occasion.

Final interviews with repeated advice as to the advantages of regular R.A.F. service were duly attended and the advice ignored. A reference with strong recommendation for a career in the civilian police was issued. I had a round of visits to various sections in order to have my clearance form signed and to collect my final wages. My calendar, now black with crossed-off days, had almost reached the end of November. Outstanding leave days had been taken and my enforced service to my country was almost complete. At last, my own demob. party time had arrived. The day I had longed for dawned and through an alcoholic haze I realised that I was once more a civilian. My longed for freedom failed to produce the anticipated euphoria. At 14.00 hours I collected my travel warrant from the duty corporal, humped my kitbag and luggage into the waiting truck, and left R.A.F. Feltwell officially for the last time.

What was I leaving behind? My girl-friend was most important, I suppose; visits to the camp cinema twice a week; lunch times spent in the NAAFI; tea-breaks in the Sally Army hut which was just outside the main camp; two Sunday night runs to the station to supervise returning servicemen and women arriving back on the 22.00 and 23.00 hours trains — duty on the last one meant missing most of Radio Luxemburg's top-twenty tunes. A prompt return could just catch the final top three: "I Believe" and "Answer Me" vied for top spot and suited my blue period of impending departure from the current true love of my life. Don't laugh, even potential muck-carters can wax sentimental on occasions. It's strange how certain hit tunes of the past trigger off memories, another example being "High Noon" which belted out of the Tannoy as we "bulled" our boots in a Hednesford billet. Whenever I hear the strains of

"I believe for every drop of rain that falls a flower grows", or "Answer me, oh my love", I am transported back into the last bitter-sweet weeks before my demob. My fellow corporals were now all National Servicemen with part of their time to complete. David Gold and Ron Atkinson were next in line for Civvy Street, and an avid Lincoln City supporter whose name I cannot recall to mind, had seven months left. The most recent in-comer was "Swannee" Swann, a lad from Norwich who had a few games for the City A team before suffering a badly-injured hand. Playing in goal he tried to save a thunderbolt from the Canaries hot shot, South African-born, Alf Ackerman, and virtually ended his hopes of a professional contract in the process.

I arrived back home complete with a full kit to be kept in good condition, just in case a re-call was necessary in those days, which were far from peaceful. By degrees the clothes and boots graduated downwards into working gear. The only remaining item is the kitbag, still with me today reminding me of those two years when I answered to the number 2540928. Strangely though that kitbag still had a part to play in the jigsaw of my life, and we will meet up with it again if and when I begin writing a third volume, "Life after Soigné.

Chapter 16
Back in Civvy Street

29 November, 1953, and I am now a free man, National Service completed and a carefree life on the farm to look forward to. What more could a man want from life? Yet before a nice home-cooked breakfast had been digested, fears and worries assailed me from all directions. Taking as a yardstick the pain and stiffness I'd suffered during that short excursion into sugar-beet chopping-out at Feltwell, I couldn't see how my soft muscles could withstand the shock of knocking sugar-beet. Experience gathered prior to R.A.F. service left me in no doubt that the work-hardened gang would leave me for dead long before dinner time. No, I couldn't face that situation this year. I must send Charlie Wilson a message via Freddie asking for day work until my flabby body hardened up. Failing that, perhaps a month's holiday until the beeting season concluded would be better. My financial situation quickly vetoed this second idea. If I was to propose marriage to the love of my life at Christmas then money was needed and double-quick at that. The hundred pounds my father had saved to set up home in 1931 wasn't a sufficient sum in 1953, especially as red velvet curtains had been mentioned, a must in that young lady's envisaged love nest. Velvet curtains may have been drawn across windows at the Hall but were never even dreamed of for a tied house. My mother's eyebrows had risen at their mention, and my thin wallet had deflated even further as other girlish dreams had followed in furnishings. No Soigné Farm pay packet would run to such extravagances which had seemed so wonderful whilst sitting in the NAAFI with a cup of tea and a romantic haze blotting out all practicalities. The mud caused by November drizzle threw back a totally different mental picture, wherein my slightly built, lady-like intended, seemed to slip away into the world I had left behind, taking her no more than modest dreams with her. What was worse, though difficult for others to comprehend, was the fact that I could not follow her, whatever my feelings. My feet were well and truly stuck in that Soigné mud for better or for worse.

It wasn't until I returned to the farm and began to odd job around that I discovered a big step forward had occurred in beet harvesting. A new type of plough had been invented. This machine, mounted by powerlift on the rear of a tractor, consisted of heavy metal bars on a frame. These bars were angled so as to push beet from one side and then the other, loosening the root before squeezing two rows into one. This method prevented clay soil being pressed on to the root, thus removing the need to knock beet prior to topping. Also the new technique made a track for wheels by the pushing of two rows into one. This simple but very efficient idea did away with the killing work involved in the knocking process. Having learned this from our two new neighbours at No. 5 and No. 4, Bill Johnson and Leslie Lloyd, I then asked to begin piecework and re-joined the gang as work began on the final field, Swaffham Breck, as near home as it was possible to get.

I palled up straight away with Leslie who had been working at Southacre as a tractor-driver until he fell out with "Flicker Bensley", the foreman. Leslie was the younger son of Wally Lloyd, blacksmith at Westacre, and was as volatile as his father; he never stopped chattering and was a cheerful, happy-go-lucky mate who would swear about anything and everything when a leg-puller wound him up. The very mention of foreman Bensley would produce a stream of highly coloured oaths designed to turn the air blue for the rest of the day. He had already received the nickname of "Flicker" before I arrived, although I never used it and called him Leslie out of respect for our comradeship destined to last throughout my remaining years at Soigné. We were to share all our piecework together and shared many a laugh both at work and over the fence.

Early December gave us a dry, sunny end to the beet season, which was very unusual. Blackie, still in command of the gang, spent all of breakfast time trying to discuss the more intimate details of the camp followers at current service camps and comparing my answers with his own observations of World War 1. Leslie Lloyd, Bill Johnson and myself made up the trio working around a long, four-wheeled trailer, one at each side and one behind. The tractor-driver pulled slowly on each time the rear topper caught up, averaging about six feet or so on a move. Occasionally a side worker with an extra thick patch of beet would begin to fall behind, in which case his mates would take a short wind to allow him to regain his rightful position. My return allowed Harry Ashby to leave in order to begin bullock-feeding at Elbreck. Two other topping gangs worked alongside us, one using the red board-sided, two-wheeled trailers and the other with horse and tumbrils. If four men worked around a conveyance, two were on the right hand side, one on the left, and one behind. Very occasionally a very loud, concerted shout of "Whoa" would rend the air, confirming the fact that one horse had pulled on too far leaving the luckless back topper a twelve foot throw in order to get his beet on board. But otherwise the horse gang was the more peaceful, and were able to hear each other's normal conversation, whereas we others had to shout above the tractor engines in order to converse. The garrulous Leslie kept up a non-stop stream of chatter with our driver just as soon as he drew level with the trailer front, whilst Bill on the opposite side chipped in occasionally with some comment, usually controversial, designed to set Leslie clacking away nineteen to the dozen. Me, well I just concentrated on keeping up behind, sometimes omitting to tap on the trailer back as soon as I had caught up in order to rest my aching back for an extra minute.

Despite the loss of back-breaking knocking, I still found the jump from lazing in the guardroom to heavy, manual work a big hurdle to clear. Being the back marker and a trailer length from the three conversationalists, my verbal contributions were limited to the change of trailers or end of row "back ups", as we called those occasional rests. The lack of conversation allowed my mind to wander back to Feltwell and the mates left behind. Were they sitting over a cup of tea and a cake in the Sally Army refreshment hut? Who was on the bank run to Brandon, armed with a heavy pistol they weren't allowed to use except in self-defence? I could dream of a slight figure in blue sitting with Ron and his girl-friend, Pat, in the NAAFI. Would I get a letter today? The anxious eyes watched for our postman or postwoman each morning. There was hope if they called at No. 6, a hope that would almost certainly be dashed by a quick glance on our sideboard at dinner time. The very observant Bill Johnson quickly interpreted my furtive glances in the postman's direction and set up a "letter watch" with the rest of the gang, with plenty of good-natured banter thrown in. Anything was pounced upon to relieve the monotony felt by those men who had been engaged in a long and hard beeting season.

I think by this time Jean Plummer had taken over the post round from Fred Sculpher who must have been well past retiring age. When Fred and his wife, Sally, gave up the post office it was taken over by Billy "Trot" Taylor and his wife, the premises moving across the road where one room of the Taylors' tied house became a small shop-cum-service counter.

In our quiet backwater any movement on the road was watched with avid interest, and whilst on the subject of postal deliveries and observation of the same, I must mention one occasion when sharp eyes saved the mail. Ted Green, Jack Bly, and Lou Abel were engaged in repairing the high front chimneys at Pretoria and their scaffold provided an excellent observation tower. The faint sound of a motor cycle chugging through the woods beyond Shortrow focused their eyes on the Westacre road. Presently the machine appeared bearing Fred Sculpher on his post round. Most old motor bikes left a trail of blue smoke behind as they laboured along, but on this occasion an unusually dense cloud billowed out from above the exhaust pipe level. As the slumped figure of our postmaster drew nearer, Lou, who had the keenest eyes, yelled out that Fred was on fire. Flickers of flame could be seen just below the big brown post-bag slung across Fred's back. Rushing down the long ladder, Lou ran to the corner, whilst his two companions waved like fury to attract the attention of our flaming postman. Hauling the bike with its tank full of petrol well clear of its rider, Lou turned, then went to help the now flaming postie. Whipping the precious post-bag off, they turned their attention to the seat of the fire, a pocket in Fred's thick Post Office issue topcoat. Coughing and swearing in equal amounts whilst beating his pocket, the cause of the fire soon became obvious to our over-heated carrier of the Royal Mail. His half-smoked pipe had been placed in a pocket on the assumption it was out, and the movement of air caused by the speed of his motor cycle had caused the tobacco to glow once more and ignite the pocket-lining. Everyone had a good laugh when the smoke cleared and the dust settled. Mrs. Sculpher, who was never lost for words especially where her husband was concerned, said, on hearing of the incident, "Serves the old bugger right. He knows he isn't supposed to smoke when on duty. It's a pity it didn't burn his arse". Scant sympathy there it would seem. I wonder if she patched his coat for him.

There was no such excitement for us that day as we worked our way across Swaffham Breck. Hook, lift, top and throw, hook, lift, top and throw was the pattern as the green beet tops attached to a sliver of crown fell away and the white root flew through the air on to the trailer. After a few days my back eased and I wished we were on the first of the season's beet fields instead of the final one. The new system of lifting had halved the agony associated with sugar-beeting and made it, for me at any rate, a rewarding occupation. As the scute rows in front of our cottages were mopped up and the season concluded I felt quite sad. I'd enjoyed the company of Leslie and Bill, their leg-pulling helping to offset the lack of letters coming from Feltwell.

At the weekend I boarded the Saturday afternoon bus to Lynn and, armed with my extra piecework money, bought a Christmas present and card for the love of my life, not realising that by the next weekend I would be left with a redundant present and no girl-friend.

Thus began a very black week in the run up to Christmas, following the familiar pattern well known to our family at that time of year. Charlie, not renowned for his vision in man management, put me with Blackie, Percy and Horrie covering mangold hales on Lower Fifty Acres. You may remember how I loved soiling up hales, be they mangold or potato variety. A whole week of dull, damp weather ensued, with no conversation outside of World War 1 remembrances, and not even a car passing on the road. By Wednesday night I would have given anything to be back in uniform. I felt I should go mad if poor old Blackie told the same tale again. A long, black winter stretched ahead with nothing it seemed to cheer my spirits. Why, oh why had I spurned the chance of regular service in the R.A.F.? After being involved with the constant comings and goings at the camp entrance it was no wonder I felt bereft.

Charlie Wilson called once a day, which hardly helped lift my gloom as the verbal exchange went as follows:

"Morning, my fellows", from Charlie.

"Morning, Charlie."

"Mucky old day again."

"Might brighten later."

"We had a fair drop of rain in the night."

"Ah, I noticed the tank by my back door was running over."

"Heard anything of poor old Jack Havers?"

"He's back in hospital; they say there's no hope."

With this last piece of sombre news Charlie spun round and set off for his bike, scraping the mud from his boots on the road before zigzagging away towards Soigné.

"We shan't see him any more today", said Blackie.

"Nor anyone else", I muttered under my breath. "He was like a breath of fresh air, I don't think."

The one person who was a breath of fresh air was Leslie Richardson when he came past in the afternoon with a load of straw for Elbreck bullocks. Slowing his Fordson tractor opposite our chain-gang, he yelled in his usual "hushed" tones, "Is that all you've done together? Them mangolds will be fruzz long before you get them covered at this rate".

Then, after fielding a barrage of the most highly-coloured ways of telling him to mind his own business, he ground his tractor into gear once more, but not before his stentorian tones rang out with, "It's no wonder Charlie said this job was beginning to stink". A huge grin showing very white teeth split his florid face from ear to lug as he sailed off down the slope towards Waterpit corner, his beret looking for all the world like a black cow pat ground on his black head. Dilberry, standing on the drawbar, made rude signs behind Young Laddie's back before hanging on for dear life as the tractor bucked in the huge pot-holes at the entrance to Elbreck Lane. We all fervently hoped Laddie's load would shake off, but our tormentor was an expert in roping and not one bale rocked off. So passed the only distraction of the day, leaving us to discuss the weather and Blackie's wartime conquests with the opposite sex.

Christmas came and went, the only highlight being two days' paid holiday that went with it. My father milked the High House cows morning and evening, and expressed his annual preference to cheese against the succulent home-reared cockerel at dinner time, but still managed to force himself to eat some, and then sawed firewood on Boxing Day. Ernie Deasley popped in from No. 7 to enjoy a glass of brandy, which Mum kept for medicinal purposes, but otherwise no festive visitors passed under our lintel. All very homely, this was the very essence of the kind of hospitality I had dreamt about for the first eighteen months of National Service. But my mood had changed causing me once more to yearn for that which I did not have. The glitter and alcohol-induced enjoyment beckoned, despoiling all my basic instincts for a contented countryman's life-style. Once again I felt as if I were a square peg in a round hole and it made me a very disagreeable person to live with for the next three months at least.

Just into New Year the mundane plod of cattle-feeding and yard-strawing was relieved by the arrival of Walter Desborough and his threshing tackle. A Fordson Major tractor had by this time replaced the colossal but eye-catching steam engine, so coal and water weren't required. For generations a wagon had been sent to Massingham Station to collect steam coal, as the hirer was required to supply fuel for this power-providing giant. Now a five-gallon drum of T.V.O. and perhaps a top-up of water for a leaky radiator was all a tractor required. Pulling in beside an oat stack on the Hulver, Walter prepared his tackle for about a fortnight's work, all that remained of the whole winter's threshing programme of a few years back. The combine harvester had almost robbed Walter of his livelihood and removed one of the filthiest jobs left on the farm.

The following morning dawned cloudy and damp with a fairly brisk south-westerly wind coming across the open field. Collecting our pitchforks from the farm, Gerald, Leslie Lloyd and myself prepared to mount the stack to release brorches and clear off the thatch. Rolling back this covering of part-decaying rye straw we let it drop away on the field side before piling it behind the wire netting put up by Horrie and Jack Curl to confuse any rats and prevent them getting away. Horrie also collected the thin nut stick brorches, tying them in a neat bundle in readiness for his thatching duties, come next harvest. Owing to a heavy cloud cover we worked away in half darkness for daylight was loath to brighten our world that morning. By eight o'clock everything was ready for action. Nobbie Easter and Walter's drum-feeder stood on top of the huge machine, which was driven by a heavy belt running from tractor to a central axle. From this primary point various smaller belts connected up to riddles and fans, all designed to reduce the flattened sheaves of oats into grain, chaff and straw, sending these separate items out of chutes on its sides. The corn was also graded so that wholesome grain was run into a separate sack to that for the thin, poor quality tail corn. Chaff was blown into large sacks on one side of the machine, whilst straw spewed out at the back where either a straw-pitcher or buncher sent it on to the straw stack. Horrie and Jack teamed up to take care of straw, whilst Blackie and Walter bagged up and weighed the oats into twelve-stone railway sacks. Lastly the chaff-sacking task was undertaken by Alfie Dann, a prime example of generations of inbreeding and resembling a character from Dickens with his short, humped figure, his collar up, and trilby hat pulled down. Alfie had walked the four or so miles from Castleacre to find employment and this was his reward.

So there I was, standing on the pitched roof of the stack, waiting for the low hum of a slowly- turning drum to accelerate into a whirring, shaking monster, ready to receive the first sheaves of the day. During my days as rat-catching schoolboy and then apprentice chaff-carter my ambition had been to work on the stack, lifting summer-bronzed sheaves where rats lurked and mice showered out into a hostile environment of dogs and thrashing sticks. I had seen heroes such as 'Lijah Bloy and Arthur Wright hauling up layer after layer of flat, golden sheaves, and with seemingly effortless ease walk across the stack to deposit them on the drum-board. To my boyhood, rose-coloured thinking, this must have been a job made in Heaven, and on a par with cutting corn using tractor and binder. To think that at long last I had reached a pinnacle in my career, monarch of all I surveyed from the top of that stack. This was real living.

Gerald took up his station at the south end of our task for the day, and I took up mine at the opposite gable, with Leslie in central position, just above Nobbie who stood ready, with shining blade, to cut the sheaf bands before his drum-feeder shook the shaggy-headed oats into the gaping mouth of an ever-hungry thresher. From there they were whipped in by revolving beaters which knocked the sun-ripened grain on to a series of riddles and shakers designed to withhold or let through, depending upon their hole size and respective duties. For half-an-hour we gradually worked down the roof, being more than able to supply the drum without undue physical effort.

A short break for breakfast allowed us to walk down to the drum-board, across the now silent monster, and down a short ladder propped alongside. Standing with army coat over my shoulders and eating a cheese sandwich allowed me to view the familiar scene. With some pride I took in the three pitchforks standing up against the sky. I, in my humble opinion, was one of the three most important men in the whole operation. The speed of the day's operation and the final finishing time would be in our hands. Our work rate would be the key to an early finish because, as mentioned in a previous chapter, one stack was a day's work and when finished the gang went home.

Everything went well as we removed the roof and the flattened stack reduced to the level of the protruding drum-board. Frequently having to slow up in order to allow Leslie to clear the middle meant that my back hardly reached sweating point. On the odd occasion when Nobbie needed to clear an overloaded board Leslie sought for some mischief to fill his time. Peeping over the stack edge he saw the hunched figure of Alfie Dann tending his chaff box below. Gently lifting a sheaf covered in spoiled grain and rat droppings, he shook it over the side above unsuspecting Alfie's head. The debris from above made our Dickensian comrade pull his hat down further and hunch deeper into his old coat. Our muffled laughter was drowned by the noise of machinery and the practical joke continued until Alfie caught sight of Leslie's grinning face over the edge. Letting out an enraged roar, our victim leapt back to shake his fist at his convulsed tormentor.

"Blast you, Lloyd, pack it up", and grabbing his pitchfork the poor old chap bayonet-charged the hanging chaff sack and shook it so violently that it came unhooked allowing oat flights to blow in a blinding cloud all over him. We laughed so much our sides ached and when a poker-faced Gerald looked down to ask whether Alfie was all right, we started all over again.

"Tell that Lloyd I'll put this fork through him if he comes down here."

"No need for him to tip that muck over you, Alfie; I shouldn't put up with it if I was you", returned one of the biggest tricksters on the farm, still keeping the straightest of faces. Needless to say, when a mid-morning break for sack-loading came, Leslie daren't come off the stack for fear of Alfie's pitchfork, discretion being considered the better part of valour. Those kinds of situations helped everyone forget the sweat, muck and grind of heavy, manual jobs and the time seemed to speed away.

By dinner time Alfie's temper had subsided, although it was noted that "Lloyd" sat at the opposite end of our group as we huddled around a straw bale fire well away from the site where one spark could have had disastrous consequences in the tinder-dry straw. Jack tried to fan the flames of Alfie's anger by remarking how much dust nestled on the brim of his hat, which brought forth more obscenities with the sole purpose of removing the last vestiges of honour from Leslie's parentage and ended with the much used phrase, "Bloody Lloyd". Eventually peace was restored, though not a long-lasting one, by a slice of Mrs. Lloyd's home-made fruit cake being passed along the line and ending in the dusty one's cavernous mouth. Thus all was forgiven before our corn stack reached a level on a par with the chaff-sacker's pitchfork.

Resuming our work after the luncheon adjournment, with the wind still gusting across an open field, we were by that time well below the drum-board level and pitching everything above our heads. It was our turn to receive a shower of loose grain, dust and rat droppings with every forkful hoisted upwards. The increased effort needed, produced more sweat on my back and highlighted my lack of work fitness in tough conditions. Finally I felt forced to divest myself of the thick jacket, which kept the cool wind from my overheating muscles, an action immediately frowned upon by my older and more experienced companions. "You'll be stiff tomorrow, my boy", they prophesied, giving a solemn shake of the head. Of course, they were right, as I found out when my bootlaces seemed to be well out of reach for tying the following morning. Normally all sweat was sealed in by layers of heavy clothes traditionally worn by East Anglian labouring men, and left there until it dried once more from body heat. My back just turned cold and certainly stiffened up causing me to realise the folly of my ways.

Horrie and Jack now looked down on us from the dizzy heights of their golden-coloured straw stack as we gathered up the last layers of flattened sheaves. Thankfully the thin layer of barley straw, forming a damp-preventing bottom layer, appeared at last. Nobbie cut the last band and then swept all loose straw and grain into the drum. Slowly the frantic hum of machinery slowed and, with a final click of belts on wheels, silence came. The day's work was almost complete. The stack bottom would now be slowly turned and the hidden rats beneath killed before they could flee to their numerous holes in the nearby bank. Being an oat stack, the rat population was greatly reduced as, for some reason, this type of grain held less attraction to the rat palate than wheat or barley. Nevertheless Soigné corner was and always had been notorious for its rat infestation amongst thorn and elm roots alongside the track, and this year was no exception. Turning the half-mouldy straw revealing an infrastructure of tunnels produced fifteen minutes of sport where pitchforks and nut sticks vied with each other to knock over as many vermin as possible. Every trouser bottom had been tied from the outset so that any rat running towards our feet was dealt a quick stamp with a heavy boot without fear of repeating Charlie Wilson's experience at Elbreck when a young rat ran up his open trouser leg. When the last forkful had been turned and the last rat knocked over we all joined forces to load the remaining bagged corn for transport to the barn. Oat sacks of twelve stones only were easily lifted by two men on to a trailer without using a stool to rest them half way up, as was the case for heavier grains. With Young Laddie seizing their tops as they came up with a swing the job was soon done. Finally the heavy metal and wooden weighing equipment, complete with weights, joined the spare, empty grain sacks in readiness for transport to Lower Thirty Acres where three barley stacks awaited our services. Knocking the worst of the accumulated dust and chaff from our clothes we picked up our bags and coats in readiness for home. Walter Desborough was already marshalling his threshing tackle for the short trip through the farmyard and up to White Gate corner. As we mounted our machines for Pretoria, Alfie Dan started out on his long trek back to Castleacre where he lived with his aunt. His father, old Dan Boldero, had re-married to a young girl whilst in his early seventies and fathered twins. Billy Dan, Alfie's elder brother, still lived at home, but our chaff-sacker had moved out to go into lodgings. His aunt, it would seem, objected to her lodger hanging around the house all day, and had sent him forth to seek gainful employment. Failing repeatedly to be taken on in the vicinity of Castleacre, he at last walked to Soigné in search of work. The Major decreed that if Boldero was prepared to walk that far for work he should be given a job. His foreman and fellow workers often doubted he deserved the Major's patronage, but were powerless to do anything about it. Here was a case of "it's not what you know, but who you know". Often Major Birkbeck would be driving towards the Hall as the humped figure of Alfie walked home. "Get in, Boldero", the Major would order, and then proceed to drive him to the far Park gates which halved the poor old chap's walking distance. Eventually a tricycle was bought, Alfie having no sense of balance for an ordinary cycle, and Hubert Watts, the Hall chauffeur given the task of teaching Alfie to ride. This was no easy thing to do as head, hands and feet had little co-ordination, but eventually Hubert's prodigy rode proudly in and out of Castleacre, thanks to Westacre Estate's answer to the Social Services.

Whilst Alfie plodded his weary way home, I was indoors preparing to rid myself of all the dust and sweat of a day's threshing. Firstly a large, zinc bath was carried in and placed before the living room fire; soft rainwater had been heated in two large saucepans on the front trivet and these were tipped in, then cooled to body temperature. Drawing the window curtains, stripping off and standing in the bath, I soaped and scrubbed the grime away, trying not to leave too many tide marks for wiping on the white bath towel. A change of shirt and underclothes allowed the others to dry in readiness for another day of dust on the morrow. Note, the soiled clothes did not go into the washing machine – the only washer we had was my mother's hands, coupled with a bar of hand-washing soap. So you see, working clothes had to last a week by sheer necessity if not by choice. The Estate coffers might run to the cost of one tricycle, but the very mention of piped water, electricity and flush toilets sent grown men reeling and reaching for the smelling salts. But there, I don't suppose the Estate management raised much dust, pen-pushing, so they wouldn't realise the personal hygiene problems of those that did. That was the way the radical thinking lady of the house at No. 6 Pretoria saw it, and her eldest son was fast coming round to a similar point of view. It was no wonder my late girl-friend shied away from our primitive infrastructure. Bathing in a pie dish and wiping one's behind on squares of newspaper in a draughty outside lavatory isn't every girl's dream, especially after having visions of red velvet curtains at every window and plush carpets on the floor.

Chapter 17
Old Seasons, New Methods

Apart from the threshing, early 1954 held nothing more exciting than an occasional trip to Norwich to see them trying to win another Division 3 South league game. Jack Eagle ran a coach from Castleacre for home matches, and this came as far as Soigné to collect Gerald and Charlie Andrews, and, after the latter took over as cowman from Dick Welham, Coddy and Terry Eagle. Coddy had moved up from Westacre to become shepherd in Charlie's place. These four were very keen supporters, only missing occasional games when work commitments intervened. By the following season brother Michael and myself became regular attenders, sharing the suffering and pain well known to Norwich supporters through the years, but having plenty of football news to discuss during the week.

A severe sporting set-back came at the annual general meeting of the Westacre Cricket Club where it was decided not to run a team the following season due to lack of members. This state of affairs came about after several older members were forced to retire through advancing years and long-term injuries. Several senior schoolboys were on the verge of becoming worthwhile cricketers, but were considered just that bit too young to compete with men. I believe it was the first time for many years that the village would be without a team which, despite only playing friendly matches, enjoyed considerable support, not least from the Birkbeck family. Captain Harry Birkbeck, who had played for the County, was president and turned out occasionally. The lack of opportunity for facing a hard cricket ball propelled at high speed did not worry me, but watching, scoring, and travelling to other villages for away matches did appeal, and I was sorry to lose that side of the game.

Leslie Lloyd, who was a keen bowls player, tried to interest me, without much luck, although I did travel with the team on warm, summer evenings, but more for something to do than sporting knowledge or support. Bowls was still considered to be an old man's sport, the place where retired cricketers spent their declining years. Leslie was the exception and set a new trend in a game that now more than ever caters for players of all ages.

By discussing summer sport, I have jumped the gun slightly. First of all, spring cultivations need be dealt with. They followed the same pattern as before National Service, namely full use of all available tractor power and stock-feeding duties being filled by we non-mechanical men using horsepower. This suited me admirably as it reunited me with horses after quite a long separation. My only mechanised jaunt came on a Saturday afternoon when one tractor-driver couldn't work and I was asked to finish harrowing-in seed on Waterpit. Seated on a Fordson Major tractor, I swept up and down the length of that field, just feeling confident enough to turn at each end and keep a moderately straight line in between. I don't think I enjoyed it quite as much as my previous "harrowing" experience with Beauty beside the peaceful haven of Soigné Wood. The noisy grind of a tractor can soon dull one's brain as well as shut out all natural country sounds. It was a novelty, but not one I craved to repeat, although riding as opposed to walking the land did have its appeal. Monday morning brought low rumblings on the grapevine that Charlie had upset the unwritten pecking order by asking me to work on Saturday afternoon. One or two labouring men with tractor-driving aspirations objected to me jumping the queue, although I had no idea there was a line of succession. My immediate reaction was to say, "Bugger the tractors, you are very welcome to shake your guts out on them", and never got on one for many a moon. The incident did confirm one fact and it was that only certain backsides were shaped for sitting on tractor seats, and mine wasn't one of them. Poor old Charlie didn't have an easy task keeping a balanced ship for a large percentage of his men tended to choose what work they did, and could be damned awkward if things panned-out differently. A new broom brought in to break this progressively constricting mould would have done a power of good. As it was things continued to decline until the tail wagged the dog and Charlie Wilson found he was hemmed in, unable to please himself or many other people either. It was a shame to see a very decent man being manipulated by those of stronger character whose sole aim was to achieve an easy working life for themselves at the expense of their workmates, and the farm as a whole. There certainly was a pecking order for muck-cart with a very different set of names at the top compared with that other order appertaining to seat jobs.

By this time an artificial fertiliser drill was in great demand. More and more bags of chemicals had been unloaded from Geoffrey Thaxton's green lorry during the winter months and piled high in the redundant stables. Having found myself under these awkward-to-handle, paper sacks on their way into store, the spring cultivation push gave me the doubtful pleasure of helping to carry them out again. Leslie Richardson was in charge of the manure drill, and we helped him load his trailer for the day every morning. This task was always accompanied by an excess of friendly banter as Young Laddie piled enough bags on to last any normal worker two days, just in case he ran out. With sweat running down his face he roared off out of the yard to spend the day covering as many acres as was possible, hardly sparing the time to burn empty bags on the headland. He always put in a day's work far beyond the call of duty. At the end of his season the drill was always dismantled and every part cleaned, then left to soak in black sump oil to prevent rusting from the corrosive content of chemicals. On one occasion Charlie wanted to send him on another job before all the cleaning was complete. "Be it on your head, Charlie", roared Laddie, "those plates will all rust and be of no use next season". "I suppose you're right, my fellow", conceded his foreman and quickly retracted his orders Of course, Leslie was correct about the rust, and Charlie knew he wouldn't find anyone else too keen to handle artificial fertiliser for such a large acreage and care for the machinery as was being done at that moment.

Warm days of late April saw us once more at muck-cart. Gerald, Jack Curl, Leslie Lloyd and myself were incarcerated in south-facing yards at High House. The trapped heat of the sun and rising heat from compacted manure made life very unpleasant. I can well remember having sandwiches of rather salty bacon, and due to a bone-dry mouth, being unable to chew and swallow. Phew! Did we long to get out into the fields for summer work. All too slowly the seedling beet showed in thin rows across the first fields sown, making our hands itch to handle a hoe for chopping-out. Leslie had arranged with his blacksmith father, Wally, to make us some new hoe heads. These heads could then be attached to the long, wooden handles already in our sheds. At last, armed with our new hoes we set off for Sixteen Acres behind Mink Belt which, rather strangely, being a north-facing field, was the first crop sown. Another change had occurred during my absence in the R.A.F. and this appertained to the piecework system for chopping-out. Instead of working all together as a gang, individual plots had been measured and staked in units of ten rows. Either working singly, or in groups, we all selected a numbered plot. Leslie Lloyd, Bill Johnson and myself teamed up together, and so took these adjoining stakes with my Uncle Will Bumfrey working alone on the next ten rows. Having entered the field from the bottom end adjacent to the Heath road, we set off towards the distant Mink Belt with myself in pole position, then Leslie, with Bill bringing up the rear. With my new hoe blade flashing in the early morning sun, the soil fairly dry and light, I made good progress, staying just ahead of Leslie without too much effort. The clink of hoe blades against stone the only sound to be heard, all heads were down and eyes concentrating on singling as many cotton-like sugar-beet seedlings as possible first time. Slowly the line of men spread out as the faster hoers left their slower workmates behind. Obviously the faster one could hoe, the more money could be earned. Before the halfway mark had been reached one smaller figure lay well out in front. Nobbie Easter was by far the fastest hoeman there, his lack of inches helping him to hoe up straight without being too far from the end of his implement. As we entered the last quarter of our rows he was already turning and on his way back. Having completed two rows and reached the bottom fence once more, it was time for breakfast. Blackie, his old head grey with experience, cautioned Nobbie to go steady until the price per hundred yards of row had been fixed.

"Mustn't let them" (Charlie Wilson and Willie Thaxton) "think the going is too good", was the veteran's advice. So, taking note of his word of warning, we carried on at a steady pace until about 11 o'clock when "they" arrived and we all gathered round to set a price. Blackie led our side of the negotiations, with Barney Hooks as support.

Willie led off with the usual opening gambit: "You've all made a good start I see".

"Yes, we wanted to get underway."

"Well, we don't want to hold you up too long over this bit of business."

"No, let's get on while it's fine, time is money with us, you know."

Please take the following prices as examples, for I can't remember what we were paid, but I can assure you no one earned enough to retire on!

Willie again: "Now, what did we pay last year, 4d a length?"

"You know very well it was 6d, Willie", a younger, impatient voice came from the back.

"Oh yes, that's right, and you fixed a very good bargain there. I think we were over-generous then. I was going to say 6d this time."

Growls of discontent rise from the back, and one younger hoeman flings his implement into the hedge and I feel my hackles rise at this same old argument.

All the time this discourse takes place Charlie is silent, an occasional kick at the ground his only contribution.

"They say they want 9d, Willie, and that's only if the going is as good as this."

"My fellows, you'll bankrupt us", burst out Charlie, "we would be better off hiring Irishmen."

"Best thing you can do then, let them buggers break their backs for nothing", that younger voice breaks in once more.

At this juncture we know the two officials will withdraw a short distance and converse in low tones, an occasional throw back of Charlie's trilby-covered head indicates a slight disagreement, but the flat cap of Willie seems to carry more weight in their private argument. Whilst this slight altercation takes place we all shuffle rather self-consciously and one or two take the opportunity to drink from their flasks.

At last negotiations recommence as Willie, all smiles, and Charlie, very sombre, walk back along the headland.

"Let's split the difference, then", says "all smiles". "If we forget about halfpennies and settle for 7d and keep the tractor hoe close in front, will that do?"

A rumble runs through the assembled company before 8d becomes their last and lowest settlement figure.

Once more Charlie's head flings back with force, giving risk to his neck muscles and almost upsetting his hat. But Willie, the veteran of many years' bargaining, suddenly appears to capitulate and shakes Blackie's hand to seal the bargain at 8d per 100 yards singled and scored.

"We know you fellows will do a good job, so we'll let you have a good price." With these generous words from the bailiff ringing in our ears we prepare for resumption of work. My hoe is retrieved from the hedge where the display of controlled histrionics had deposited it, and off up the field we all hoed. As I went, my thoughts turned over the events just witnessed. Had I been in any way instrumental in the final price settlement, which seemed, on the face, to have come down fractionally on our side of the fence? The further I hoed and the more I thought, tended to sow doubts into the mind. By the time we turned and prepared to hoe back, I was convinced that what I had just witnessed, was part of a carefully orchestrated farce, and 8p per 100 yards' hard graft was the preconceived price, carried in that old fox Willie Thaxton's head, well before he had left High House, safe in the knowledge that men living in tied houses, combined with those aged over 60 who would be asking for favours to be done on arable-cropped allotments at Castleacre, could bring very little force to bear on the argument. But what of we few single, free men, were we to continue this subservient bargaining? Our only earnings were in the pay-packet. Even with a subsidised rent, low-price milk, and free firewood, or use of farm implements, those aforementioned employees were very poorly paid. What of us who enjoyed none of these perks and needed to make full financial use of the prime time in our labouring lives? We technically worked for an even lower rate of pay. Yes, my thinking began to manufacture a hair shirt, which grew coarser with time, and eventually caused an unbearable irritant and the parting of the ways for me and Soigné Farm.

Enough of looking into the future, there is work to be done and lots of 8d per 100 yards to be earned. The crop had been tractor-hoed using static blades set along bars on a powerlift frame on the rear of a tractor. Brum Chase and Georgie Wright had set up their respective machines as near the precious beet seedlings as possible. By steering the tractor accurately they made a very good job of killing weeds, although even then at least two inches remained in our rows. Also, the two rows adjacent to the track compressed by the heavy tractor wheel, were hard and often in a slight depression, making singling much more difficult. These problems became accentuated as the season progressed, plants and weeds larger and field conditions drier. In saying this, let me take nothing away from those two drivers' skill, for we were lucky to have these very conscientious workmates ahead of us. The art of chopping-out at speed is in the initial strike. Hit hard with the first chop thus causing the smaller plants in the group to fall sideways, leaving the larger seedling, or "cock" plant upright. A second chop through the row ahead of the cock plant will clear the ground, with the exception of a small wedge behind the plant. Now the urge is to leave this and proceed with all speed to the next plant, but it's a percentage bet that contained in the tiny wedge of soil is a weed seed. If left this seed will blossom into a tall, very healthy thistle or fat hen by the time you return to "score" the crop in approximately four weeks. I always pushed this soil away from the back, leaving one prime beet seedling with clear soil all round. If a second thread-like beet refuses to be parted from its mate, then it was left, for time was of the essence when on piecework.

I found I could always hoe easier if I led my two mates and endeavoured to keep pole position. If by chance Leslie had a length of already single plants and surged ahead, I only had to wait for one of the numerous passing 'planes to fly over. Leslie, who was an aeroplane enthusiast, would stop to give us the make, a short potted history, and likely destination. This enabled us to speed up and leave him once more trailing the field, usually swearing well at our retreating backs. Some wag would spout, "Come on, Flicker, you're not at Southacre now". Leslie's work rate would increase along with the variety in choice of swear words. At dinner time, a rest was taken in the shade of hedgerow trees, with our sacks spread amongst curled bracken fronds just emerging. Very little disturbance comes from traffic on the adjoining Gayton to Massingham road, maybe one car passing in the forty minutes we lay there. As one we rose up at 12.40, Will expressing his oft' repeated phrase, "There's no rest for the wicked".

The sun now fast reaching its zenith for the day pours down on us, and as we bend forward, reflected heat hits our faces. The tiny seedlings wilt under this rising heat making separation more difficult, but on the plus side no mud adheres to our blades blunting that first clean cut so essential to this job.

By mid-afternoon we reach our bags once more for a much-needed drink. Will, working the next plot to us, had struggled a bit in keeping pace. We took a leisurely drink and my uncle, arriving fractionally later, had just poured the last of his tea from a flask when, with a wink and a nod, we immediately set off again in an attempt to make him swear. "I'm buggered", says Will, "hent we got time to have a drink now?" "Time is money for us, Will", we three younger bloods explain. "It's alright for you rich old bachelors." Hoeing furiously, we don't quite catch his mumbled reply through a mouthful of lukewarm tea — but you can be sure it wasn't anything complimentary. Of course, there was no need for him to go at our speed as the one idea of individual plots was to allow each hoeman to set his own pace. I think Will felt he needed company on the long haul from Massingham Heath to Mink Belt.

The sixteen-acre field was soon covered by the score or so men. As each numbered plot was completed, its hoer carefully noted the number, and then submitted it to the foreman, who, having previously measured its length, worked out the money to be paid. We would draw at the rate of 6d per 100 yards, and leave 2d for the scoring later. Our next stop was Lower Thirty Acres, working there the week before the Whit Monday Bank Holiday. On Friday the afternoon was very warm and we worked in shirt sleeves.

Old Seasons, New Methods

Returning to the Walton Green Lane end where our clothes had been left, and about half-way across there suddenly blew up a very keen north-easterly movement of air. I felt the almost knife-like cooling across my back and shoulders, but thought nothing of it. By Saturday morning a severe gnawing pain lay across my shoulders and I hardly knew how to wield the hoe. Thankfully, Sunday and Monday allowed treatment to ease the discomfort and by work resumption on Tuesday most of the pain and stiffness had gone. From then on I always worked with a long-sleeved jersey tied round my middle in readiness to shield my back from similar rapid cooling. I learned the hard way why fast bowlers always don their long sweaters at the completion of each of their overs. Our elder companions still wore a waistcoat and this, although opened at the front, always remained to protect the back on such occasions.

It was about half-way through the season when we worked a plot next to the ultra-fast hoer, Nobbie Easter. Nobbie hardly ever started work before 8 o'clock and left off at half past three, earning more than we plodders even then. I remember he rode an old Panther motor cycle that had belonged to one of the Birkbeck sons, then my Uncle John before Nobbie purchased it and set about restoring it to very efficient working order.

"I wish I could hoe like you, Nobbie", I said. "You make it look so easy."

"Well", he replied, "you want to open that hoe head first of all." Seizing my hoe, he put the head between two, closely-growing ash saplings and pulled on the handle. This rather alarming pressure opened the angle between blade and handle by about two inches

"There we are, you can keep your back straight now", he told me.

I was amazed at the difference it made and that realigned tool stayed with me throughout my hoeing career.

Gradually we worked our way through all sugar-beet fields, then mangolds and marrow-stemmed kale. The object of the whole exercise from management point of view was to leave a single plant every six inches, free from weeds and couch grass. This pattern was said to give the heaviest weight of beet per acre when harvested. I must admit my rows were of beet at around nine inches average, which, on the good soil of Soigné gave beet with bigger roots, which were easier to harvest and, in my humble opinion, the same weight of crop. Certainly the scoring or second round of work undertaken in sequence immediately after singling finished was an easy trip. Those workers who left a large number of doubles and weeds the first time had an horrendous job trying to tame a thick jungle. I found the ease of scoring well worth the extra effort put in when the land was clear and weeds easy to locate. Let me just explain that there were no sprays for use on weed infestation in broad-leaved crops such as sugar-beet at that time.

Any limited chemical spraying used on corn crops was carried out by Bob Clarke who, quite early in his career, indicated he was not built for hand hoeing. So it was that Bob took on the early spraying duties and miraculously lived to tell the tale. Sitting on an open tractor seat (cabs hadn't reached our neck of the woods) and with a tank fitted close behind by powerlift, Bob probably took in lungs full of poison whenever the wind travelled faster than he did. Of course there was a limited warning printed on the metal containers alongside mixing quantities, but no one realised how lethal some of the new sprays were. Perhaps Bob was supplied with rubber gloves, but I fear little else in the way of protection. The very first experiment with a spray was conducted during the war on Squires field where a heavy infestation of docks was treated with sulphuric acid. This corrosive material came in large glass carboys surrounded with straw, and contained in a metal casket. The sprayed acid remained on the large expanse of dock leaf, but ran down the narrow-leaved wheat crop. The docks burned up and died down, whilst the wheat thrived with little or no competition. I expect the sprayer was supplied by the War-ag. I know the empty carboys remained lying in the field hedge for many years until the metal caskets rusted and the glass was broken. Note the lack of care taken to dispose of such child-unfriendly items, and I doubt if any more protective measures were employed when Bob began work with his tiny sprayer.

Leslie Richardson continued with his artificial-manure drill, spreading a top dressing on all grain crops. As previously mentioned, Brum Chase and Georgie Wright tractor-hoed the root crops before and after they had been chopped out. Mechanical hoeing continued until it was impossible to run tractor wheels between the rows. A final trip through the crop with a cultivator tine, down each row centre, broke up the hard pan caused by heavy wheels, thus allowing moisture to feed hungry roots, as opposed to running off into bare headlands. After this, the field, with its overall covering of large, green leaves, was closed to work and the beet crop left to manufacture sugar until yellowing foliage in the autumn indicated it was time for harvesting. The view from a convenient gateway often showed strips of heavy weed infestation where lesser hoemen had "slipped the collar" in making a poor job of cleaning their plot on the second visit. This inferior work carried the label "a good piece of slubbery", indicating a lazy workman. Tall weeds, such as thistles, fat hen and an occasional dock were very obvious; creeping plants, namely crab grass and twitch, strangled at ground level, leaching goodness from the beet. Weed infestation had, of course, increased due to combining where weed seeds spread back on the land grew like cress under ideal, well-manured conditions prepared for root crops. As the last of the kale crop was singled and cleaned, often with plants already six inches or more in height, in iron-hard ground, we gladly hung up our hoes for the season. The next time we entered the root fields would be late September when our sugar-beet hooks would be the only tools needed by us for three months at least.

Hay crops were now at their best for harvesting. Tractor-drawn grass cutters were still used on Soigné, although power-driven, tractor-mounted machines were widely available. Changes were taking place in the gathering of hay though, and the age-old method of loose material being cocked and then carted, had been superseded by baling. These oblong parcels were then stood on end, in groups, to dry out a little more before stacking in the field corner as tradition decreed. Lifting and conveying was easier and slightly less dusty, but stacking had its problems. Corners had to be tied in to prevent bales sliding out, and the completed structure resembled a heap rather than a thing of pride and beauty standing four-square for all to admire. Difficulty also arose in thatching, which was almost impossible, although by covering first with a load of loose straw, a semi-pitched roof was produced. As no Dutch barns existed, efforts were made to use large, brick-built barns such as Rats Hall and High House. Hauling heavy bales to the roof in dusty, airless conditions was terrible, and we field men had the best of a bargain then. At that time silage hadn't entered the winter-feed equation, at Soigné anyway, but an experimental clamp was tried in the bottom corner of the Hulver at a later stage. I wasn't engaged in this venture, as was the case with anything new — only the select few superior brains were allowed to take part. We at-a-distance spectators were amazed to see a tractor running up and down the sloping heap of green grass, and buckets of molasses being tipped sparingly over its surface. Buck-rakes were used to convey the grass from field to clamp, and the whole exercise caused many a disbelieving shake of a grizzled head as to the wisdom of "making hay like that". I cannot recall if this first silage clamp was covered, but I do remember the soggy, black extremities of the area. Against all expectations, cattle seemed to like this foul-looking, high-smelling, silage when fed it on cold, winter pastures. Not so keen was my mother who declared my boots smelt worse than pig muck and decreed they spend the night in the shed. My clothes weren't much better, but luckily neither they nor myself were banished to such extremities of the family home.

So the summer passed with the majority of time spent in gang-work, and the company lifted my spirits and slowly dissolved my yearning to re-enter the R.A.F.. Leslie persuaded me to accompany the bowls club on away matches in lieu of cricket, which had been suspended for the season, as previously mentioned. Not the height of excitement I suppose, but it was the case of any port in a storm, and the pint at close of play was always enjoyable. Leslie was good company, and Joe Bly, now retired from cricket anyway, always made me welcome.

Harvest came and went. The traditional harvest was fast disappearing. Combines were here to stay, taking a bigger slice of the crop each year, with eventually bindering confined to feed oats, and an occasional field of wheat or barley. With the decline in the number of stacks, thatching straw became almost a thing of the past. Only straw bales were left to be cleared on piecework, and, despite quite a good price per acre being paid, extra harvest money for those unconnected with combining became almost non-existent.

Just one story I omitted to tell came when we were chopping-out on Little Ashbreck. The demob. of the last corporal in my batch at Feltwell came around in June. Biking off after work, I planned to join in the celebrations, which lasted 'til quite a late hour. Being unable to mount my cycle safely afterwards, I spent the night on the floor of the guardroom billet. Boy, was I stiff next morning as I tried to clear my head and return for work. Arriving well hung-over, I tried valiantly to single all those double and treble beet I saw before my bloodshot eyes. When a semi-eclipse of the sun took place later I thought the end of the world had come as an answer to my prayers for deliverance from my head-splitting torture. It was then I realised the sheer futility of heavy drinking, and vowed to mend my ways. With that celebratory hangover I said farewell to Feltwell and cut all ties with the R.A.F. and settled down to life once more at Soigné.

Chapter 18
Heroes in Yellow and Green

The summer of 1954 saw the start of a new venture at Soigné. Continued advance by the combine harvester meant that more and more grain flooded the market in late July and August keeping prices relatively low, except for high quality, malting barley. On-farm storage also became a must, and so new ideas had to be implemented. First of all a huge hole was excavated in front of the barn by a building firm from Gayton. The very fact of Ted Green and his band of Estate maintenance men being augmented by outside contractors raised eyebrows amongst the old brigade. Various theories were put forward by hoers as they cycled through the farmyard en route to far flung beet crops, as to the purpose of the aforementioned hole. Geoffrey Thaxton informed us on good authority that a pit to hold loose corn was the answer, and this reservoir would feed a dresser to be constructed on the upper barn floor. Any new moves in age-old custom were used to the full as grist for our mill of discussion, and this project was no exception. Older men saw this rapid progress into bulk handling of corn as an end to traditional harvest, and the final nail in the coffin of their lifelong skills in stacking, thatching, and also winter employment with the threshing tackle. Their worst fears were, of course, realised, although not in that first year. Younger, labouring men saw the disappearance of extra piecework money, for with the exception of straw bales, there would be nothing to clear from the land. Harvest was classed as the best hope for a bonus if weather conditions were good. Only men with mechanical aspirations seemed to view these progressions with any kind of hope on the financial side. Dawn to dusk tractor-driving, or machine-operating, as barn men, would certainly benefit the élite, or so it seemed at those headland discussion forums. "We shall be in the money", ribbed Artie Keeley who hoed with Geoffrey Thaxton and John Bumfrey. Artie liked to have a foot in each camp when there was money to be earned, and never wasted a chance to rub we labourers up the wrong way with his sly sense of humour.

Eventually the steep, concrete-sided pit was finished, and dressing machinery set up inside the barn. Two bright-red, two-wheeled tipping trailers arrived, complete with tin-covered floors. The scene was set for Soigné Farm to enter the mechanical age with a vengeance, although that first year was a bit of a struggle, with too many men getting in each other's way; but eventually a settled picture emerged, with Will Bumfrey being in charge of the corn-bagging, and Gerald Andrews supplying the main manual support, when able to steer his sack barrow around the army of "lookers-on", who hung about this new toy. If memory serves me correctly, tractors driven by Brum Chase and Georgie Wright hauled the new trailers to and from the combines, winding the high-sided bodies upwards into a tipping position over the pit by means of a manually-operated handle. Hydraulic tippers hadn't been considered, mainly on the basis of extra cost, I imagine. Artie Keeley and Bob Clarke drove the large, red, Massey Harris combines round and round those fields of barley, with trailers running alongside to receive threshed grain driven out by an auger from the holding tank whilst on the move. No need to stop in order to fill sacks now. Harvest was on the march at Soigné, with machines pushing manual labour into the background.

Following the combines came a straw baler, which gathered up the fluffy rows of loose straw and rammed it into oblong bales before tying lengthways with two, thick, twine strings holding the whole together. Each bale was deposited on to the ground in much the same way as shoofs had been behind the binder, only at a larger distance apart. After carting a few acres of oats and wheat, we labouring gang set about clearing these bales for winter bedding, stacking them in heaps; one couldn't call them stacks, as they were of little use in resisting autumn and winter rainfall. The skill had gone overnight, and with it any pride in a job well and neatly done. Clear the field and get the money was the only incentive. To be fair, Willie and Charlie gave us a good price per acre to help compensate for our loss of earning power associated with a real traditional corn harvest. I doubt we lost out at all really, for most harvests showed very little profit to the workers after a spell of wet weather which came in most years. Leslie Lloyd and I pitched bales, and Gerry Deasley loaded. In spite of the long distances walked, the job was very enjoyable with good, clean air, no pressure, and plenty of jovial banter to pass the time. Gerry did "download" occasionally, but the field gang could easily keep pace with stackers who struggled to tie corners in order to keep some semblance of shape to their heaps. I didn't realise this would be my last harvest outside in God's fresh air with sunshine warming my back. I enjoyed it as we waited, almost snoozing, for an empty trailer to come out. Pitching was the best job as both loading and stacking were carried out by manhandling the bales, which cut and scratched hands and soon wore holes in trouser legs constantly in contact with rough bale sides. Some dust and pheasant droppings descended as the bale passed upside-down above your head, but this was a small price to pay for being able to use a fork. An occasional extra-heavy bale, collected under a wood side, needed a two-pronged attack, and in such cases Leslie and I joined forces to avoid the risk of rupture, which was a constant fear amongst younger men, whose older workmates had been forced to wear an uncomfortable support for many years, as a result of rash lifting in their youth. Dotted amongst the fields of golden stubble, the green canopy of beet rows began to

Heroes in Yellow and Green

show yellow-edged leaves, and the next harvest beckoned, but with the promise of mud where our boots now kicked up dust. But at least there was no fear of beet mechanisation taking the bread from our mouths. Clay soil and heavy-wheeled harvesters did not go well together, so our beet hooks had no redundancy look about them. What a joy! We could spend the next three months mud-covered, numb-fingered and aching, but earning a living just above the minimum wage.

Often in spring and autumn we would work in the garden before taking our main meal of the day, in order to make the most of shrinking or limited daylight. On these occasions Mum would make us a cup of Ovaltine before gardening began. One afternoon I prepared to come for my drink when the Rev. Thornton came in at the gate. Taking rapid evasive action, I remained hidden amongst the bean rows until his retreating figure allowed me access to my fast-cooling drink. Whether the Rev. smelt the beverage, I don't know, but a few days later I was seated in the living room consuming this strength-providing liquid when his skeletal figure passed the window. Thinking the worst of the reverend gentleman, and classing church and squire (they were in-laws) as my Tory enemies, I burst out, "Here's that .... old parson again. He must have smelt my Ovaltine". "Shut up, he'll hear you", hissed my mother, and with a bang of the door left me muttering obscenities about the ruling classes and their C. of E. stooges in particular. Thrusting aside any delusions of etiquette, she kept the parson on the doorstep and breathed a sigh of relief when he went. Meanwhile, her communistic son, whose political leanings were bearing further and further to the left, sat nursing an empty mug as well as thoughts on the possible future overthrow of the establishment.

I had always been proud of the fact that my father was a member of the N.U.A.W., as were his brothers and myself, of course. Horrie Everard had invited me to attend monthly Union meetings at the reading room, where Don Clarke from Castleacre collected subscriptions and produced the up to date union news. The attendance rarely exceeded Don, Horrie and myself, although members came in to pay their subs and then left on the pretext of more urgent business. Seeing my interest in trade union work, Don arranged for me to attend a week's course at Esher in Surrey, where N.U.A.W. work and policies were discussed under the guidance of Bro. Edgar Pill, a very large man in stature, whose political views were definitely a bright red. I enjoyed the week, and came back with, in my opinion, a much-improved view on Soigné Farm piecework procedures and workers' bargaining powers. My involvement in trade union affairs had begun, and was to continue not only as a fully paid up member of a union all my working life, but with posts ranging from Oxon. County Chairman in the N.U.A.W. to senior shop-steward for the Transport and General Workers. Promotion at work never entered my head, fair deals for the men always coming to the forefront. These two things failed to gel for me to make promotional progress, so it was the bottom rungs of the ladder, with flat cap and heavy boots, which kept me true to my roots. Don't go away with the idea that I ran around waving a red flag at this juncture, but thoughts of social injustice began to seriously undermine my enjoyment of a simplistic country life with which the majority of my contemporaries were basically content.

So it was off to the beet fields once more by mid-September, trying to make the most of dry days with mist in the morning and warm sunshine in the afternoon. Price-fixing again took several days as Willie and Charlie were conspicuous by their absence whilst we remained under a tight rein in the perfect beeting conditions of light land provided by the field behind Mink Belt where our chopping-out price farce had been enacted in May. Tempers became fractious and Blackie came under fire for not forcing the issue by demanding a meeting, but eventually our two commanders found time from their "busy" schedule and the usual pricing game went through its paces, but with more acrimony than on previous occasions. "All smiles" looked hurt at our stubborn refusal to fall in with his preconceived idea of a fair price, whilst Charlie did more than his fair share of ground kicking to show his displeasure.

The dreary autumn months were helped along by our fortnightly trips to Carrow Road. Saturday dinner was gobbled down as we washed, changed and ate in the thirty minutes between leaving work at twelve, and catching Jack Eagle's coach at twelve-thirty. This dire situation was necessary during the shortest days, for floodlights hadn't arrived for Norwich City, necessitating a 2.15 kick-off in order to finish the game in natural daylight. We noticed that Charlie always gave us a pile of work to be completed on the Saturday mornings of match days, safe in the knowledge we would bust a gut to be finished by 12 o'clock. After a tortuous coach journey to Norwich, which was filled with anxious clock-watching, we would rush down to the ground in a muck sweat, and then freeze for the rest of the afternoon, getting only a scant degree of excitement from the performance of our heroes, as their league position sank progressively from third in 1952 to twelfth in 1955. A record of thirty-one goals from Ralph Hunt in 1956 lifted us to seventh place, but this feat only flattered to deceive as they crashed to rock-bottom the next year. After spending the intervening days in moaning and criticism, we wouldn't miss a game, for nothing must stand between us and that coach on match days. Come hell or high water, we took our place in the Barclay Stand behind the goal, to cheer Ron Ashman as he led the Canaries out to do battle. On one bitterly cold afternoon Sammy Chung, playing wing-half for Norwich, went into a tackle and unluckily broke his leg. The bone snapped like a gunshot, and I promptly fainted into the arms of a very surprised stranger standing behind me. No kiss of life came from a luscious blonde nearby, so there was no happy ending to report.

Heroes in Yellow and Green

Fierce arguments raged as to the merits of various players. Coddy Eagle was adamant that Terry Bly, an up-and-coming local lad, should play centre-forward in place of Ralph Hunt, even in his record-breaking season. We championed the man in possession, and rubbished Coddy's opinions. But hindsight tells me that after Terry Bly's prolific scoring for Peterborough, which enabled them to gain Football League status, Coddy had more than a point. Don't ask why Coddy's hero was transferred to a near rival team because, like so many vexing questions about Norwich City, both then and now, there seems to be no feasible answer. Our men always play their best football after transferring to other teams. Another infuriating fact was that my father always claimed to know more about the game by reading the "Pink Un" football paper than we did after watching it from the terraces. The green and yellow, knitted scarf worn with such pride on those trips still hangs over my bedroom mirror, unworn these days due mainly to a few moth-holes collected over the years, but a symbol of lifelong support in exile for our beloved Canaries.

The winter brought its usual spell of snow, with the risk of roads blocked by drifting. Pantry shelves were kept well stocked with food, and the coal heap in our shed corner held several hundredweights. Wood sawing by hand was still a Sunday morning ritual. One Saturday morning stands out in my memory as blizzard conditions blew in from the north-east. Having biked to work at 7 a.m., we battled through increasing wind and snow to feed and bed down cattle before the weekend. Meanwhile, Ezra Boldero struggled to Soigné with the week's groceries in Joplin's van. Rushing round to Charlie Andrews' house as fast as his short legs could wade through the snow, he dumped the grocery box on the table, refused to stop for any money, and made for the gate in order to get back home before drifts closed the road. Charlie, always looking for a wind-up, called Ezra back. "Suppose you haven't got a pair of shoe laces on the van, Ezra?" "Shoe laces", ground out the notoriously short-tempered roundsman, "you want shoe laces on a day like this?" "Well, I could do with a pair", wheezed Charlie as Ezra slammed the van door and set off for Castleacre, with grinding gears as well as teeth, not appreciating Charlie's wicked sense of humour. By twelve o'clock the road was already closing up, forcing us to drag our bikes along the field back to Pretoria. The driven snow, forced along by a near gale-force wind, seemed to cut half my face away, and frozen hands half carried the wretched bike back home. Adding insult to injury, my father remarked that only a fool would have taken a bike out on such a morning. Of course, as usual, he was right.

It seemed as if the senior members of our Bumfrey family hated snow in any shape or form, but this didn't extend to us of the younger generation. A good fall of snow helped to relieve the monotonous round of cattle-feeding, home, bed, and then work again. Snowball fights broke out as soon as Charlie

Wilson's back was turned. Leslie Lloyd had a vicious throwing arm, with missiles projected at prodigious speed over long distances. One snowy morning Leslie and myself followed Will across the yard, and my mate couldn't resist a shot at my uncle's retreating figure. The well-aimed missile struck just below Will's cap, and slid down the back of his collar. Whirling round with murder in his eyes, the victim mouthed obscenities at an unknown perpetrator of the attack. With swift reactions, Leslie and myself straightened our faces, pretending to take evasive action from an imaginary attack coming from a distance. "It's those buggers in the barn", I burst out, hoping to save Leslie's life by this ploy. "I'll put this bloody fork through them if I go across there", fumed Will, before continuing on his path through the cart-shed, followed closely by we two very chastened minions. Leslie never repeated his shot at Will, although we others often felt the sting of his unerring aim with a rock-hard snowball.

We younger men always worked on the principle that bikes were made for riding. At the first hint of ice on the road Freddie and Will would leave their machines in the shed and take to Shanks' pony. Their youthful family members risked life and limb to move on two wheels. One icy morning we biked to Soigné in pitch-black conditions, with only a weak dynamo-driven light on the front. As we swept into the cart-shed, Charlie Wilson remarked how lucky we were to stay in the saddle. As it grew lighter we found the yard surface like a sheet of glass, and had great difficulty to stand up, let alone ride a bike. The very fact that we couldn't see the icy surface had enabled us to keep our balance earlier, I suppose.

Another balancing act we carried out was to stand upright on flat-bottomed trailers whilst travelling from job to job. That morning I stood four-square, leaning on a pitchfork, waiting for Gerry to turn the conveyance and set off for Elbreck. Gerry leapt on to his machine, whipped it around on the icy surface, and sent me spinning off. More by luck than judgement, I landed on one knee, avoiding the flying pitchfork tines, and went sliding a fair distance across the ice. Amid cheers from a watching audience, I rose gingerly and limped off to my mate who had stopped further up the yard when, out of the corner of his eye, he saw me sliding off at an angle to his wheel-spinning tractor. Gerry was most upset and apologetic, but the fault was entirely mine for taking up such a foolhardy posture in the first place. This near brush with injury did not deter me, or any other reckless youth, from dicing with death on moving trailers. Health and safety never entered our silly heads, although we urged our trade union to enforce safety guards on machinery and other farm implements, especially power take-off shafts which were death traps for anyone wearing loose clothes in close proximity to them, as they turned at high speed.

Around this time, mechanised transport became more common. Georgie Wright, Leslie Lloyd and Harry Reynolds became car owners; Charlie Wilson went forth by car to take up his Methodist Chapel preaching appointments on Sundays; Jack Curl had bought Derek Winner's motorbike when he left to join the Navy, so he rode in from The Warren; Bob and Frank Clarke had cars, and John Bumfrey and Nobbie Easter their motor cycles. However, eyebrows were raised in surprise when Blackie Wright, Percy Barnes and Barney Hooks rode in from Castleacre on auto-cycles, each displaying pristine "L" plates front and back. All we pedal-cyclists held back to give them maximum road space when they pedalled furiously to start their machines, and then wobbled away in a cloud of blue exhaust smoke. Sometimes over-enthusiasm on the choke lever could cause the spark plug to soot up. This meant removal of the same with a plug spanner, and copious wiping, and cleaning of the offending vital part. Possibly, with this flotilla of machines in mind, the Major had cattle grids installed at all park gates, so there was nothing to detain this brave trio from speeding up past the Hall and away to their homes in the next village. At a slower speed would follow Alfie Dan on his tricycle, hunched over the handlebars, with spindly legs pushing the pedals round. Of the scores of men from Castleacre who used to work at Soigné when horses ruled the agricultural world, only these four intrepid workers remained.

Another great leap forward into civilisation had come with the advent of mains electricity delivered via new pylons to Pretoria and Soigné. Obviously the corn-dresser was driven by it, and as a by-product we had our houses connected to it. Light and energy on the pull of a switch at long last! An electric cooker with oven, which baked irrespective of wind direction; an electric razor, my life-long ambition, or at least from teenage years; a radiogram purchased to replace the wireless with its dry batteries and acid accumulator; an electric iron to replace Mum's flat irons and ironing-box; even a small washing machine, demonstrated and installed by Derek Hazell from Castleacre, the Hoover rep. for our area. This last labour-saving device became necessary after my mother's illness and a considerable stay in hospital. Would you believe it, she now wanted piped water and flush toilet! Was this mother of mine a descendant of Oliver Twist so renowned in asking for more? Well, the second half of the essential services wasn't too far behind, and piped water with bathroom and toilet made life considerably easier for her at a time when her health wasn't at its best. Coupled with that, Granny Eke's strong physique began to fail after eighty years' sheer hard work, so Mum spent time caring for her at Briston, which meant we fended for ourselves. Needless to say, the new labour-saving devices were a boon. The saying goes that the Lord provides neither too early nor too late — well, that promise held good for us at this time, but whether it was the Lord in Heaven or the lord of the manor who instigated the providing, I'm not sure, and maybe it was a little of each.

As mentioned in earlier chapters, our toilet facility prior to these new innovations consisted of an outside lavatory with a bucket placed under a wooden seat structure. My father found the new flush toilet to be set lower than his lifelong wooden one, and expressed concern over this fact, declaring he felt more comfortable on the latter and would continue to use it. After years of agitating to get an indoor flush toilet, my mother couldn't believe her ears, and after a sharp exchange of words, mostly aimed at questioning Dad's sanity, and that of the Bumfrey family males as a whole, regarding modern progress, she threatened to take the axe and demolish the offending wooden structure, and possibly her husband as well if he was enthroned upon it at the time. So it came to pass that under duress, my father learned how to perform his bodily functions on a toilet pan set at the same level as those of all his fellow countrymen and women. This slight altercation caused many a laugh during the days ahead.

It was during these momentous days of modern progress on the Estate that Dad too began to suffer signs of mental fatigue and poor health. After a lifetime of seven-day-a-week work with cattle he felt a change would do him good. A suggestion to Willie Thaxton that the cowman's post at High House be relinquished, and labouring work be taken up out on the farm, was met with undisguised shock and horror. High House without Fred Bumfrey was unthinkable, mainly because the two men had worked together there for so long. "Just like brothers", Geoff Thaxton once described them. "In everything except pay", Dad had quipped. Eventually, after a prolonged bout of poor health, Dad joined the Soigné labouring gang, although I myself had misgivings as to his physical strength at 50-odd, being able to take on the heavy work involved. Still, it seemed to be the better of two evils, and on the plus side the chronic indigestion he had suffered ever since I could remember disappeared overnight, and had presumably been caused by cattle smells settling on his stomach. Freddie took to his new environment, new as regards workmates and change of scenery, like a duck to water. He had reverted to his "Alfred Lewis" days of the early thirties, and as very little had changed in working practice, with the exception of tractor power, he met with little difficulty. A few horses remained to remind him of past days, and he spent much of his time odd-jobbing around, with an old mare for company, able to enjoy his weekends with a trip to Lynn with Bro. Will or to Norwich football ground with Michael and myself. Strangely, the High House set up continued to function with a German named Hans moving in to continue hand-milking the cows, supplying milk for the Hall. Doubtless Willie and family missed Dad as he had been much more than a cowman over the years. It was the end of an era in which the Bumfrey and Thaxton families had been very closely tied. No more Saturday morning bets on the forthcoming results of Norwich City on Dad's side and Arsenal for Geoff Thaxton. Huge stakes of one hand-rolled cigarette were put up against the outcome of matches, at twenty minutes to five. If Freddie won he could roll a fag from Geoff's "makings", the result

Heroes in Yellow and Green

being a smoke at least three times thicker than the sparrow's leg made from his own tobacco tin. Geoff always claimed Freddie kept his thumb on the tobacco in his own tin when the results went against him, preventing the Arsenal supporter from taking too much. No longer could Cecil Wright, the Ipswich man, lay in wait for his Norwich opposite number when the Town won and City lost. When losing, our intrepid cowman held his milk pails tightly to prevent clanking, thus avoiding alerting Cecil to his arrival at the dairy. Still, at least he could get first-hand information by attending each game and not annoy us by pontificating with facts gleaned from the "Pink Un" reporters.

Our recreational pursuits, in winter at any rate, revolved mainly around football and the cinema. Alternate Saturday evenings were spent in one of the three King's Lynn cinemas. Catching the late afternoon bus from Westacre, leaving our bikes in an outhouse at the keeper's cottage, No. 1 River Road, Gerry and Collie Deasley, Michael and myself, John Thaxton, and occasionally Gerald from Soigné would queue for the film of our choice in freezing conditions. No wind was ever warm in Lynn, but a lazy north-easter, blowing off the river, went through the thickest coat. The warmth of the circle and excitement generated by the latest film soon cast aside any such discomforts suffered during time spent queueing. A different story, however, appertained at Swaffham where a midweek bus travelled via Pretoria, especially for cinema buffs. No need to queue there, for the barn of a building was rarely more than quarter-full. The temperature inside resembled that of a deep-freeze store, and patrons either sat huddled in thick overcoats, or, in the case of courting couples, both lovers inside one thermal covering. Quite why we left our blazing firesides to endure such torture, I just cannot begin to imagine.

To end this chapter I must recount one more story connected with this mausoleum. Young Jack Eagle always collected our fares on arrival at Swaffham, parking his coach opposite the cinema. Slowly filing down the centre aisle, I found myself at the rear of the line. All my mates duly paid their half-crowns, and as it was pouring with rain, raced across the road and were about to disappear inside the building. Feeling in my pocket for change, I discovered the loose coins fell short of the required amount. My hand then went to my wallet-pocket, and panic − it was empty. My money must still lie on the dressing table at home. "Oh, I haven't any money, Jack." "That's all right, pay me next time, Derek", said Jack, who knew us all well enough to trust us implicitly. Thanking him again, I stepped down and allowed the coach to pull away before proceeding. Then the awful thought struck me. My mates had disappeared into the cinema, and I was outside with no money. Frantically I tore into the foyer and arrived just as they collected their tickets and prepared to enter the main cinema. "Wait a minute", I yelled, "I've left my wallet at home". "Ha, ha", they shot back, "pull the other one, it's got bells on", and away they went, still laughing at, as they thought, my attempted leg-pull. Pushing past the doorman, I just managed to grab Michael's arm, and pull him back. "It's true", I said, "my wallet is at home". After a good chuckle at the thoughts of me almost spending two and a half hours mooching the wet Swaffham streets practically penniless, he bought my ticket and in we went. I think our gang derived more merriment from my dilemma than from the comedy film. The joke about leaving one's wallet at home had been tried so many times that, on the one true occasion, they all thought it was the old tale of "wolf" being cried once again.

Chapter 19
More Muck-Cart and Merriment

With each succeeding year at Soigné the winter months became more of a soul-destroying drag for me. At the completion of the beet harvest, shortly before Christmas, the opportunity of gang-work almost totally disappeared until chopping-out began in May. Threshing, although the filthiest job imaginable, had given some opportunity for a get-together of labour, but by this time it was almost a thing of the past. Working with one companion for weeks on end can be very trying, unless that person happens to be a good mate, or very garrulous as was Leslie Lloyd, on both counts. Usually all sources of conversation had been exhausted by half past eight, owing to the fact that so little happened or changed around us, and the rest of the day held a succession of pregnant silences that almost drove me mad. Perhaps it was me, or perhaps it was others, but I became progressively more dissatisfied and critical of life at work and at home. If it hadn't been for our football trips I fear my sanity would have cracked. Being trapped between a desperate need to break out from the walled-in world of Westacre, and the lack of willpower and opportunity to do so, became almost unbearable to live with. One more hearing of Blackie's so oft-repeated tales would have been enough to tip the balance, I fear.

    Obviously there were times when a flicker of sunlight lit the gloom of those seemingly endless dull days. One season, immediately after beeting had been completed, I was sent with Geoff Thaxton in order to assist him in loading his lorry with beet, then ride to Lynn and bring back a load of ash to be used in the construction of a hard tennis court at the Hall. I still cannot imagine how or why I was chosen for this semi-élite job, but there we are, my luck changed for a short time. Geoff picked me up at Pretoria as he passed en route for the beet hale at the Long Plantation corner of Big Ashbreck. Having been apprenticed to this job prior to National Service, in the days of Sommerfeld and Thomas contract lorries, it held no terrors for me. Geoff was also very adept at throwing heavy forkfuls of beet up on to a high-sided lorry, as he had been filling the load single-handed every day since the season began. All the Thaxton family were good company and Geoff was no exception. Our lorry was loaded by breakfast time, and after a leisurely snack taken in the lorry cab, we would set off to Lynn Sugar-beet factory. To get outside the Estate confines was a pleasure in itself, but to be paid for it as well was a double bonus.

Joining the long queue of loaded vehicles waiting to enter the factory gates, we eventually reached the weighbridge where Geoffrey Edrich, the Lancashire batsman and one of the four brothers from that famous Norfolk cricketing family, worked during the winter months. After documents were exchanged, our load was removed by strong jets of water, so no manual labour was involved. Then, off to South Lynn station we went, where a loaded truck awaited us, and with it a couple of hours' heavy work with shovels. Now, some railway trucks were designed with a side door which let down completely, giving a clear throwing space once the standing area had been cleared; others had a wide bar along the top which remained in place once the door itself had been let down. This accursed bar meant each swing of the shovel either had to go under it, or over the top. Every time this awkward operation took place half the shovel contents hit the obstruction and fell down on the line below. Life for the labouring man was never easy, but it seemed as if railway design left a lot to be desired, especially when your shovel repeatedly struck inch-thick pieces of plank nailed over holes in the truck bottom. These obstructions always seemed to be strategically placed in the position where a dry runnel of ash continually came to rest. Sometimes the fine, black ash was wet, and although heavier, it kept its place better. It was dry material and high wind that made life very unpleasant for we two slaves.

Still, I enjoyed these days of virtual freedom and was very sorry when the last load of beet entered the factory, and the pile of power-station ash was deemed to be sufficient for laying a tennis court within the high garden walls of the Hall. Whether the lack of sufficient hand labour in the gardens helped the ageing head gardener, George Wright, come to terms with this sacrilegious take-over of centuries-old, hand-tilled garden I'm not sure. But things were changing in and around High House, and the reason was the sudden death of Major Birkbeck on 16 August, 1956. The Major left three daughters, two of whom were married and farmed in Kenya, and two surviving sons, the elder, Captain Harry Birkbeck inheriting the Estate. On the day of the funeral all harvest work ceased on the farms to enable us all to attend the service and interment at Westacre church. The small building was crowded, and I recall we stood outside under the ancient archway leading down to Abbey House. It was a sad day, even to a person such as myself who harboured thoughts of full nationalisation of land, and worker-participation on all farms. The Major was a gentleman, much respected by his own class, and by those employed by him, but he lived to a certain extent in an ivory tower feeding off information supplied by those who tended to tell him that which he most wished to hear, or which they thought he did — that's how it seemed to we employees who sat below the salt, in the age-old set-up of Estate pecking order. With Captain Birkbeck moving up to Westacre High House (the Hall) and Mr. Cameron taking up residence in the Abbey House, a new regime came to power. Willie

More Muck-Cart and Merriment

and Charlie were now to take orders from two men learning the farming trade as they went along, realising that changes had to be made in order to remain solvent, whilst at the same time retaining the old pattern of Estate life. How do you radically change the workings of an institution without causing ripples? I believe the younger element of farm employees would have gone along with change if the leadership could have convinced them of its eventual success, leading to better wages and living conditions. As it was, those with "cushy numbers" did their utmost to hang on to them by resisting any new ideas, although, let's face it, there were very few of the latter at Soigné, if my memory serves me correctly. Most of us just worked from day to day, making the most of whichever way the cookie crumbled, and still regarded the Estate as an institution on which outside influences had no effect. Jobs, though not of the highest order, would always be there even if things were left to run themselves. As far as I was concerned, there was no promotion to work towards, no cash incentives, apart from perhaps 6d an acre extra per annum on piecework. The whole set-up was in a rut, and I personally sank into the deepest rut of all.

The first springtime after my father came back to farm work at Soigné saw him take up his hoe, which had virtually rested in the shed since the early thirties, to join the majority of men at chopping-out sugar-beet. Commencing work on a ten-acre field adjacent to Rats Hall, he appeared to enjoy the company as he partnered brother Will on their individual plots. But the joy was short-lived when his feet began to swell and his work rate fell behind. Pressed by my mother to visit the doctor at Swaffham, he came back with a supposedly clean bill of health, with the doctor, who shall remain nameless, insinuating that he was attempting to "swing the lead". To say my mother was furious is an understatement, because we all knew Fred Bumfrey would attempt to rise from his deathbed in order to get to work. Soaked with sweat and weak, this was in fact what he did, giving us on the field the hardest job to persuade him to go back home. Grandad Bumfrey, now long retired, came from No. 9 to visit him. When he came downstairs, he said to my very worried mother, "Allah, he's got rheumatic fever". Poor Grandad had every reason to recognise the symptoms, as his youngest son, Stanley, had contracted and died from it at the age of fourteen. The doctor was sent for, and luckily this time Dr. Hall-Smith came to confirm the fact that indeed Dad had rheumatic fever. With the illness, only very minimum movement was advised for fear of heart damage in the patient. We were mortified that a doctor had sent him out to work after failing to recognise symptoms so plainly visible to a retired farm worker. There was no form of redress in those days, apart from never allowing that particular doctor near any of us again. My father did eventually recover his health, but never to a very high standard. His death from a major heart attack before he reached retirement age could possibly have sprung from those exertions on that beet field beside the site of his old home, Rats Hall. My personal opinion was then, and still is, that the physician who wrongly diagnosed my father's condition, allowed the fact of his occasional invitation to shoot on the Estate to cloud his judgement. I believe he really did think he was doing the Estate a favour by sending a shirker, in his opinion, back to work where he belonged. Don't forget, under the pre-war, anti-trade union "them and us" mentality, horses could be sick, but not labourers. These thoughts and conclusions, which were not without foundation I can assure you, helped fuel my determination to bring a day of reckoning for the employer and his professional toadies. Karl Marx and thoughts of Lenin and Trotsky were fast becoming my bedtime reading. Years later I realised just how naive I was at that time in believing there was a sharp, dividing line between those who employ and those who are employed. Many was the time in the future when I saw my so-called working comrades bought off with trifles and false promises in a far easier manner than were uneducated natives who traded land for beads and trinkets.

These last few insights into my past thinking should help to pinpoint the reasons why my enjoyment of a country lifestyle began to wane at that particular juncture in my chequered career.

Before I leave this rather sad year in our lives, may I be allowed to point out that I have always been proud of my father and, in a way, envied his very simple outlook and expectancy from life. He had his bed down in the front room to avoid the strain of stairs, and I always took him a cup of tea before going off to work. The sad, almost pathetic look in his eyes reminded me of an elderly, faithful dog, who could no longer go for a walk with younger successors, and who was being left at home. The worry about his physical and mental state made me snappy, and I have always hated myself for my hard-hearted replies as I tried to shake him out of himself, and to point out that going to work wasn't the be all and end all of life, because to him it was. What a reward for all the effort involved in doing extra work in order to give me a better education. It must have seemed to him that I had turned out to be a boor of a son when, in fact, I was a very worried young man, albeit a square peg in a round hole, sunk in a rut, which seemed to get deeper every day.

One way I found to break out of my "nose to the grindstone" existence was to take a week's holiday at Butlin's Holiday Camp, Filey. Gerry Deasley and myself went on the first occasion, when the sun shone every day and we enjoyed ourselves immensely. On the second trip we persuaded John Thaxton to accompany us, and we had even more fun, even if the sea mist hid the sun every day bar one. Renting a three-bed chalet, we really let our hair down. One night saw John and bed carried out on to the grass between the chalet rows – great fun for two of us, if not altogether for John, although he was a good sport. The first morning we were there John padded off across the grass in search of the toilet. After a short interval John failed to re-appear, and on

More Muck-Cart and Merriment

hearing a disturbance further along the line, we peeped out of our door. There, about three doors down, stood a red-faced, pyjama-clad figure, bending at the keyhole and yelling, "Open up, you buggers, I'm freezing out here". After another sustained rattling of the door handle, the apparition, who was none other than our mate, looked up and saw our grinning faces. John had forgotten our chalet number, and was trying someone else's door handle. Turning even redder in the face, he flew into our chalet and slammed the door, swearing profusely, whilst we literally rolled around the floor laughing. What a shot for "Candid Camera"! As we imagined the frightened occupants of the other chalet cowering under bedclothes to protect them from a raving lunatic, our laughter became more and more uncontrollable. I don't think I have ever seen anything funnier in my life than the shot of John swearing through that keyhole.

How soon we would have sobered up had we known of the traumatic accident that had just taken the life of a Thaxton family member. Ted, or Titch as we knew him, my erstwhile twin of High House days, took a short cut through the Abbey Farm on, I believe, the Saturday evening. Passing close to the parked timber drag, fully loaded and secured with chains, a ten million to one chance caused a chain link to fracture, releasing tree trunks down on Ted. He was, of course, fatally injured, and the news was kept from us until Cyril Goose, John's stepfather, met him off the Lynn bus as we returned. We were all dumbstruck, as Ted was a mate from schooldays through to work. After a few years in the Navy he returned to drive a high-geared, ex-Air Ministry, Fordson tractor, and sometimes a second lorry for the farm. He wasn't long married to a lovely girl from London who remained living, incidentally, in the cottage hard by the Park gates, where Geoff and his wife, Mary, lived for years after as her neighbour. We never went for another bachelor holiday — it didn't seem right somehow, for Ted's untimely death stayed with us all for many years. I had known Ted from my very earliest memories, and I treasure most the memory of him drying my tears and fetching me a replacement when I broke my Jubilee mug bearing the heads of King George V and Queen Mary. We were waiting for the ice-cream man, and playing on an old horse-rake; Ted, like all the Thaxtons, was kind-hearted, and we enjoyed many a laugh together over the years.

I'm afraid this chapter has turned out to be rather bitter-sweet, a little like life really, I suppose. As there were quite a number of we younger men around the farm, life couldn't be without its laughs for long. One such incident occurred after an evening trip to Norwich football, when floodlights had been installed. The devious plot was hatched before Michael and myself set off on the coach, when a reel of thin, tying-wire and some pliers were secreted inside our front hedge. Now Leslie Lloyd and Bill Johnson shared a front gate which, unlike ours, hung open all the time. After dismounting from the coach, and noisily proceeding round to our back door, we crept back to the wire and pliers, and proceeded to wind the former round Leslie's closed gate, before securing the ends in a tight twist.

Speeding to work in the dark the next morning, we stood at the back of our cart-shed awaiting Leslie's late arrival. As later discourse revealed, Leslie had lain-in, not an unknown occurrence, and Bill Johnson came out first to find the wired gate. Entering into the joke, he went back indoors to await the explosion, which was bound to happen any minute. Down the passage tore Leslie, hitting the gate with his front wheel. When nothing gave, and he found the reason for this, a torrent of unprintable expletives rent the morning air. By the time our hero had found wire snips and freed the gate, he was really late, and arrived sweating, swearing hell and damnation on the perpetrator of this fiendish and job-threatening trick. Charlie Wilson quickly removed himself from the fusillade of swear words, and took refuge with the tractor-drivers across the yard, where he rather under-remarked that Leslie Lloyd seemed to be in a taking over something that morning. Meanwhile, Leslie asked me if I'd seen anyone about when we came back from Norwich. "No", I lied, "but I did notice your gate was closed". "It must have been that Gerry Deasley", burst out our man, and promptly rushed across the yard to where the innocent Gerry stood laughing with Charlie. More hot language hit the cool morning air, and Charlie once more sought refuge for his Chapel preacher's ear-drums, and fled to the barn. Naturally, and truthfully, Gerry denied all knowledge of the heinous crime for which he was blamed, and reverberations rumbled around the yards for most of that day. We never let on, we daren't I might add, and Leslie never knew for certain who played that trick on him. But, when our neighbour, Bill Johnson, recounted his observations of the morning, our sides ached once more. Leslie was another good-hearted mate, but with a very short fuse, making him a natural butt for our wicked little jokes. Turning his gate upside down didn't bring such a spontaneous response, as he never even noticed until Michael pointed it out to him almost a month later. "Your gate looks funny with the points downwards, Leslie. Must be a job to fasten it up", the poker-faced Michael volunteered, having tired of waiting for Leslie to give vent about it. "Well, I'm buggered, Mike, somebody must have done that last night or I would have noticed it. It's a pity I didn't catch them at it and put my toe into their arse". Needless to say, there were plenty more expletives to go with those few lines. "Let me help you put it up the right way", suggested that ever-helpful brother of mine. "It's a mystery how these things get done". "Ah, I'll catch them, Mike, even if I have to sit up all night to do it". We suspended the gate tricks and hoped Leslie wouldn't sit up on too many nights hoping to catch his pranksters, and consequently lie in the next morning.

Muck-carting from bullock yards still filled quite a bit of our time. As indicated earlier, there was only a certain type of man designed for this task, and myself, Leslie Lloyd, Jack Curl and Gerald Andrews came top of this

More Muck-Cart and Merriment

particular pecking order. As it seemed to be only we four on the roster, as more people became infirm or excused from hard labour, bullocks and pigs produced more muck than we could remove in a season. To combat this unfortunate trend, Charlie took on four, temporary labourers from Castleacre, namely Lou Creed, Charlie Wright, and two Ellis brothers. They worked at High House on a day-work basis, with a Soigné labourer unloading at the heap and leading the horses from Soigné each day. I had this honour for a time, and I found it pretty hard going. Still, the ride between farms at the start and end of the day was some compensation.

The four of us home-grown, muck-fillers were pretty wiry, and well-honed physically. Gerald, without doubt, was the strongest, and although using a very short-tined fork, could lift twice the normal weight of wet manure. One day Willie Thaxton called in at Elbreck to check on our progress and, after a few words, said to Gerald, "It's about time you bought a new fork with decent tines". Quick as a flash our mate replied, "You'd find this one quite big enough if you had to use it all day, Willie". To give the bailiff credit, he saw the funny side of this rather sharp reply, and had to laughingly agree that Gerald had a point. I think he'd said it more for conversational purposes than criticism, as Willie of all people knew a good workman when he saw one, and Gerald was of the best.

A few days later, at the same venue, the sun was hot and we were tired. So tired was I that a rest in one of the suspended, long food hoppers seemed a good idea, whilst the empty trailer reversed into position. Continuing to sprawl on my back, with eyes closed, I failed to observe Charlie Wilson striding into the yard. A hissed, "Hie up, Charlie's about", from Leslie galvanised me into action, but try as I might, I found it impossible to get out of my improvised bed. The sudden movements caused it to swing like a hammock. The sight of my foreman's eyes protruding like organ stops at the sight of a labourer prostrate in a bullock's food trough started me laughing, which neither helped my efforts to stand up, nor Charlie's temper. "My fellah, what's going on here? You aren't at Butlin's Holiday Camp now". Flinging himself round, he stomped away, his exaggerated swing registering displeasure and, I suspect, partly hiding a grin, for it must have been an amusing sight. It's not every day one sees a pair of size nine, manure-covered boots flailing the air, and their owner upside-down in a wooden hammock.

Whilst on the subject of Charlie Wilson's sudden spurts of action from a standing start, I must recall an hilariously funny incident which took place one morning. As already mentioned, we gathered in the cart-shed each morning to receive orders for the day. Charlie walked down from his house, and after a few words, generally gave out the individual orders. It was the custom to tarry a few minutes after the orders were given, and if the foreman considered these minutes had been exceeded, he would begin to cough and kick the floor in the hope these signals would be interpreted without further need for words. On this morning in question, everyone seemed dilatory and slow to move out. Charlie's kicks became slightly more vigorous, and eventually his agitation became such that he launched himself forward to stride across the yard. Unfortunately his wellington boot failed to propel him forward, and instead he slipped backwards on a patch of spilled tractor oil. Suddenly seventeen stone of farm foreman crashed, face down, on the earth-packed floor, his trilby hat rolling across the yard. Silence, and then laughter, started by one whose sense of humour was easily tickled, spread like wildfire. Blackie, with quickly adjusted, poker face, rushed to his foreman's aid, although his efforts to help the stricken man resembled a tugboat raising the Titanic. Remonstrating at we convulsed and unsympathetic morons, with the aside, "It's nothing to laugh at, Charlie could have hurt himself", Blackie had the hardest job in the world to keep a straight face. As he remarked later, "The wind went out of him like a burst tyre". After retrieving his muddy trilby and ramming it back over his shiny, white, bald pate, our fallen hero had just enough breath left to bark out, "Get to your work, my fellahs, there's been enough time wasted already". Needing no second bidding, we fled to a safe haven where we could laugh ourselves sick at the funniest sight we could remember. How the mighty was fallen. I wonder whether he preached a sermon on the fall of Goliath or the walls of Jericho tumbling down at the next chapel meeting. You see, we weren't just ordinary morons, but irreligious ones — to boot. Luckily Charlie suffered no physical injury, although there was no doubt that his pride took a bit of a tumble, but the replayed versions of that incident brightened our lives for quite a few days after.

During the winter months Barney Hooks spent his time between tending the barn machinery and the carpenter's shop. Barley meal had to be ground for pigs, and oats rolled for horses. But, apart from meal dust or sawdust from his workbench, the neat little figure of Mr. Hooks kept pristine clean. With a thick, woodworker's pencil behind his ear, and boxwood measuring stick to hand, he repaired sheep troughs and trailer bottoms, and carried out any rough carpentry jobs needed for the farm. On one occasion he replaced a shaft on Charlie Wilson's large garden wheelbarrow. The replacement handle had been cut out at Westacre on the Estate saw-bench. Who provided the template to guide them I don't know, but the resultant handle bore little resemblance to the one left on the barrow. After doing his best with the refurbishment, Barney passed it fit for use. Leslie Lloyd and myself were conscripted to muck and dig the foreman's vegetable garden. Loading the massive barrow with rotted muck, I set off across the soft garden and promptly turned it over, as Barney's unevenly-set shaft twisted in my grasp. Trial and error indicated that only half loads could be negotiated if a rupture or twisted gut was to be avoided. Much ridicule was poured upon the carpenter's efforts by we two diggers. What

More Muck-Cart and Merriment 217

right had I, who had spent five years in the school carpenter's shop producing only a scissor rack, to criticise? I knew as much about carpentry as a pig knows about a Sunday. Leslie, the son of a blacksmith, may have been more of a tradesman than me, but not much, I fear. A great deal of leg-pulling ensued over the self-tipping wheelbarrow with one handle a good six inches lower than the other.

Good quality, country life depended a lot on the fact that the young naturally helped the old, and the strong helped the weak. But, for this system to work without friction, a fair balance in ages had to be maintained in the workforce. In pre-war years this had been relatively easy as no one left their village, and consequently a progression through the age and health spectrum held steady after the awful hiccough left by the First World War, when a complete generation of young men disappeared. By the mid-nineteen-fifties a severe imbalance began to develop in the true labouring staff. As the majority of youth came of age, they siphoned off on to tractor seats, so that no reinforcements came to replace ageing labourers. Full mechanisation hadn't arrived, which meant there were more and more labouring tasks to be filled by a very limited number of men in their physical prime. This, coupled with a rapidly developing trend towards certain employees selecting their own types of work, meant that a growing bitterness crept into the workplace. It wouldn't have been so bad if harder work meant higher wages, but there was very little financial reflection for those who were prepared to sweat. With Horrie, Percy and Blackie, by this time well past sixty, spending their winters on permanent hedging duties, Barney in the carpenter's shop, and the remainder of staff either mechanised or stock-feeding, there was a dearth of muck-fillers. Jack Curl, Gerald, Leslie Lloyd and myself had the dubious honour of filling these posts. All remained well with Charlie's labour distribution until one of the muck quartet failed to turn up for work due to illness. Charles scratched his head as he deliberated on this problem. How could he fill the vacant and very necessary post? Everyone had left the yard, and were well spread over the entire farm. My fellah, what a dilemma! But wait, the penny dropped as a solution sprang to mind. This unheard-of, mind-boggling course of action is summed up in the following poem, written at the time by the author, and retained by his mother as one of her son's first literary masterpieces. It was aptly entitled, "The Ballad of Barney Hooks", or "The Muck-carter's Revenge.

> *'Twas on a sunny Monday morn' that this event took place,*
> *It was so monumental that it shook the human race.*
> *The trouble was, or so I'm told, begun by men of muck,*
> *They all decided to stay at home, they did it just for luck.*

More Muck-Cart and Merriment

Poor Charlie looked around his shed and wondered how to cope,
  He scratched his head and kicked the floor, and almost gave up hope.
Then suddenly a ray of light lit up his darkening gloom,
  A brainstorm of a high degree that sealed our hero's doom.
Barney was the man in mind, we mean our Barney Hooks,
  The greatest little carpenter upon the Soigné books.
He stood his ground with back erect, his boots as bright could be,
  As smart a little carpenter as you could wish to see.
How could you send this man to muck to make his boots all smelly?
  To do a thing like that to him would turn most men to jelly.
But Charlie marched across the yard, his fingers crossed for luck,
  And hollered, in a cultured voice, "Hey, Barney, yoke for muck".
Poor Barney stood with mouth agape, his fingers twitching slowly,
  For never in his sixty years had he a job so lowly.
He then fetched out his tattered "states", the moths had left their mark,
  For sixty years is quite a time to leave them in the dark.
His fork had death-watch beetle, and was eaten up with rust,
  The poor old tool had lost its shine, and looked just fit to bust.
But Barney stuck out at his task, despite the constant chidings,
  From Laddie and his tractor gang who spread the day's good tidings.
And, as a labourer good and true, he never flinched from duty,
  Making his muck-heap nice and high — in fact he made a beauty.
So now, to end this sorry tale, all you men upon the books,
  Please pray that Charlie never plays this trick again on Mr. Hooks.

After reading that little ditty I'm sure all readers will understand why I, the author, didn't give up my day job, but carried on for the time being as a labourer in a rapidly developing, mechanical, agricultural world.

Chapter 20
Almost the End, but not Quite

As mentioned in previous chapters, we younger element in the sugar-beeting gang were fast becoming disenchanted with Blackie's leadership as "lord". But it was one thing to find people eager to criticise, and another to find somebody willing to take over from him whom they condemned. This was very much the case with our company, for no one in the central age group stepped forward to fill the "lord's" post when Blackie Wright stepped down. Eventually, the post fell to me, the youngest member, but, according to all my workmates, the only one educationally qualified to take over. Of course, this was a smokescreen to cover the fact that no one else wanted such a thankless task. Strangely, after stressing the fact of my shyness throughout this book and its predecessor, I felt pleased to be chosen, and full of confidence in my ability to carry out the job.

The first field we entered that season was Pretoria Breck. Bearing in mind my training under Blackie, I passed the message along for everyone to curb his speed until the price per acre had been agreed. As neither Charlie nor Willie appeared on the first two days, I sensed a trial of strength was about to take place. After sending a message, via Bro. Michael, to Charlie, requesting his attendance, and getting no joy, my hackles began to rise, for I knew everyone's eyes were upon me. Finally, a message arrived to the effect that Charles and Willie would arrive to sort it out on Thursday morning, that being the soonest their heavy commitments would allow them to come. By eleven o'clock I knew very well they were setting me up, so drastic action was needed. After hasty consultation between we "young bloods", it was decided to down tools at eleven-thirty, and take dinner early, but for all intents and purposes to be on strike until the management met their obligations to set a price. We hadn't been seated for more than five minutes before Charlie drove past, and on seeing the field empty, tractors silent, and everyone sitting down, he accelerated rapidly and drove hell-for-leather towards High House. Minutes later he returned with Willie Thaxton, both looking flustered, and the latter, who was always the spokesman, asked why we had stopped work. "Oh", I said, "we are on strike until such a time as you condescend to negotiate a price". "Derek, you know you can trust us to be fair. Have we ever let you down?" asked Willie. I fear my reply wasn't over-complimentary, so bargaining began on rather a ragged note, but for once the ball was in our court. Quite quickly a sensible price was arrived at, and we shook hands. "Now, don't let this sort of thing happen again, Derek", said Willie, as if correcting an errant child.

Almost the End, but not Quite

Needless to say, I glared back at him with some venom, and went back to my dinner, dry-mouthed, but happy in the knowledge that I had gained a moral victory in our first skirmish. A few of the elder statesmen held a wishy-washy conversation with the two officials in an effort to thaw the situation, but it petered out and our bailiff and foreman left the field in pensive mood as they considered this new confrontational attitude by their workmen. Life was never going to be quite so easy-going again. For better or for worse, the "I'll scratch your back if you'll scratch mine" mould had been broken. My back wasn't for scratching, and they had learned that fact the hard way.

Despite this slight altercation, life continued in its rather mundane way. Winter passed without any major upsets, apart from a bout of bad temper on my part on New Year's Day. Having spent almost two years at R.A.F. Feltwell in the company of many Scots personnel, I had followed their tradition of celebrating New Year's Eve. Being eager to initiate our local lads in this tradition, I had foolishly increased my normal limited intake of alcohol in the form of whisky, which, in turn, had left me with a bad head. Banishment to loading pig muck outside the farrowing sties did little to improve my temper any more than the mild, drizzly conditions overhead. At about 9.30 the weight of rain increased slightly, and we decided to seek shelter in Charlie Andrews' tin meal-shed. Sitting in a semi-stupor, watching the rain drip off the sloping roofs, my cosy little world was suddenly shattered by a tornado of size 12 boots squelching outside as they carried our irate foreman into view.

"What's all this, my fellows? What's the stoppage for?" Apparently he had missed the passage of loaded trailers passing through the yard en route to the muck-heap on the Hulver.

"Can't you see it's raining?" came my growled reply. "We aren't paid enough to get wet through".

Throwing his head back and belly out, Charlie nearly blew me over, and in my fragile state this wouldn't have taken much doing. "Master, there's not enough rain to wet a cat's back". Having to grudgingly agree, we went forth once more to continue our thankless task.

This incident remains vividly in my mind, as it was then I made a resolution not to drink whisky again, and I've kept to my vow so strictly that even the most severe head cold will not tempt me to a tot with lemon on medicinal grounds.

It was around this time that we played football on Sunday afternoons. Setting up a pitch on the rough pasture alongside Charlie Andrews' house – he had by this time moved into the semi-detached dwelling vacated by Dick Welham – we divided our limited numbers into two teams. Rushing around in hobnail boots soon reduced us to spots of grease, but also released all our pent-up frustrations as we re-enacted the games witnessed at Carrow Road the previous afternoon. Charlie Andrews often joined in for a short time, but was confined to goalie owing to his "wonky" knee. He was the only goalkeeper in the history of our national game to play in wellington boots! I recall that, after the first game, my legs were so stiff on Monday I couldn't even lift them high enough to clear a ploughed-out beet row. Those aching muscles were a small price to pay for all the fun we had.

Shortly after the installation of electricity, both Gerry Deasley and myself bought radiograms. This innovation coincided with the import of rock and roll from America. When Bill Haley and the Comets came on the scene, our senior family members threw their hands up in horror. Uncle Will Bumfrey considered we were selling our souls to the devil when we dared to mention a proposed trip to Lynn's Pilot Cinema where their first film was to be shown. Rock Around The Clock echoed out of Gerry's house on Sunday mornings, its loudness causing Mrs. Deasley's saucepans to rattle in the kitchen. I must say, my music was much more controlled, owing mainly to the fact my mother kept a firm hand on the volume control. Little Richard and Wee Willie Harris were slightly less noisy at No. 6, Pretoria. Mum was very neighbour-conscious, and anyway we didn't wish to disturb Bill Johnson at No. 5 who always slept in and then enjoyed cold fish and chips on Sunday morning, having bought them from Billy Harrison's shop in Castleacre the previous evening. This was one curious habit we couldn't quite understand or come to terms with, but everyone to his own customs, I suppose.

Looking back I now realise our friend and colleague, Gerry Deasley, was a man with ideas far beyond his time. Not only did he shake the fittings in the house with the 1990s-style volume of music, he once suggested it would be a good idea if one could go into town wearing a pair of working overalls or boiler-suit. If, like me, you have witnessed torn jeans and patched denim jackets being purchased from top fashion shops, you will realise our mate was a prophet for a future no one, except him, even dreamed about. He was certainly his own man, as one episode plainly pointed out. This involved his black beret for which he searched the lower part of the house in vain as he prepared for work. Setting off for Soigné in the unheard of state that left his head uncovered, he was at a loss as to the whereabouts of his missing, grease-covered headgear. Later that morning his mother discovered it lying on his pillow. Apparently it was so much a part of his anatomy that he had gone to bed without realising it was still on his head. We had a good laugh with him over that little oversight. We presumed he had removed his wellingtons and boiler-suit before settling down to rest.

We spent quite a lot of our time working with Gerry, Michael, John Thaxton, or Terry Eagle. All these young tractor-drivers were engaged at some time or other in providing trailers for we labouring gang to fill with beet, cattle fodder, straw, or muck, depending upon the season. On one warm, late spring day, we were all confined and sweating in an enclosed yard at High House, mucking-out partially-trodden cattle bedding. Much of it was dry under the shed, and Gerald came across an abandoned clutch of hen's eggs. There wasn't much doubt that they were well rotten, and the question arose as to how we could use them to cause the most chaos. The most effective place seemed to be under the thick sack acting as Terry Eagle's tractor seat cushion. Plans were laid to lure the unsuspecting recipient of our trick out of the yard, whilst the eggs were placed under the sack. When loading had been completed, Terry climbed inside his canvas cab, flopped down on the seat, and, after engaging first gear, began to ease the machine out of the yard. Suddenly he stopped and came hurtling out of his cab, coughing and gagging as the rotten egg gas spread from beneath his seat. Boy, did that reek! We were helpless with laughter, and poor Terry was green around his gills. There was much swearing between retches as his dinner threatened to regurgitate. After some of the awful smell began to recede we were faced with a fresh problem, namely how to render the tractor cab habitable once more. Terry flatly refused to enter the gas zone, so we perpetrators of the crime were forced to help clear up the mess we had made. As the tractor had been abandoned in the yard gateway, no work could be done until it had been moved. As luck would have it, Charlie Wilson had called earlier in the day, so we were safe from any prying eyes checking on our progress. Gerald managed to hook the sack off Terry's seat with the help of his muck-fork. A dinner-bag also came out by the same method. After borrowing one of my father's pig swill buckets, we proceeded to hurl buckets of water, obtained from a scum-covered cattle trough, on to the metal seat, in an effort to remove as much rotten egg as possible. By degrees the air became less foul, enabling us to use a near-hairless yard broom to finish the job. Then, returning the bucket, we borrowed a meal sack for Terry to sit on, and eventually wheels turned and work resumed.

After mentioning a cab on Terry's tractor, I must use a paragraph in tracing the acquisition of cabs at Soigné. As post-war restrictions receded, tractor manufacturers each tried to upstage one another by producing machines of greater power and versatility. No one seemed to give much thought to the operator who was expected to sit for hours on a poorly-sprung, metal seat, whilst exposed to all weathers. Two folded, thick, railway corn sacks did a sterling job as cushions. At night they were spread over the tractor radiator, which acted as a drying rack, until the water therein cooled. As cabs began to appear on other farms, Bob Clarke made suggestions that these modern efforts to improve the lot of tractor-drivers should be used at Soigné. The cost, of course, put the idea on hold immediately, but Bob, being both persistent and of an inventive state of mind, then suggested they make their own from sheet tin and perspex. So Bob and Artie Keeley set out to construct one for Bob's Fordson Major, and Artie's larger and more powerful International. The work progressed slowly in a large shed-cum-workshop just inside Lightning Breck, adjacent to the Clarkes' house. The results were quite good considering the limited tools available, and were fully workable, having sliding side-windows and a hand-operated windscreen wiper. Presumably the cost was more expensive or on a par with factory made models, so work ceased after those two passed off the production line. Soon afterwards canvas cabs arrived, again with Perspex windows, and these were stretched over a metal framework. Admittedly, they kept out most of the rain, but draughts entered and circulated quite freely, making life on the seat only slightly more comfortable, I fear. Cold was the tractor-driver's worst enemy, as sitting for three or so hours at a time between meal breaks could freeze the very bone marrow, no matter how many layers of clothes were worn. Thermal clothes were practically unknown, although some ex-R.A.F. pilots' wear could be bought at the Army and Navy Stores. On wet days, thick army coats soaked up water which eventually dripped down the legs, or allowed it to seep under your sacking seat. A tractor-driver's life wasn't always a happy one, although we labouring types reckoned that if they were too lazy to work like us, they deserved to sit and freeze. We gave scant credit for their skill, but weren't averse to easing our muscles when that skill made our work easier.

One way in which we gained considerably by these skills was at chopping-out time. A tractor-hoe, complete with small discs designed to cut soil away from each side of a beet row, had been introduced. A man sat on the hoe to steer the machine as close as possible to the line of tiny seedlings, thus leaving them sitting up on a ridge. This, in turn, made our task as hoe-men a great deal easier. Michael spent most of his time on the hoe behind either Georgie Wright or Norman Chase. Either combination made a good team, so we were very lucky on that count.

The beet-singling season always brought the most fun as almost all the Soigné staff were somehow involved. Artie Keeley, John Bumfrey and Geoff Thaxton hoed together, and the latter kept up a good line in chatter as the hand hoes clinked away as blade met small flint stones, many of which were turned up by the then modern ideas of deep ploughing for beet crops. Artie and John spent their winter months ploughing these fields, using a mill-sail method which involved starting in the field centre then ploughing outwards with unploughed corners worked last, hence the name mill-sail, these four corners resembling the sails of a windmill. Where the first two furrows were turned on top of one another in the centre, a slight rise occurred, even after all field cultivations were concluded. This rise always brought clever remarks from Geoffrey, such as, "Here we go over Mount Everest", or, "Knock the snow off your hoe, boys". As these observations were made to discredit the ploughman's skill, John took exception to them, and threatened Geoff accordingly. One occasion on Twenty-five Acres a free-standing cattle trough, left from the days when permanent pasture covered the field, gave John the idea of holding his tormentor's head under water until he turned blue. This threat tended to silence Geoff for a time. Another time my uncle took a swing at Geoff's spindly legs with his hoe, threatening to break them if he made one more derogatory remark. John's hot temper was well-known and one marvelled at Geoffrey as he took his life in his hands every time we crossed "the mountain range".

Geoffrey wasn't the only one to liven things up on those warm, sunny days. Gerald Andrews couldn't stay quiet for long, and he really came into his own when we were scoring on the Top Hulver. As we were all taking a welcome rest under shady trees, he spotted a wasps' nest in the grassy bank. Noting its close proximity to the older members of our party, he tipped us the wink to move slowly away, before he sidled towards the tiny hole through which the wasps entered and left their nest underground. Grasping his hoe on the very end of its shaft, he then made two strikes at the entrance, ripping soil and grass away. Then, taking a few very swift sideways steps, he left the way open for a cloud of very angry wasps to attack the nearest human beings they met up with. The evacuation of that area was swift, as our comrades suddenly realised they were being dive-bombed by a yellow and black cloud, hell-bent on extracting revenge for the desecration of their home. Strangely, none of those veterans saw the funny side of it, whilst we of a more tender age laughed our silly heads off. In fact, "Mr. Bloody Dilberry" came in for much criticism for his choice of stupid joke from those whose five minutes' rest had been disturbed.

When hoeing commenced, the pitch-halfpenny season also came into its own. As soon as dinner had been bolted down, some of the younger bloods would clear a level patch on the headland, stick a shut-knife up in the ground, and the game would begin. Each, in turn, would try to pitch his two halfpennies as close to the knife as possible. The art was to get one's halfpenny to land flat, just in front of the target, and then have enough force for it to slide forwards. Occasionally the coin would land on its edge, then roll away, accompanied by catcalls from opponents. The player whose coin landed closest to the knife picked up all coins, and then tossed them, keeping all heads as his winnings. The second man then tossed the remainder, and this went on down the line until all money had been won. Arguments often ensued over whose coin lay in pole position, and Geoffrey had a strange saying if he felt a decision went against him of "Cheats never tribe", which presumably meant that cheats never prosper. I used to lie in the shade and listen to the coins chinking, and the cheer when someone scooped "a hat full", that being when every coin fell head up on the first toss. An indescribable joy was mine when stretched out on my sack and able to rest those over-worked muscles in the warmth of a summer's day, surrounded by soothing smells of bruised grass and shaken pollen. Not for me the scramble for copper coins on the dusty ground — my heaven lay in watching the shimmering heat-haze through half-closed eyes,

Almost the End, but not Quite

and hoping my watch hands were still a long way short of twenty minutes to one. At that time, of course, bags were re-packed, hot hoe handles grasped, and a living earned once more out in the searing heat of a June afternoon.

Every Saturday afternoon during May, June and July meant a cricket match. Our season was limited by the fact that harvest work took precedence during the month of August. Matches were usually of a friendly variety, although towards the end of my time at Westacre we entered a north Norfolk league, which meant we played several villages out towards the coast, which was very pleasant. Although I played only as a stopgap reserve, I was very involved with the team, and spent most games with the scorer's pencil, which I enjoyed far better than receiving that hard, red ball, propelled at me with force from less than twenty-two yards. Not that this scoring lark was without incident or danger, far from it, especially when we played our local rivals from East Walton. The name of Petch comes to mind when cricket and East Walton are mentioned in the same breath. Young Fred Petch played alongside Frank and Maurice, who were his cousins, I believe. It was the latter name that struck fear into the hearts of batsmen up and down the County, for "Moke", as he was known, was a fearsome, fast bowler who attacked batsmen or wickets, just depending which of the two got in the way of the ball first. I am reminded of the first local derby in which I was unfortunate enough to play. When Moke came on, just before tea, I swiped wildly at his first ball and lost middle stump, much to my relief. My brother, Michael, came in next, being a youngster just left school, and defended valiantly by playing the remaining five balls back to the bowler with a very straight bat. This resistance so infuriated Maurice that he spent the tea interval marching round, issuing threats that indicated poor Michael would be decapitated for sure as soon as hostilities resumed. But for once Moke was frustrated, as that straight bat hung around for quite a while, enabling other batsmen to grind out a few more runs. Unfortunately the Westacre record in local derby matches wasn't too good at that time, but, as run makers John Thaxton and Brian Reynolds matured, combined with good bowlers in Michael Bumfrey and Terry Eagle, things looked up. Gerald Andrews as captain, Derek Curl and Peter Welham formed the backbone of the team for those lean years; Tom Abel kept wicket as a veteran, whilst we lesser lights made up the rest.

Before leaving the cricket field we must mention the lady reputed to be East Walton's trump card. Rumour had it that she scored more runs for Walton than her two sons put together. But no one mentioned this within earshot of the lady or they may well have been decapitated before facing that demon fast bowler. I always enjoyed scoring with her, or was it against her? She may have erred occasionally on the generous side in recording her team's runs, but she never once took offence when I pointed out this fact, nor I when she inferred my score-book was wrong. It was much more enjoyable than trying to keep score with half-interested boys who had to be told what to do. I remember one especially thick lad who I had to help repeatedly with his book. Over tea his father came and accused me of cheating, to which I took exception, and was on the point of indulging in a bout of fisticuffs from which I'm sure I would have come off second best. Luckily for me, big brother Michael and John Thaxton stepped in to extract an apology from him on pain of a good hiding if he didn't step back. Typically, he then went back and blamed his son for not doing his job properly. I just hope our man had been into bat and didn't have to face our fastest bowler in a mean mood. Michael was, and still is, very easy-going, but not a man to be crossed if you happen to be in the wrong.

It was during the latter days of my stay in Westacre that I had an urge to attend church on Sunday mornings. Four of us had attended Harvest Festival on one occasion when church and chapel combined. Our poor foreman almost fell out of his pew as we marched in. He couldn't have looked more surprised if a gentleman with horns and a forked tail had opened the big church door. I cannot remember what inspired me to go, it was so out of character, but a new parson, Canon Caley, had taken up the post for Westacre and East Walton. He was a very welcoming and sincere man. I never managed to find which book we were supposed to be using, but I enjoyed sitting in that pretty, little, sunlit church. When I left the village he remarked, "What a pity Derek is leaving; he was such a good influence on the younger members of the village". I fear that if it was a true report of his statement, the lifelong pact between Estate and church was broken at that point, for not many in the hierarchy of the former considered my influence to be anything approaching "good". Occasional visits to Reggie Eggleton's shoe repair shop helped fuel my resentment of the "bloodsucking rich". Reggie, you will remember, carried a personal crusade against all those born with the proverbial "silver spoon" in their mouths, and he found a ready disciple in me. His worldly-wise advice also swayed me to persuade my dad that the hard work in growing extra potatoes on a stack bottom was false economy when Reggie Eggleton could buy them cheaply for us from the Fens. No sooner had my superior knowledge been put to the test than the season turned out to be one of shortage, sending prices through the roof. I wasn't allowed to forget my gaffe thereafter. You would have thought my lesson would have been learned and Reggie's silver-tongued utterances taken with a pinch of salt but I'm afraid it was not so.

A day trip by coach to Great Yarmouth was celebrated with a run on the big dipper. Poor Terry Eagle turned green, and I must admit I felt almost as bad as he looked. When we stopped in East Dereham for a pint on the return journey, I won a goose in a raffle; I carried it home by the neck — it was dead, of course — and then, not having any idea what to do with it, as Mum and Dad were over at Briston visiting Granny Eke, we took it to Ivy and left her to deal with plucking and drawing it.

Almost the End, but not Quite

The second year of corn dressing in Soigné barn saw me drafted in as assistant to Gerald. Owing to shortage of ground storage space, all corn sacks had to be "topped" which meant lifting a second sack upright above the first. Uncle Will Bumfrey estimated the required weight of each sack before removing it from the machine; Gerald and myself weighed them, adding or withdrawing a small amount until our weighing machine balanced. The top was then tied securely with binder string. On one occasion my mate pulled the tie so hard that the string broke, and his fist, suddenly released, hit me in the midriff with such force I was temporarily winded. The air went out of me even faster than it did from Charlie Wilson when he crashed in the cart-shed. It was very hard work, with little ventilation or through draught. A very fine dust from the machinery was always present, and we had no idea we were breathing lungs full of the dust capable of causing that killer disease, farmer's lung. We two who moved all over the upper barn floor were more fortunate than Will who took the full force of it, and did in fact die from a condition very akin to that which shortly after became recognised as farmer's lung.

Despite the heavy lifting and arm-tearing pain, as each "topper" turned back over our entwined, bare arms, we had a lot of fun during harvest. We worked long hours, as did the combine-drivers and trailer men. Young Laddie was, by this time, one of the latter, and he came with exaggerated tales about the heroic exploits worked by men at the Abbey Farm. Their dresser staff moved twice the weight of grain we did, and that with a workforce of pensioners, to boot. He would stand on the edge of the grain pit and yell up at us, "Come on, together, you bin asleep up there. Billy Briston would have finished this lot at the Abbey and gone home by now". We would look out of the aperture beside the dresser and shout back, "Bugger off, Yellocks, and mind your own business". His sweat-and dust-covered face would give us a big grin, and suggest he asked the combines to stop for an hour or two so that we could catch up. It was all very good-humoured and helped to chivvy the job along.

One day, as Gerald and myself set off with our sack barrows to wheel and stack at the far end of the barn, a fallen sack of barley blocked our way at the top of the stairs. Thinking it was strange that an apparently safely-stored sack of grain should slide down, we stopped, lifted it up, and then continued on our way. A few minutes later, as we weighed and tied the next couple for wheeling, I saw out of the corner of my eye a black beret ducking down below the floor level. I then had a good idea how our path became blocked on the previous run.

Creeping towards the stairwell I waited, and sure enough up came Laddie's arm to pull down the sack once more. Leaping forward, I swung my boot as if to kick the offending arm, and consequently Leslie shot back. He lost his footing on the worn, wooden stairs, and fell into Charlie Andrews' open-topped meal bags underneath. Emerging from the dust cloud, Laddie limped away, covered in barley meal, as we two stood laughing at the stair top. Thank goodness those sacks were there, or else the innocent joke could have ended in tragedy. We finished up as top dogs that time, but not for long, as he was soon back goading us for lack of effort once more.

Captain Birkbeck could be seen on occasions standing outside looking into the grain pit. We made up a thought bubble for him, similar to those seen in cartoon strips; it read, "Mine, all mine, and some that is not here, that also will I bring and make it mine". Well, there was a lot more to come until the top floor of the barn was full to overflowing. This upper, wooden floor was set on timber pillars, the whole being constructed inside chalk and flint walls of the old barn. There was no other way all that weight could have been supported. I believe we worked on flat rate wages, plus overtime, and collected a bonus at the end of harvest — much sweat and effort for scant reward really, but the laughs we had were many, and the comradeship was second to none. Gerald and I worked well in tandem; Will, so methodical, kept us in order, and with Laddie, Charlie Andrews and Geoff Thaxton, our lorry-driver, popping in and out, life was never dull. In fact, we were always sorry when harvest was over and our little gang broke up.

There are still some stories to tell about my life on Soigné Farm, tales that must be committed to print and not left to die in the memory. Most of the wonderful country characters who worked there have been mentioned, but a few more wait patiently in the wings. I sincerely hope I will be given the opportunity to write a third volume concluding my working days at Soigné, and then extend to cover my experiences ranging from Agricultural College to Co-op delicatessen hand, and mink farmer to builder's merchant yard foreman.

Why did I ring so many changes in my work? Well, I made myself a golden rule never to remain working where I wasn't happy, and if circumstances changed, I pressed a self-destruct button which burned all boats and bridges, forcing me to set out for pastures new.

This was to happen at Soigné in the very near future, but the telling must wait for another book. Perhaps I shall call it "Life After Soigné". I know it will be fun to write, so I just hope you will enjoy reading it.